IDEOLOGY & CHANGE:

RADICALISM AND FUNDAMENTALISM IN AMERICA

William McPherson
LEWIS AND CLARK COLLEGE

 NATIONAL PRESS BOOKS

Copyright © 1973 by William McPherson
First edition 1973

Library of Congress Catalog Card Number:
73-77390
International Standard Book Numbers:
0-87484-263-8 (paper)
0-87484-264-6 (cloth)

Manufactured in
the United States of America

National Press Books
850 Hansen Way
Palo Alto, California 94304

This book was set in Caledonia and Helvetica
by CBM Type and was printed and bound by
George Banta Co. Book designer was
Nancy Sears and cover designer was Jim
M'Guinness. Editors were Alden C. Paine
and Gene Tanke, and Michelle Hogan
supervised production.

CONTENTS

Part II RADICALISM AND FUNDAMENTALISM

Part III IDEOLOGY AND PROPAGANDA

Part IV OLD AND NEW RHETORICS

EPILOGUE

PREFACE

Ideology, as expressed through propaganda, is the most clearly discernible product of social movements; movements have other ultimate purposes, of course, but their routine activities and public relations programs are often concentrated on propaganda work. Analyzing ideology and propaganda would therefore seem to be a major task for social scientists; however, since the pioneering work of Harold Lasswell,[1] propaganda analysis has seldom been used in the study of social movements. Work has been done in the theories of social change and collective behavior, but little effort has been devoted to classifying and discussing propaganda themes.[2]

With the revival of interest in social movements as a result of events in the 1960's, the study of propaganda has been enjoying a resurgence. This is due partly to a rediscovery of the sociology of knowledge and partly to concern over the unforeseen effects of social change. Social movements are usually defined in terms of social change—whether they promote or inhibit change[3]—and the effects of their programs for change may extend far beyond their own membership. Propaganda is the principal vehicle for extending this influence.

Analyses of both ideology and change require comparative models. The propaganda themes of any one social movement, or a congeries of similar movements (such as radical movements), are predetermined by their intellectual orientation. Thus, for example, radicals will tend to agree on some of the Marxist assumptions about class conflict even when they disagree on the specific forms taken by that conflict. From such affinities it is possible to analyze ideology only within a narrow range of propaganda themes. To study a broader range of propaganda, and thus to discern the basic themes common to all social movements, it is necessary to compare propaganda messages which express quite different ideological commitments. One of the criticisms of the "authoritarian personality" studies is that they concentrated on the psychological mechanisms of "fascism," to the exclusion of similar mechanisms in communism.[4] Follow-up studies have attempted to correct this oversight by extending the concepts of authoritarianism to such diverse groups as Communist Party members, Catholics, and others.[5] From these criticisms and studies has emerged an interest in the parallels between the ideologies of the "left" and the "right." It is not enough to suggest, for example, that there are similar mechanisms involved in the ideology of the Socialist Worker's Party and that of the Christian Crusade; the reasons for such a similarity must be explored. This exploration is undertaken in Parts Three and Four of this book; beginning with Chapter Nine, the similarities between different ideologies are explored with the use of theoretical concepts and historical illustrations.

Before examples of propaganda from specific movements are presented, however, Parts One and Two describe the movements themselves, and their origins and leadership. This first half of the book, which is intended to meet the need for historically comparative studies, presents the argument for historical and biographical studies in sociology and then illustrates the uses of history and biography with examples from specific movements. The need for historically comparative studies comes, of course, from the definition of social movements as organizations dedicated to the promotion or prevention of change. Change, as Marx and Mills and others have noted, is a historical process that is often understandable only in retrospect. Many of the best studies of social movements have been historical case studies, in which specific movements are examined for their role in causing or reflecting great social upheavals. (It is often difficult to separate cause from effect in these analyses, because the dynamics of social change are such that the role of any one leader or group is not always clear.)

It should be apparent, from these remarks and from an examination of the table of contents, that this book is based on a study of parallels in ideology, history, and biography.[6] The use of parallelism in the study of social movements is not new, but I believe that this book will contribute to that study in two ways. First, the parallels will emerge as much from the source material—that is, the readings—as from the editorial material. This should encourage the student to try his own analyses in testing the validity of the concepts. Second, the organization of the book, and particularly the concepts introduced in Chapter Nine, permit a two-way analysis of parallelism: old versus new and radicalism versus fundamentalism. Historical changes can be analyzed in tandem by examining both old radical movements and old fundamentalist movements in comparison to their newer counterparts. Thus, instead of simply comparing the "old left" and the "new left," as many have done,[7] this book strives to extend the analysis by comparing old and new radicals to old and new fundamentalists. Thus, for example, the older movements of both types tend to have a different structure and leadership than the newer movements of both types. Further, there are similarities in ideology between the older movements on one hand and the newer movements on the other that would be overlooked if only one type of movement were analyzed. Also, changes between older and newer movements will become evident when we examine the two different "traditions," which social movements have followed, radicalism and fundamentalism. Hence a four-way comparison, as used here, should add another dimension to existing comparative studies.

Many of the historical sources on social movements included here were suggested by Seymour Martin Lipset, who has guided my research from its earliest phases to the present. Some of the early phases were supported by the Anti-Defamation League of B'nai B'rith and the Milton Fund of Boston. Some of the later phases were supported by a Pomona College Faculty Research grant. The concepts used in Parts Three and Four were developed and discussed at a National Science Foundation Summer Institute at the University of Ohio in 1971. They were further refined for a paper delivered at the 1972 meetings of the Pacific Sociological Association under the chairmanship of Ralph Turner. Alden Paine, publisher for National Press Books, has made a number of helpful comments on the book. Corinne Bybee, secretary to the Department of Sociology and Anthropology at Pomona College, has been both efficient and patient in her work on my manuscripts and correspondence connected with the book.

Wm. McP.

[1]Harold Lasswell and Daniel Lerner, *World Revolutionary Elites* (Cambridge, Mass.: Massachusetts Institute of Technology, 1965);
Lasswell and Associates, *The Language of Politics* (New York: Science Editions, 1966).

[2]Neil J. Smelser, *Theory of Collective Behavior* (New York: Free Press, 1962).

[3]Ralph Turner and Lewis Killian, *Collective Behavior*, Second Edition (Englewood Cliffs, N. J.: Prentice-Hall, 1972), p. 246.

[4]Edward Shils, "Authoritarianism: 'Right' and 'Left'," in R. Christie and M. Jahoda, eds., *Studies in the Scope and Method of 'The Authoritarian Personality'* (Glencoe: The Free Press, 1954), pp. 24-29.

[5]Milton Rokeach, *The Open and Closed Mind* (New York: Basic Books, 1960).

[6]My original work on this basis was a Ph.D. thesis under the direction of Seymour Martin Lipset. William McPherson, "Parallels in Extremist Ideology," Harvard University, 1967.

[7]The entire issue of the *Journal of Social Issues*, Vol. 27, No. 1, 1971, was based on this comparative approach to radicalism.

PART I

HISTORY
AND
BIOGRAPHY

HISTORY AND BIOGRAPHY IN THE STUDY OF SOCIAL MOVEMENTS

WILLIAM McPHERSON
SOURCE: Written for this volume.

As a specialization in sociology, history, and political science, the field of social movements is underdeveloped. Movements are studied as adjuncts to collective behavior and political behavior, not as proper subjects of study in themselves. Movements are usually treated as phases in social processes rather than as viable social groups. Thus the literature on social movements, especially in the form of professional studies, is less extensive than that of other fields and the methodology is underdeveloped.

Interest in social movements in now sufficiently high to warrant study of the movements in themselves. Social movements are not political parties (except nominally, as in the case of the Communist Party), nor are they ephemeral phenomena such as crowds or mobs. They are defined as "collectivities" formed to "promote or resist a change in the society."[1] This definition is taken from a discussion which stresses the stability and permanence of movements in comparison with other types of collective behavior. Ideology is the key to understanding the stability of social movements, according to Turner and Killian. Ideologies can include such diverse philosophies as fascism and communism, Christianity and Buddhism, women's liberation and ecology. It is the expression of these ideologies in specific groups, under specific leaders, that permits the social scientist to study movements empirically.

Many excellent case studies of social movements as groups, and of their leaders as individuals, have been done by historians and biographers. Other social scientists have neglected these studies in favor of the more sweeping discussions and commentaries on social movements as mass phenomena. This is unfortunate, because sociologists from Marx to Mills, including the classical theorists Weber, Durkheim, and Pareto, have demonstrated the value of historical studies. One of Mills's principal criticisms of contemporary sociology has been directed at its neglect of history.[2] Only recently has sociology begun to rectify this neglect, partly as a result of Mills's influence.

HISTORY

Since change is the defining characteristic of social movements, historical analysis is a principal mode of studying movements. Some of the best studies have been written by historians and by sociologists writing in the historical mode. Because of the interests of intellectuals in radicalism, many of these studies are concerned with radical movements. For example, Irving Howe and Lewis Coser wrote a definitive history of the American Communist Party,[3] and Daniel Bell has written one of the best hsitorical studies of American socialism.[4] Both Coser and Bell are sociologists, but historians have also written analytic studies of radicalism. The historical orientation has benefited sociologists and the sociological orientation has benefited historians working in the area of social movements.

Studies of radicalism suffered a decline in the 1950's, but with the emergence of the "new left" in the 1960's there has been a renewed interest in leftist movements. Sociologists, including Irving Horowitz,[5] Seymour Martin Lipset,[6] and Richard Flacks[7] have analyzed the social background and the ideology of student radicals and other new leftists. Interest in the student radicals is prompted by their presence on the campuses where many of the scholars reside; it is also prompted by a renewed interest in Marxism in social theory courses. Reinterpretations of the Marxist influences in sociology have been stimulated by the rediscovery of the "early Marx" by student radicals who disagree with orthodox Marxism. Thus the emergence of the new left, a historical development, has become an important intellectual development.

While radicalism remains a topic of interest to most intellectuals, Christian fundamentalism is more relevant to core American values. The combination of historical and sociological studies in the literature on American religion is especially fruitful. It has produced studies which analyze the paradox of the unifying and divisive effects of religion. Historically, the Protestant ethic is regarded as the primary source of economic, social, and political values.[8] The translation of Protestant doctrines into political values has resulted in a form of political fundamentalism which is found in nativist movements of the nineteenth and twentieth centuries.[9]

The Protestant sources of American religion and values have provided grist for intellectual analyses of both unity and divisiveness in American history. The stress on unity has resulted from an analysis of high-level values, while the stress on divisiveness has resulted from an analysis of religious and political movements. It is the stress on divisiveness which we will be concerned with here. "Political fundamentalism" is the ideological mix of religious and political values found in the nativist movements of the nineteenth century, such as the Native American Party (the 'Know-Nothings') and the Ku Klux Klan (which survives into the twentieth century). It is found today in groups which are openly fundamentalist in their religion and politics, such as the Christian Crusade, and in groups where fundamentalism is the assumption hidden behind a relatively sophisticated political ideology, such as the John Birch Society.

It can be useful, in analyzing recent trends in American social movements, to posit fundamentalism as the underlying sociohistorical factor. Some of the tenets of fundamentalism—literal interpretation of the Bible, apocalyptic beliefs about the Second Coming of Christ, and a revivalistic mode—are found today in movements described variously as "Jesus Freaks," "Jesus People," or "new fundamentalists." The classification of these movements as fundamentalist is fruitful in a historical sense because they can be analyzed in terms of their roots in the fundamentalist religions. It also enables us to see how the "Jesus Freaks," despite their counter-cultural style, may well represent a continuity with past fundamentalist movements such as the Christian Crusade. Thus even though the Christian Crusade is currently viable, we might anticipate its decline and eventual replacement by the newer fundamentalist movements.

Historical perspective enables us to relate recent social movements to their roots in the past and to their future roles in society. It also enables us to discover the similarities and differences in social movements. Thus we can see that there are ideological affinities between older radical movements such as the Communist Party and newer radical movements such as the Students for a Democratic Society,[10] and we can see that there are similar continuities between older and newer fundamentalist groups. At the same time, the older movements of both types share certain organizational features because of their historical growth and development, and these features distinguish them from newer movements. Thus, for example, the U.S. Communist Party attained its largest membership and greatest national influence in the 1940's and has now fallen to an insignificant sectarian level. Similarly, the John Birch Society was once much larger and more influential than it is today; since reaching its zenith during the 1964 Presidential campaign, it has lost members and prestige.[11] The rise and fall of social movements is a fascinating historical phenomenon, but it also has sociological implications. Movements tend to "freeze" values by expressing them in a specific ideology which is relevant to one era or period of history but not to another. Thus, for example, the Communist Party version of American society is more appropriate to the relatively unregulated economy of the pre-Depression era than to the highly regulated business community of today. Ideology has been defined as the "conversion of ideas into social levers"[12] or the combination of "factual propositions and value judgments."[13] As these definitions imply, ideology is a mixture of abstract values and concrete social prescriptions; the values may be enduring but the social prescriptions tend to be time-bound. Thus the "movement" of social movements tends to leave some groups behind, clinging to familiar tenets and statements of belief but losing touch with their constituencies.

Ultimately, the historical significance of social movements lies in the impact they have on the larger society. The ideologies of movements express the discontents and aspirations of the members, and for a time they also express the interests of a wider constituency. When a society is undergoing change some segments will be "ahead of the times" and others will be left behind in the backwash of change. The historical context of the ideology is critical to its effect on the society; change can be facilitated or retarded by the operation of belief systems in the social system. Thus it is necessary to study the history of social movements in order to analyze their impact on society.

BIOGRAPHY

In the collective-behavior conception of social movements, individuals in the mass membership might be considered insignificant. However, as Turner and Killian and others indicate, the stability of organized social movements permits individual leaders to emerge and to lead a "following."[14] The influence of the leader may extend far beyond the membership to shape the history and culture of the society in which he operates. Leaders of social movements become "heroes" with lasting impact on the political and religious life of the world.[15]

Just as history can be a rich source for the study of specific movements, biography can be valuable for research on individual leaders. The lives of Lenin, Trotsky, and Stalin are studied to enrich our understanding of the Russian Revolution.[16] In American history, Eugene V. Debs and William Z. Foster demonstrate, in the course of their lives, the transition from labor agitation to Marxist ideology in the socialist movement.[17] It is one of the ironies of radicalism that movements which advocate the solidarity of workers and the strength of numbers often produce more "stars" and celebrities than other movements. The new radicals depend heavily on media exposure for their impact on society; this has inevitably made "stars" out of the spokesmen of the new left. Tom Hayden, David Dellinger, Bobby Seale, and Huey P. Newton have become "household words" because of their activities; their followings fluctuate in size and influence, but they remain well known to the public. Two of the new radicals, Abbie Hoffman and Jerry Rubin, even created a Youth International Party (Yippies) to exploit the appetite of the media for sensational, staged events. Biography is essential for the study of the new radicals because many of the organized movements, such as the Students for a Democratic Society, have dissipated. The importance of the new radicals lies more in their individual experiences than in their organizational successes.

Fundamentalist movements, as mentioned previously, embody historical expressions of the Protestant ethic; individual American leaders in the past and present symbolize it in their own lives. Historically, men such as Cotton Mather and Benjamin Franklin represent religious and secular expressions of the work ethic.[18] Contemporary fundamentalist movements also have leaders whose lives symbolize the political and religious aspects of the Protestant ethic. Billy James Hargis, the leader of the Christian Crusade, is in the tradition of the Puritan preachers, warning an apostate people of the damnation that awaits those who stray from the straight and narrow. Hargis's ideology equates Communism with belief in Satan; his simplistic dualism is typical of fundamentalist beliefs. Some of the leaders of the "Jesus Freaks," such as Duane Pederson, the leader of the Hollywood "Jesus People," also employ dualism in their preaching. Today Pederson is a minister preaching to the long-haired youth of Southern California; a few years ago he was a drug user and night-club entertainer. He experienced the total conversion typical of the fundamentalist believer, a conversion experience which follows from the dualistic, heaven-hell, either-or mode of fundamentalist ideology. Robert Welch, on the other hand, is a "secular fundamentalist" in the tradition of Benjamin Franklin. He is a successful businessman who turned to politics to conduct a moral crusade against a government he saw as tyrannical. While he is not a fundamentalist preacher, he is a political fundamentalist and his life embodies the "moral crusader" role described by Orrin Klapp.[19] Welch does not belong to a fundamentalist church, but his family background is fundamentalist[20] and his writings, notably *The Blue Book*, are full of references to the "Christian basis" of Western civilization. Thus the biography of Robert Welch demonstrates the affinity of political and religious fundamentalism, even when the expression of fundamentalism in a specific movement such as the John Birch Society is obscured by an ostensibly non-sectarian ideology.

The use of biography in the study of social movements enables us to focus the analysis on significant personal events as well as on the larger historical context of the movements. Social movements can be seen as vehicles for personal crusades; those which do not build a base or structure that extends beyond the fiefdom of the leader may not last long. But, as Max Weber has suggested, the resolution of a succession crisis may permit a movement to become a bureaucracy and thus perpetuate itself in the image of the founder. The founding leader may thus leave an indelible impression on a movement, and through it on society. His life may serve as an example to members of the movement or as a source of the myths and legends of the movement. His charismatic authority may be used to justify discipline in the movement, and it may be shared by other leaders in the movement through a bestowal of titles and privileges. In other words, the biography of the leader may be an important source of information on the movement.

Leaders and members of social movements may be reticent to reveal much about themselves to the inquisitive social scientist, but the information about their lives is sometimes available in their biographies. Thus Robert Welch admits his cynicism about politics in *The Blue Book*, and the John Birch Society attracts members with a similar disposition. Eldridge Cleaver confesses to a life of crime in *Soul on Ice*, and the Black Panther Party develops a theory of America as a "criminal system" in which society, not the individual, is responsible for crime. Duane Pederson frankly admits his past use of drugs in *The Jesus People*, and many of his followers are reformed drug addicts. Of course, autobiographical material is offered selectively, and often helps the movement build legends and myths around its leaders. However, it can be cross-checked with scholarly biographies, and when these are available they are reprinted along with the autobiographies in Part Two.

CONCLUSION

Separately, history and biography are useful sources of information on social movements; together, they are indispensable. As C. Wright Mills contends, without the historical context of leadership, biographical studies become psychoanalytic curiosities. Without biographical details, historical analysis of social movements is impersonal and abstract.

In the remainder of Part One, the issues raised in this chapter are discussed at greater length by C. Wright Mills, Seymour Martin Lipset, and Sidney Hook. Mills discusses the reasons for the neglect of history and biography in postwar sociology. Lipset suggests areas in which history and sociology might benefit from an interchange of concepts and methods. Hook vividly describes the role of hero in history, in a way which suggests the intensity of leadership influences in social movements, and thus the need for biographical studies.

---

[1]Ralph Turner and Lewis Killian, *Collective Behavior* (Englewood Cliffs, N.J.: Prentice-Hall, 1972), p. 246.

[2]C. Wright Mills, "The Uses of History," from *The Sociological Imagination* (New York: Oxford University Press, 1959). Excerpted in Chapter Two of this volume.

[3]Irving Howe and Lewis Coser, *The American Communist Party* (New York: Praeger, 1962). Excerpted in Chapter Five of this volume.

[4]Daniel Bell, "The Background and Development of Marxian Socialism in the U.S.," in *Socialism in American Life*, ed. by D. Egbert and S. Persons (Princeton, N.J.: Princeton University Press, 1952). Excerpted in Chapter Five of this volume.

[5]Irving Horowitz, *The Struggle is the Message* (Berkeley: Glendessary Press, 1970).

[6]Seymour Martin Lipset, *Rebellion in the University* (Boston: Little, Brown and Co., 1972). See also S. M. Lipset, and P. Altbach, eds., *Students in Revolt* (Boston: Houghton-Mifflin Co., 1969).

[7]Richard Flacks, "Revolt of the Youth Intelligentsia," in *The New American Revolution*, ed. by Roderick Aya and Norman Miller (New York: Free Press, 1971).

[8]Will Herberg, *Protestant, Catholic, Jew* (New York: Doubleday, 1955); David Riesman and associates, *The Lonely Crowd* (New Haven: Yale University Press, 1951).

[9]Richard Hofstadter, *Anti-Intellectualism in American Life* (New York: Alfred A. Knopf, 1963); Seymour Martin Lipset and Earl Raab, *The Politics of Unreason* (New York: Harper and Row, 1970).

[10]Peter Stuart, "Revolution Turned Middle-Aged," *Christian Science Monitor*, June 26, 1969. Excerpted in Chapter Five of this book.

[11]A. Forster and B. Epstein, *The Radical Right* (New York: Vintage Books, 1967); Gerald Schomp, *Birchism Was My Business* (New York: Macmillan Co., 1970).

[12]Daniel Bell, *The End of Ideology* (New York: Free Press, 1960). Excerpted in Part Three.

[13]Raymond Aron, *The Opium of the Intellectuals* (London: Martin Secker and Warburg, Ltd., 1957), p. 236.

[14]Turner and Killian, *Collective Behavior*, p. 246.

[15]Sidney Hook, *The Hero in History* (Boston: Beacon Press, 1955). Excerpted in Chapter Four.

[16]Bertram Wolfe, *Three Who Made a Revolution* (New York: Delta Books, 1964).

[17]Biographies of Debs, by H. Wayne Morgan, and Foster, by Paul F. Douglass, are excerpted in Chapter Five.

[18]This distinction was suggested by Professor Robert Bellah in personal communication.

[19]Orrin Klapp, *Collective Search for Identity* (New York: Holt, Rinehart and Winston, 1969). Excerpted in Chapter Ten.

[20]J. Allen Broyles, *The John Birch Society* (Boston: Beacon Press, 1964).

THE USES OF HISTORY

This chapter, taken from a book which firmly established Mills's reputation as a critic of American sociology, is a reassertion of the classic tradition in sociology. The classic tradition emphasizes the historical dynamics of political and religious change, as in the studies of the Protestant ethic by Max Weber. Mills finds conventional sociology shortsighted in both directions—past and future—because of its neglect of history. He recognizes that the historical record can be selective and incomplete, but he argues that sociology cannot afford to neglect history because of its faults. Mills's own work is based on historical and biographical sources.

His study of the "power elite" is based on biographical data, and his study of changes in the composition of the middle class is based on historical data.

Mills was a "new radical" in much of his thinking and writing. Although he disavowed orthodox Marxism, he did reawaken interest in the historical and dynamic processes that Marx analyzed. Mills's emphasis on biography might offend orthodox Marxists who regard the individual as an instrument of historical forces; however, many of the new radicals would agree with Mills's emphasis on the role of the individual in social change.

C. WRIGHT MILLS

SOURCE: *From* The Sociological Imagination *by C. Wright Mills. Copyright © 1959 by Oxford University Press, Inc., Reprinted by permission.*

Social science deals with problems of biography, of history, and of their intersections within social structures. That these three—biography, history, society—are the coordinate points of the proper study of man has been a major platform on which I have stood when criticizing several current schools of sociology whose practitioners have abandoned this classic tradition. The problems of our time—which now include the problem of man's very nature —cannot be stated adequately without consistent practice of the view that history is the shank of social study, and recognition of the need to develop further a psychology of man that is sociologically grounded and historically relevant. Without use of history and without an historical sense of psychological matters, the social scientist cannot adequately state the kinds of problems that ought now to be the orienting points of his studies.

I

The weary debate over whether or not historical study is or should be considered a social science is neither important nor interesting. The conclusion depends so clearly upon what kinds of historians and what kinds of social scientists you are talking about. Some historians are clearly compilers of alleged fact, which they try to refrain from "interpreting"; they are involved, often fruitfully, in some fragment of history and seem unwilling to locate it within any larger range of events. Some are beyond history, lost—often fruitfully so—in trans-historical visions of the coming doom or the coming glory. History as a discipline does invite grubbing for detail, but it also encourages a widening of one's view to embrace epochal pivotal events in the development of social structures.

Perhaps most historians are concerned with "making sure of the facts" needed to understand the historical transformation of social institutions, and with interpreting such facts, usually by means of narratives. Many historians, moreover, do not hesitate to take up in their studies any and every area of social life. Their scope is thus that of social science, although like other social scientists, they may specialize in political history or economic history or the history of ideas. In so far as historians study types of institutions they tend to emphasize changes over some span of time and to work in a non-comparative way; whereas the work of many social scientists in studying types of institutions has been more comparative than historical. But surely this difference is merely one of emphasis and of specialization within a common task.

Many American historians, just now, are very much influenced by the conceptions, problems, and methods of the several social sciences. Barzun and Graff have recently suggested that perhaps "social scientists keep urging historians to modernize their technique" because "social scientists are too busy to read history" and "they do not recognize their own materials when presented in a different pattern."[1]

There are of course more problems of method in any work of history than many historians usually dream of. But nowadays some of them do dream, not so much of method as of epistemology—and in a manner that can only result in a curious retreat from historical reality. The influence upon some historians of certain kinds of "social science" is often quite unfortunate, but it is an influence which is not, as yet, wide enough to require lengthy discussion here.

The master task of the historian is to keep the human record straight, but that is indeed a deceptively simple statement of aim. The historian represents the organized memory of mankind, and that memory, as written history, is enormously malleable. It changes, often quite drastically, from one generation of historians to another—and not merely because more detailed research later introduces new facts and documents into the record. It changes also because of changes in the points of interest and the current framework within which the record is built. These are the criteria of selection from the innumerable facts available, and at the same time the leading interpretations of their meaning. The historian cannot avoid making a selection of facts, although he may attempt to disclaim it by keeping his interpretations slim and circumspect. We did not need George Orwell's imaginative projection in order to know how easily history may be distorted in the process of its continual rewriting, although his *1984* made it dramatically emphatic, and, let us hope, properly frightened some of our historian colleagues.

All these perils of the historian's enterprise make it one of the most theoretical of the human disciplines, which makes the calm unawareness of many historians all the more impressive. Impressive, yes; but also rather unsettling. I suppose there have been periods in which perspectives were rigid and monolithic and in which historians could remain unaware of the themes taken for granted. But ours is not such a period; if historians have no "theory," they may provide materials for the writing of history, but they cannot themselves write it. They can entertain, but they cannot keep the record straight. That task now requires explicit attention to much more than "the facts."

The productions of historians may be thought of as a great file indispensable to all social science—I believe this a true and fruitful view. History as a discipline is also sometimes considered to contain all social science—but only by a few misguided "humanists." More fundamental than either view is the idea that every social science—or better, every well-considered social study—requires an historical scope of conception and a full use of historical materials. This simple notion is the major idea for which I am arguing.

At the beginning, perhaps we should confront one frequent objection to the use of historical materials by social scientists: It is held that such materials are not precise or even known fully enough to permit their use in comparisons with the better confirmed and more exact contemporary materials available. This object does of course point to a very worrisome problem of social inquiry, but it has force only if one limits the kinds of information admitted. As I have already argued, the requirements of one's problem, rather than the limitations of any one rigid method, should be and have been the classic social analyst's paramount consideration. The objection, moreover, is relevant only for certain problems and may, in fact, frequently be turned around: For many problems we can obtain adequate information only about the past. The fact of official and unofficial secrecy, and the widespread use of public relations, are contemporary facts which surely must be taken into account as we judge the reliability of information about the past and about the present. This objection, in a word, is merely another version of the methodological inhibition, and often a feature of the "know-nothing" ideology of the politically quiescent.

II

More important than the extent to which historians are social scientists, or how they should behave, is the still more controversial point that the social sciences are themselves historical disciplines. To fulfill their tasks, or even to state them well, social scientists must use the materials of history. Unless one assumes some trans-historical theory of the nature of history, or that man in society is a non-historical entity, no social science can be assumed to transcend history. All sociology worthy of the name is "historical sociology." It is, in Paul Sweezy's excellent phrase, an attempt to write "the present as history." There are several reasons for this intimate relation of history and sociology:

(1) In our very statement of what-is-to-be-explained, we need the fuller range that can be provided only by knowledge of the historical varieties of human society. That a given question—the relations of forms of nationalism with types of militarism, e.g.— must often be given a different answer when it is asked of different societies and periods means that the question itself often needs to be re-formulated. We need the variety provided by history in order even to ask sociological questions properly, much less to answer them. The answers or explanations we would offer are often, if not usually, in terms of comparisons. Comparisons are required in order to understand what may be the essential conditions of whatever we are trying to understand, whether forms of slavery or specific meanings of crime, types of family or peasant communities or collective farms. We must observe whatever we are interested in under a variety of circumstances. Otherwise we are limited to flat description.

To go beyond that, we must study the available range of social structures, including the historical as well as the contemporary. If we do not take into account the range, which does not of course mean all existing cases, our statements cannot be empirically adequate. Such regularities or relations as may obtain among several features of society cannot be clearly discerned. Historical types, in short, are a very important part of what we are studying; they are also indispensable to our explanations of it. To eliminate such materials—the record of all that man has done and become— from our studies would be like pretending to study the process of birth but ignoring motherhood.

If we limit ourselves to one national unit of one contemporary (usually Western) society, we cannot possibly hope to catch many really fundamental differences among human types and social institutions. This general truth has one rather specific meaning for work in social science: In the cross-section moment of any one society there may often be so many common denominators of belief, value, institutional form, that no matter how detailed and precise our study, we will not find truly significant differences among the people and institutions at this one moment in this one society. In fact, the one-time-and-one-locale studies often assume or imply a homogeneity which, if true, very much needs *to be taken as a problem*. It cannot fruitfully be reduced, as it so often is in current research practice, to a problem of sampling procedure. It cannot be formulated as a problem within the terms of one moment and one locale.

Societies seem to differ with respect to the range of variation of specific phenomena within them as well as, in a more general way, with respect to their degree of social homogeneity. As Morris Ginsberg has remarked, if something we are studying "exhibits sufficient individual variations within the same society, or at the same period of time, it may be possible to establish real connections without going outside that society or period."[2] That is often true, but usually it is not so certain that it may simply be assumed; to know whether or not it is true, we must often design our studies as comparisons of social structures. To do that in an adequate way usually requires that we make use of the variety provided by history. The problem of social homogeneity—as in the modern mass society, or, in contrast, as in the traditional society—cannot even be properly stated, much less adequately solved, unless we consider in a comparative way the range of contemporary and historical societies.

The meaning, for example, of such key themes of political science as "public" and "public opinion" cannot be made clear without such work. If we do not take a fuller range into our study, we often condemn ourselves to shallow and misleading results. I do not suppose, for example, that anyone would argue with the statement that the fact of political indifference is one of the major facts of the contemporary political scene in Western societies. Yet in those studies of "the political psychology of voters" which are non-comparative and non-historical we do not find even a classification of "voters"—or of "political men"—that really takes into account such indifference. In fact, the historically specific idea of such political indifference, and much less its meaning, cannot be formulated in the usual terms of such voting studies.

To say of peasants of the pre-industrial world that they are "politically indifferent" does not carry the same meaning as to say the same of man in modern mass society. For one thing, the importance of political institutions to ways of life and their conditions are quite different in the two types of society. For another thing, the formal opportunity to become politically engaged differs. And for another, the expectation of political involvement raised by the entire course of bourgeois democracy in the modern West has not always been raised in the pre-industrial world. To understand "political indifference," to explain it, to grasp its meaning for modern societies requires that we consider the quite various types and conditions of indifference, and to do that we must examine historical and comparative materials.

(2) A-historical studies usually tend to be static or very short-term studies of limited milieux. That is only to be expected, for we more readily become aware of larger structures when they are changing, and we are likely to become aware of such changes only when we broaden our view to include a suitable historical span. Our chance to understand how smaller milieux and larger structures interact, and our chance to understand the larger causes at work in these limited milieux thus require us to deal with historical materials. Awareness of structure, in all the meanings of this central term, as well as adequate statement of the troubles and problems of limited milieux, require that we recognize and that we practice the social sciences as historical disciplines.

Not only are our chances of becoming aware of structure increased by historical work; we cannot hope to understand any single society, even as a static affair, without the use of historical materials. The image of any society is an historically specific image. What Marx called the "principle of historical specificity" refers, first, to a guide-line: any given society is to be understood in terms of the specific period in which it exists. However "period" may be defined, the institutions, the ideologies, the types of men and women prevailing in any given period constitute something of a unique pattern. This does not mean that such an historical type cannot be compared with others, and certainly not that the pattern can be grasped only intuitively. But it does mean—and this is the second reference of the principle—that within this historical type various mechanisms of change come to some specific kind of intersection. These mechanisms, whick Karl Mannheim—following John Stuart Mill—called "principia media," are the very mechanisms that the social scientist, concerned with social structure, wishes to grasp.

Early social theorists tried to formulate invariant laws of society—laws that would hold of all societies, just as the abstracted procedures of physical science had led to laws that cut beneath the qualitative richness of "nature." There is, I believe, no "law" stated by any social scientist that is trans-historical, that must not be understood as having to do with the specific structure of some period. Other "laws" turn out to be empty abstractions or quite confused tautologies. The only meaning of "social laws" or even of "social regularities" is such *principia media* as we may discover, or if you wish, construct, for a social structure within an historically specific era. We do not know any universal principles of historical change; the mechanisms of change we do know vary with the social structure we are examining. For historical change is change of social structures, of the relations among their component parts. Just as there is a variety of social structures, there is a variety of principles of historical change.

(3) That knowledge of the history of a society is often indispensable to its understanding becomes quite clear to any economist or political scientist or sociologist once he leaves his advanced industrial nation to examine the institutions in some different social structure—in the Middle East, in Asia, in Africa. In the study of "his own country" he has often smuggled in the history; knowledge of it is embodied in the very conceptions with which he works. When he takes up a fuller range, when he compares, he becomes more aware of the historical as intrinsic to what he wants to understand and not merely as "general background."

In our time problems of the Western societies are almost inevitably problems of the world. It is perhaps one defining characteristic of our period that it is one in which for the first time the varieties of social worlds it contains are in serious, rapid, and obvious interplay. The study of our period must be a comparative examination of these worlds and of their interactions. Perhaps that is why what was once the anthropologist's exotic preserve, has become the world's "underdeveloped countries," which economists no less than political scientists and sociologists regularly include among their objects of study. That is why some of the very best sociology being done today is work on world areas and regions.

Comparative study and historical study are very deeply involved with each other. You cannot understand the underdeveloped, the Communist, the capitalist political economies as they exist in the world today by flat, timeless comparisons. You must expand the temporal reach of your analysis. To understand and to explain the comparative facts as they lie before you today, you must know the historical phases and the historical reasons for varying rates and varying directions of development and lack of development. You must know, for example, why the colonies founded by Westerners in North America and Australia in the sixteenth and seventeenth centuries became in due course industrially flourishing capitalist societies, but those in India, Latin America, and Africa remained impoverished, peasant, and underdeveloped right up into the twentieth century.

Thus the historical viewpoint leads to the comparative study of societies: you cannot understand or explain the major phases through which any modern Western nation has passed, or the shape that it assumes today, solely in terms of its own national history. I do not mean merely that in historical reality it has interacted with the development of other societies; I mean also that the mind cannot even formulate the historical and sociological problems of this one social structure without understanding them in contrast and in comparison with other societies.

(4) Even if our work is not explicitly comparative—even if we are concerned with some limited area of one national social structure—we need historical materials. Only by an act of abstraction that unnecessarily violates social reality can we try to freeze some knife-edge moment. We may of course construct such static glimpses or even panoramas, but we cannot conclude our work with such constructions. Knowing that what we are studying is subject to change, on the simplest of descriptive levels, we must ask: What are the salient trends? To answer that question we must make a statement of at least "from what" and "to what."

Our statement of trend may be very short-term or of epochal length; that will of course depend upon our purpose. But usually, in work of any scale, we find a need for trends of considerable length. Longer-term trends are usually needed if only in order to overcome historical provincialism: the assumption that the present is a sort of autonomous creation.

If we want to understand the dynamic changes in a contemporary social structure, we must try to discern its longer-run developments, and in terms of them ask: What are the mechanics by which these trends have occurred, by which the structure of this society is changing? It is in questions such as these that our concern with trends comes to a climax. The climax has to do with the historical transition from one epoch to another and with what we may call the structure of an epoch.

The social scientist wishes to understand the nature of the present epoch, to outline its structure and to discern the major forces at work within it. Each epoch, when properly defined, is "an intelligible field of study" that reveals mechanics of history-making peculiar to it. The role of power elites, for example, in the making of history, varies according to the extent to which the institutional means of decisions are centralized.

The notion of the structure and dynamics of "the modern period," and of such essential and unique features as it may have, is central, although often unacknowledged, to the social sciences. Political scientists study the modern state; economists, modern capitalism. Sociologists—especially in their dialectic with Marxism—pose many of their problems in terms of "the characteristics of modern times," and anthropologists use their sensibilities to the modern world in their examinations of pre-literate societies. Perhaps most classic problems of modern social science—of political science and economics no less than of sociology—have, in fact, had to do with one rather specific historical interpretation: the interpretation of the rise, the components, the shape, of the urban industrial societies of The Modern West—usually in contrast with The Feudal Era.

Many of the conceptions most commonly used in social science have to do with the historical transition from the rural community of feudal times to the urban society of the modern age: Maine's "status" and "contract," Tönnies's "community" and "society," Weber's "status" and "class," St. Simon's "three stages," Spencer's "military" and "industrial," Pareto's "circulation of elites," Cooley's "primary and secondary groups," Durkheim's "mechanical" and "organic," Redfield's "folk" and "urban," Becker's "sacred" and "secular," Lasswell's "bargaining society" and "garrison state"—these, no matter how generalized in use, are all historically-rooted conceptions. Even those who believe they do not work historically, generally reveal by their use of such terms some notion of historical trends and even a sense of period.

It is in terms of this alertness to the shape and the dynamics of "the modern period," and to the nature of its crises, that the social scientist's standard concern with "trends" ought to be understood. We study trends in an attempt to go behind events and to make orderly sense of them. In such studies we often try to focus on each trend just a little ahead of where it is now, and more importantly, to see all the trends at once, as moving parts of the total structure of the period. It is, of course, intellectually easier (and politically more advisable) to acknowledge one trend at a time, keeping them scattered, as it were, than to make the effort to see them all together. To the literary empiricist. writing balanced little essays, first on this and then on that, any attempt to "see it whole" often seems an "extremist exaggeration."

There *are* of course many intellectual dangers in the attempt to "see it whole." For one thing, what one man sees as a whole, another sees as only a part, and sometimes, for lack of synoptic vision, the attempt becomes overwhelmed by the need for description. The attempt may of course be biased, but I do not think any more so than the selection of precisely examinable detail without reference to any idea of any whole, for such selection must be arbitrary. In historically oriented work, we are also liable to confuse "prediction" with "description." These two, however, are not to be sharply separated, and they are not the only ways of looking at trends. We can examine trends in an effort to answer the question "where are we going?"—and that is what social scientists are often trying to do. In doing so, we are trying to study history rather than to retreat into it, to pay attention to contemporary trends without being "merely journalistic," to gauge the future of these trends without being merely prophetic. All this is hard to do. We must remember that we *are* dealing with historical materials; that they do change very rapidly; that there are countertrends. And we have always to balance the immediacy of the knife-edge present with the generality needed to bring out the meaning of specific trends for the period as a whole. But above all, the social scientist is trying to see the several major trends together—structurally, rather than as happenings in a scatter of milieux, adding up to nothing new, in fact not adding up at all. This is the aim that lends to the study of trends its relevance to the understanding of a period, and which demands full and adroit use of the materials of history.

III

There is one "use of history," rather common in social science to-day, that is, in fact, more a ritual than a genuine use. I refer to the dull little padding known as "sketching in the historical back-ground," with which studies of contemporary society are often prefaced, and to the ad hoc procedure known as "giving an his-torical explanation." Such explanations, resting upon the past of a single society, are seldom adequate. There are three points which should be made about them:

First, I think we must accept the point that we must often study history in order to get rid of it. By this I mean that what are often taken as historical explanations would better be taken as part of the statement of that which is to be explained.. Rather than "ex-plain" something as "persistence from the past," we ought to ask, "Why has it persisted?" Usually we will find that the answer varies according to the phases through which whatever we are studying has gone; for each of these phases we may then attempt to find out what role it has played, and how and why it passed on to the next phase.

Second, in work on a contemporary society, I think it is very often a good rule first to attempt to explain its contemporary features in terms of their contemporary function. This means to locate them, to see them as parts of and even as due to other features of their contemporary setting. If only to define them, to delimit them clearly, to make their components more specific, it is best to begin with a more or less narrow—although still of course historical—span.

In their work on the adult problems of individuals, some neo-Freudians—most clearly perhaps Karen Horney—seem to have come to the use of a similar order of procedure. One works back to the genetic, biographical causes only after having exhausted the contemporary features and setting of the character. And of course, a classic debate on the whole matter has occurred be-tween the functional and the historical schools of anthropology. One reason for it, I suppose, is that "historical explanations" so often become conservative ideologies: institutions have taken a long time to evolve, and accordingly they are not to be tampered with hastily. Another is that historical consciousness so often be-comes the root of one kind of radical ideology: institutions are after all transitory; accordingly these particular institutions are not eternal or "natural" to man; they too will change. Both these views often rest upon a kind of historical determinism or even inevitability that may easily lead to a quiescent posture—and a mistaken conception of how history has been and how it can be made. I do not want to mute such historical sense as I have worked hard to acquire, but neither do I want to prop up my ways of explanation with conservative or radical uses of the notion of historical fate. I do not accept "fate" as a universal historical category, as I shall explain later on.

My final point is even more controversial, but if it is true, it is of considerable importance: I believe that periods and societies differ in respect to whether or not understanding them requires direct references to "historical factors." The historical nature of a given society in a given period may be such that "the historical past" is only indirectly relevant to its understanding.

It is, of course, quite clear that to understand a slow-moving society, trapped for centuries in a cycle of poverty and tradition and disease and ignorance, requires that we study the historical ground, and the persistent historical mechanisms of its terrible entrapment in its own history. Explanation of that cycle, and of the mechanics of each of its phases, requires a very deep-going historical analysis. What is to be explained, first of all, is the mechanism of the full cycle.

But the United States, for example, or the north-western European nations, or Australia, in their present condition, are not trapped in any iron cycle of history. That kind of cycle—as in the desert world of Ibn Khaldoun[3]—does not grip them. All attempts to understand them in such terms, it seems to me, have failed, and tend in fact to become trans-historical nonsense.

The *relevance* of history, in short, is itself subject to the principle of historical specificity. "Everything," to be sure, may be said always to have "come out of the past," but the meaning of that phrase—"to come out of the past"—is what is at issue. Sometimes there are quite new things in the world, which is to say that "history" does and "history" does not "repeat itself"; it depends upon the social structure and upon the period with whose history we are concerned.[4]

That this sociological principle may be applicable to the United

States today, that ours may be a society in a period for which historical explanations are less relevant than for many other societies and periods, goes far, I believe, to help us to understand several important features of American social science: (1) why many social scientists, concerned only with contemporary Western societies or, even more narrowly, only with the United States, consider historical study irrelevant to their work; (2) why some historians talk now, rather wildly it seems to me, about Scientific History and attempt in their work to use highly formalist, even explicitly a-historical, techniques; (3) why other historians so often give us the impression, especially in the Sunday supplements, that history is indeed bunk, that it is a myth-making about the past for current ideological uses, both liberal and conservative. The past of the United States is indeed a wonderful source for happy images; and—if I am correct about the contemporary irrelevance of much history—that very fact makes such ideological use of history all the easier.

The relevance of historical work to the tasks and to the promise of social science is not, of course, confined to "historical explanations" of this one "American type" of social structure. Moreover, this notion of the varying relevance of historical explanation is itself an historical idea, which must be debated and tested on historical grounds. Even for this one type of contemporary society, the irrelevance of history can easily be pushed too far. It is only by comparative studies that we can become aware of the *absence* of certain historical phases from a society, which is often quite essential to understanding its contemporary shape. The absence of a Feudal Era is an essential condition of many features of American society, among them the character of its elite and its extreme fluidity of status, which has so often been confused with lack of class structure and "lack of class consciousness." Social scientists may—in fact, many now do—attempt to retreat from history by means of undue formality of concept and technique. But these attempts require them to make assumptions about the nature of history and of society that are neither fruitful nor true. Such a retreat from history makes it impossible—and I choose the word with care—to understand precisely the most contemporary features of this one society, which is an historical structure that we cannot hope to understand unless we are guided by the sociological principle of historical specificity.

IV

The problems of social and historical psychology are in many ways the most intriguing that we can study today. It is in this area that the major intellectual traditions of our times, in fact of Western civilization, now come to a most exciting confluence. It is in this area that "the nature of human nature"—the generic image of man, inherited from the Enlightenment—has in our time been brought into question by the rise of totalitarian governments, by ethnographic relativism, by discovery of the great potential of irrationality in man, and by the very rapidity with which men and women can apparently be historically transformed.

We have come to see that the biographies of men and women, the kinds of individuals they variously become, cannot be understood without reference to the historical structures in which the milieux of their everyday life are organized. Historical transformations carry meanings not only for individual ways of life, but for the very character—the limits and possibilities of the human being. As the history-making unit, the dynamic nation-state is also the unit within which the variety of men and women are selected and formed, liberated and repressed—it is the man-making unit. That is one reason why struggles between nations and between blocs of nations are also struggles over the types of human beings that will eventually prevail in the Middle East, in India, in China, in the United States; that is why culture and politics are now so intimately related; and that is why there is such need and such demand for the sociological imagination. For we cannot adequately understand "man" as an isolated biological creature, as a bundle of reflexes or a set of instincts, as an "intelligible field" or a system in and of itself. Whatever else he may be, man is a social and an historical actor who must be understood, if at all, in close and intricate interplay with social and historical structures.

There is, of course, no end of arguments about the relations between "psychology" and "the social sciences." Most of the arguments have been formal attempts to integrate a variety of ideas about "the individual" and "the group." No doubt they are all useful, in some way, to somebody; fortunately, in our attempt to formulate here the scope of social science, they need not concern us. However psychologists may define their field of work, the economist, the sociologist, the political scientist, the anthropologist, and the historian, in their studies of human society, must make assumptions about "human nature." These assumptions now usually fall into the borderline discipline of "social psychology."

Interest in this area has increased because psychology, like history, is so fundamental to work in social sciences that in so far as psychologists have not turned to the problems involved, social scientists have become their own psychologists. Economists, long the most formalized of social scientists, have become aware that the old "economic man," hedonistic and calculating, can no longer be assumed as the psychological foundation of an adequate study of economic institutions. Within anthropology there has grown up a strong interest in "personality and culture"; within sociology as well as psychology, "social psychology" is now a busy field of study.

In reaction to these intellectual developments, some psychologists have taken up a variety of work in "social psychology," others have attempted, in a variety of ways, to re-define psychology, so as to retain a field of study apart from obviously social factors, and some have confined their activities to work in human physiology. I do not wish to examine here the academic specialties within psychology—a field now greatly torn and split—much less to judge them.

There is one style of psychological reflection which has not usually been taken up explicitly by academic psychologists but which none the less has exerted influence upon them—as well as upon our entire intellectual life. In psychoanalysis, and especially in the work of Freud himself, the problem of the nature of human nature is stated in its broadest bearings. During the last generation, in brief, two steps forward have been taken by the less rigid of the psychoanalysts and those influenced by them:

First, the physiology of the individual organism was transcended, and there began the study of those little family circles in which such dreadful melodramas occur. Freud may be said to have discovered from an unexpected viewpoint—the medical— the analysis of the individual in his parental family. Of course, the "influence" of the family upon man had been noticed; what was new was that as a social institution it became, in Freud's view, intrinsic to the inner character and life-fate of the individual.

Second, the social element in the lens of psychoanalysis was greatly broadened, especially by what must be called sociological work on the super-ego. In America, to the psychoanalytic tradition was joined one having quite different sources, which came to early flower in the social behaviorism of George H. Mead. But then a limitation or a hesitancy set in. The small-scale setting of "interpersonal relations" is now clearly seen; the broader context in which these relations themselves, and hence the individual himself, are situated has not been. There are, of course, exceptions, notably Erich Fromm, who has related economic and religious institutions and traced out their meanings for types of individuals. One reason for the general hesitancy is the limited social role of the analyst: his work and his perspective are professionally tied to the individual patient; the problems of which he can readily become aware, under the specialized conditions of his practice, are limited. Unfortunately, psychoanalysis has not become a firm and integral part of academic research.[5]

The next step forward in psychoanalytic studies is to do fully for other institutional areas what Freud began to do so magnificently for kinship institutions of a selected type. What is needed is the idea of social structure as a composition of institutional orders, each of which we must study psychologically as Freud studied certain kinship institutions. In psychiatry—the actual therapy of "interpersonal" relations—we have already begun to raise questions about a troublesome central point: the tendency to root values and norms in the supposed needs of the individuals *per se*. But if the individual's very nature cannot be understood without close reference to social reality, then we must analyze it in such reference. Such analysis includes not only the locating of the individual, as a biographical entity, within various interpersonal milieux—but the locating of these milieux within the social structures which they form.

V

On the basis of developments in psychoanalysis, as well as in social psychology as a whole, it is now possible to state briefly the psychological concerns of the social sciences. I list here, in the barest of summary, only those propositions which I take as the most fruitful hunches, or, at the least, as legitimate assumptions on the part of the working social scientist.[6]

The life of an individual cannot be adequately understood without references to the institutions within which his biography is enacted. For this biography records the acquiring, dropping, modifying, and in a very intimate way, the moving from one role to another. One is a child in a certain kind of family, one is a playmate in a certain kind of child's group, a student, a workman, a foreman, a general, a mother. Much of human life consists of playing such roles within specific institutions. To understand the biography of an individual, we must understand the significance and meaning of the roles he has played and does play; to understand these roles we must understand the institutions of which they are a part.

But the view of man as a social creature enables us to go much deeper than merely the external biography as a sequence of social roles. Such a view requires us to understand the most internal and "psychological" features of man: in particular, his self-image and his conscience and indeed the very growth of his mind. It may well be that the most radical discovery within recent psychology and social science is the discovery of how so many of the most intimate features of the person are socially patterned and even implanted. Within the broad limits of the glandular and nervous apparatus, the emotions of fear and hatred and love and rage, in all their varieties, must be understood in close and continual reference to the social biography and the social context in which they are experienced and expressed. Within the broad limits of the physiology of the sense organs, our very perception of the physical world, the colors we discriminate, the smells we become aware of, the noises we hear, are socially patterned and socially circumscribed. The motivations of men, and even the varying extents to which various types of men are typically aware of them, are to be understood in terms of the vocabularies of motive that prevail in a society and of social changes and confusions among such vocabularies.

The biography and the character of the individual cannot be understood merely in terms of milieux, and certainly not entirely in terms of the early environments—those of the infant and the child. Adequate understanding requires that we grasp the interplay of these intimate settings with their larger structural framework, and that we take into account the transformations of this framework, and the consequent effects upon milieux. When we understand social structures and structural changes as they bear upon more intimate scenes and experiences, we are able to understand the causes of individual conduct and feelings of which men in specific milieux are themselves unaware. The test of an adequate conception of any type of man cannot rest upon whether individuals of this type find it pleasantly in line with their own self-images. Since they live in restricted milieux, men do not and cannot be expected to know all the causes of their condition and the limits of their selfhood. Groups of men who have truly adequate views of themselves and of their own social positions are indeed rare. To assume the contrary, as is often done by virtue of the very methods used by some social scientists, is to assume a degree of rational self-consciousness and self-knowledge that not even eighteenth-century psychologists would allow. Max Weber's idea of "The Puritan Man," of his motives and of his function within religious and economic institutions, enables us to understand him better than he understood himself: Weber's use of the notion of structure enabled him to transcend "the individual's" own awareness of himself and his milieux.

The relevance of earlier experience, "the weight" of childhood in the psychology of adult character, is itself relative to the type of childhood and the type of social biography that prevail in various societies. It is, for example, now apparent that the role of "the father" in the building of a personality must be stated within the limits of specific types of families, and in terms of the place such families occupy within the social structure of which these families are a part.

The idea of social structure cannot be built up only from ideas or facts about a specific series of individuals and their reactions to their milieux. Attempts to explain social and historical events on the basis of psychological theories about "the individual" often rest upon the assumption that society is nothing but a great scatter of individuals and that, accordingly, if we know all about these "atoms" we can in some way add up the information and thus know about society. It is not a fruitful assumption. In fact, we cannot even know what is more elemental about "the individual" by any psychological study of him as a socially isolated creature. Except in the abstract building of models, which of course may be useful, the economist cannot assume The Economic Man; nor can the psychiatrist of family life (and practically all psychiatrists are, in fact, specialists of this one social area) assume the classical Oedipal Man. For just as the structural relations of economic and political roles are now often decisive for understanding the economic conduct of individuals, so are the great changes, since Victorian fatherhood, in the roles within the family and in the family's location as an institution within modern societies.

The principle of historical specificity holds for psychology as well as for the social sciences. Even quite intimate features of man's inner life are best formulated as problems within specific historical contexts. To realize that this is an entirely reasonable assumption, one has only to reflect for a moment upon the wide variety of men and women that is displayed in the course of human history. Psychologists, as well as social scientists, should indeed think well before finishing any sentences the subject of which is "man."

The human variety is such that no "elemental" psychologies, no theory of "instincts," no principles of "basic human nature" of which we know, enables us to account for the enormous human variety of types and individuals. Anything that can be asserted about man apart from what is inherent in the social-historical realities of human life will refer merely to the wide biological limits and potentialities of the human species. But within these limits and rising out of these potentialities, a panorama of human types confronts us. To attempt to explain it in terms of a theory of "basic human nature" is to confine human history itself in some arid little cage of Concepts about "human nature"—as often as not constructed from some precise and irrelevant trivialities about mice in a maze.

Barzun and Graff remark that "The title of Dr. Kinsey's famous book *Sexual Behavior in the Human Male* is a striking instance of a hidden—and in this case false—assumption: the book is not about human males, but about men in the United States in the mid-twentieth century. . . . The very idea of human nature is an assumption of social science and to say that it forms the subject of its reports is to beg the fundamental question. There may be nothing but 'human culture,' a highly mutable affair."[7]

The idea of some "human nature" common to man as man is a violation of the social and historical specificity that careful work in the human studies requires; at the very least, it is an abstraction that social students have not earned the right to make. Surely we ought occasionally to remember that in truth we do not know much about man, and that all the knowledge we do have does not entirely remove the element of mystery that surrounds his variety as it is revealed in history and biography. Sometimes we do want to wallow in that mystery, to feel that we are, after all, a part of it, and perhaps we should; but being men of the West, we will inevitably also study the human variety, which for us means removing the mystery from our view of it. In doing so, let us not forget what it is we are studying and how little we know of man, of history, of biography, and of the societies of which we are at once creatures and creators.

---

[1]Jacques Barzun and Henry Graff, *The Modern Researcher*, New York, Harcourt, Brace, 1957, p. 221.

[2]Morris Ginsberg, *Essays in Sociology and Social Philosophy*, Vol. II, 39, London, Heinemann, 1956.

[3]See Muhsin Mahdi, *Ibn Khaldoun's Philosophy of History*, London, George Allen & Unwin, 1957; and *Historical Essays*, London, Macmillan, 1957, which contains H. R. Trevor-Roper's revealing comment on it.

[4]I note supportive reasoning in an excellent account of types of labor history, for example, by Walter Galenson: "... the marginal revenue from cultivating the older ground is apt to be small ... in the absence of ... important new material. ... But this is not the only justification for concentrating upon more recent events. The contemporary labor movement differs not only quantitatively but qualitatively from that of thirty years ago. Prior to the 1930's it was sectarian in character; its decisions were not a major economic factor, and it was concerned more with narrow internal problems than with national policy." (Walter Galenson, 'Reflections on the Writing of Labor History,' *Industrial and Labor Relations Review*, October, 1957.) In connection with anthropology, of course, the debate between "functional" and "historical" explanations has long been under way. More often than not anthropologists must be functional because they cannot find out anything about the history of the "cultures" they examine. They really must try to explain the present by the present, seeking explanations in the meaningful interrelations of various contemporary features of a society. For a recent perceptive discussion, see Ernest Gellner, "Time and Theory in Social Anthrolopogy," *Mind*, April 1958.

[5]Another major reason for the tendency to apotheosize "interpersonal relations" is the sponge-like quality and limitations of the word "culture," in terms of which much of the social in man's depths has been recognized and asserted. In contrast with social structure, the concept "culture" is one of the spongiest words in social science, although, perhaps for that reason, in the hands of an expert, enormously useful. In practice, the conception of "culture" is more often a loose reference to social milieux plus "tradition" than an adequate idea of social structure.

[6]For detailed discussion of the point of view expressed here, See Gerth and Mills, *Character and Social Structure*, New York, Harcourt, Brace, 1953.

[7]Barzun and Graff, *The Modern Researcher*, New York, Harcourt, Brace, 1957, pp. 222-223.

HISTORY AND SOCIOLOGY: SOME METHODOLOGICAL CONSIDERATIONS

Lipset here responds to Mills's criticism of American sociology (in Chapter Two) by observing that many sociologists have begun to use historical materials. Lipset, like Mills, notes some of the methodological faults of history. He goes on to suggest that historians adopt concepts and methods from Sociology, e.g. 'reference group' concepts and survey methods. He also suggests that one of the most fertile areas of overlap between history and sociology is the study of social movements. Because they combine religious and political ideology, they are instructive for the study of social and political value conflicts.

Conflict is a sign of social change, and many radical sociologists have analyzed conflict for its role in economic and political changes. Ironically, Mills overlooked much of the conflict that historians have documented. He despaired of finding meaningful conflict in American society. Lipset, on the other hand, found significance in the religious and political conflicts of American history.

SEYMOUR MARTIN LIPSET

SOURCE: From pp. 20–33, "History and Sociology: Some Methodological Considerations," by Seymour M. Lipset, in Sociology and History: Methods, Vol. I, edited by Richard Hofstadter and Seymour Martin Lipset. Copyright © Basic Books, Inc., Publishers, New York, 1968.

American sociology has been criticized for having departed from the historical concerns of its nineteenth century European founders. This departure was characterized by a shift from a macroscopic to a more microscopic focus on society, from studies of social change and aspects of total societies, viewed in a historical and comparative perspective, to the study of interpersonal relations, the structure of small groups, and the analysis of the decision-making process, accompanied by an emphasis on improving the quantitative methodology appropriate to these topics. This change suggested to its critics that modern sociology had lost contact with its original intellectual traditions. The writings of men such as Alexis de Tocqueville, Max Weber, Robert Michels, and Vilfredo Pareto were apparently of contemporary interest only insofar as they had attempted to specify functional relationships and social psychological processes of the type that interested latter-day sociologists.

There are many examples which indicate ways in which sociological research has made major errors by ignoring historical evidence. Oscar Handlin and Stephan Thernstrom have given us an illustration of the weakness of an ahistorical sociology when they demonstrate how W. Lloyd Warner misinterpreted a number of patterns in his Yankee City series of studies of a New England community by relying on contemporary reports concerning past patterns and ignoring the actual history of the community as available in documentory sources.[1] Thernstrom has also pointed out the weakness of many assumptions made about rates of social mobility. He indicates that both sociologists and historians have erred in their interpretations concerning the extent of social mobility in mid-nineteenth-century America by relying either on impressionistic accounts by contemporaries concerning the presumed high rates of upward movement, or on logical deductions concerning an inherent need for a high mobility rate in a rapidly expanding economic system. His detailed quantitative analysis of the actual movement of unskilled workers in Newburyport, Massachusetts, a century ago, suggests a rate of mobility that is lower than has been found in studies of contemporary communities.

THE REVIVAL OF HISTORICAL AND COMPARATIVE SOCIOLOGY

In the last decade, the situation with respect to sociological concern with historical topics has begun to change. There has been a significant revival of historical and comparative sociology. This revival has taken many forms, including interest in the sociology of science, concern with the determinants of change in intellectual life, interest in the evolution of national values, study of past patterns of electoral behavior, analysis of changes in religious life, and the like. The growth of interest in such problems is so recent that many with an interest in sociology, including some in the profession itself, are unaware of the extent to which leading sociologists have become involved in these fields of inquiry.

A significant source of the renewed interest in historical and comparative sociology has been the emergence of the body of inquiry which has been called the sociology of development. This term refers to interest in the processes which affect propensities to "modernize" total societies. As a field of research, it parallels the work of economists on problems of economic development. And just as economists concerned with economic development have recognized that much of what is conventionally termed "economic history" is actually the study of economic development, and that generalizations concerning economic development which are relevant to contemporary "developing economies" can be tested by reference to the past history of developed economies, so sociologists interested in problems of societal modernization and nation building in Africa and Asia have come to understand that the "old states" of the world have much to tell us about these problems. In sociology, as in economics, interest in comparative development has involved a renewed concern with historical analysis.[2]

The re-emergence of historical and comparative sociology does not reflect any general feeling on the part of sociologists that the emphases on quantitative techniques, rigorous methodology, and systematic theory, which have characterized the work of the discipline in recent decades, were misguided. If there is any criticism of these efforts, it is only that they had the temporary effect of narrowing the focus of concern from the macroscopic (total society) to microscopic (small unit) problems, and from concern with patterns of social change to the analysis of the processes determining group behavior, regardless of time or place. In a sense the swing back to the macroscopic and the historical involves an effort to relate the new methodological and theoretical developments to the analysis of total social systems and social change. Much of the logic of inquiry developed and tested with respect to experimental and microscopic sociology and to analysis of current contemporary processes has proven applicable to macroscopic research, including comparative and historical.

SOCIOLOGICAL APPROACHES

If the sociologist has erred in the past by ignoring historical data, the historian has erred in the eyes of the sociologists by ignoring concepts and methods which are as available and useful to the historian as to the sociologist. This does not mean that sociologists seek to turn historians into historical sociologists. From an ideal-typical point of view, the task of the sociologist is to formulate general hypotheses, hopefully set within a larger theoretical framework, and to test them. His interest in the way in which a nation such as the United States formulated a national identity is to specify propositions about the general processes involved in the creation of national identities in new nations. Similarly, his concern with changes in the patterns of American religious participation is to formulate and test hypotheses about the function of religion for other institutions and the social system as a whole. The sociologist of religion seeks to locate the conditions under which chiliastic religion occurs, what kinds of people are attracted to it, what happens to the sects and their adherents under various conditions, and so on. These are clearly not the problems of the historian. History must be concerned with the analysis of the particular set of events or processes. Where the sociologist looks for concepts which subsume a variety of particular descriptive categories, the historian must remain close to the actual happenings and avoid statements which, though linking behavior at one time or place to that elsewhere, lead to a distortion in the description of what occurred in the set of circumstances being analyzed. As Lewis Namier has put it:

"The subject matter of history is human affairs, men in action, things which have happened and how they happened; concrete events fixed in time and space, and their grounding in the thoughts and feelings of men—not things universal and generalized; events as complex and diversified as the men who wrought them, those rational beings whose knowledge is seldom sufficient, whose ideas are but distantly related to reality, and who are never moved by reason alone."[3]

To use concepts and methods developed in sociology or in the other social sciences, however, does not turn the historian into a systematizing social scientist. Rather, these offer him sets of categories with which to order historical materials and possibly enhance the power of his interpretive or causal explanations. Thus, looking at the findings of social science may give a particular historian certain ideas as to types of data to collect which may be pertinent to his problem. For example, in recent years students of stratification have formulated the concept of status discrepancy as an explanatory variable. Status discrepancy refers to situations in which individuals or groups are ranked at different levels of prestige or reward on various dimensions of stratification. A college graduate who is a manual worker is high on one dimension—education—but low on the other—occupation. A political boss may be much higher on the power dimension than he is on prestige. College professors may be higher in prestige than they are in income, and so on.

The students of status discrepancy have postulated that those who are in discrepant positions will behave differently in specific ways from those whose statuses are congruent, i.e., all relatively on the same level. It has been suggested, for example, that individuals subject to status discrepancies are likely to be more liberal politically than others who are in the same income, occupational, or other stratification category as themselves. They are also more likely to react in extreme fashion with respect to political and religious behavior. Clearly, a concept such as this may be of use to the historian. It indicates the need to consider the possibility that the varying status positions might explain the deviation from expected behavior of some individuals or groups in the past. I do not suggest that the sociologist can furnish the historian with certain definite facts to incorporate into his analysis; just the opposite is true—the sociologist is complicating the work of the historian by indicating that he ought to examine even more factors because evidence drawn from sociological studies suggests that these may be relevant.

To take another example, work in sociology and social psychology on attitudes has indicated that the conventional contemporary American definition of liberalism (which assumes that to be liberal means to support socioeconomic policies which favor redistribution of community resources in favor of the underprivileged, the welfare state, trade unions, civil rights for Negroes and other minority groups, civil liberties for unpopular minorities, internationalism, liberal immigration policies and so forth) turns out to create major analytical problems when the actual attitudes of samples of the general population are examined. Opinion studies suggest that there are at least two dimensions of liberalism, economic and noneconomic. The first refers to support for welfare-state reforms, trade unions, planning, redistributive tax policies; the second includes backing for civil rights, civil liberties, internationalism, and similar issues.[4] Moreover the evidence indicates that the less income people have, the more likely they are to be liberal on economic issues, while higher education is closely correlated with noneconomic liberalism. Since the better educated are generally more well-to-do than those with less education, one finds that poor and less-educated people are liberal on economic issues and illiberal on noneconomic ones, while well-educated and well-to-do people tend to be liberal on noneconomic measures and illiberal on economic ones.[5] There are, of course, many who are liberal on both; such a position characterizes the intellectual community and is the policy fostered by the liberal wing of the Democratic party and organizations such as trade unions and civil rights groups which support the liberal coalition. There are those who are illiberal on both dimensions; these include Southern conservatives, lower class Republicans, and many right-wing organizations and political leaders.

The significance of this distinction for the historian is fairly obvious. It should be possible to discover to what extent similar variations existed in the past. Thus, as one illustration, this distinction may be reflected in the fact that in debates over the suffrage in New York State, Federalists and Whigs favored equal suffrage rights for Negroes and whites (noneconomic liberalism), but the Federalists sought to preserve a property franchise (economic class illiberalism). The Democrats, on the other hand, opposed a property requirement, but showed little interest in Negro suffrage.[6] The hypothesis would suggest that xenophobia, nativism, and anti-Catholicism had a strong appeal to less-educated lower-class persons all during the nineteenth century. Thus, the Whig and Republican alliances with nativist and "Know-Nothing" elements may have been their primary means of securing lower-class support away from the Democrats.[7] Such hypotheses might be tested by analyses of the various referenda conducted before, as well as after, the Civil War, which dealt with issues of Negro rights, as well as with suffrage rights for the foreign-born, prohibition, and other noneconomic issues.

In urging that historians apply generalizations developed in contemporary analysis to the past, I am not suggesting that they should assume that such propositions have always been valid, or even that the same relationships among different factors will probably help account for given past events. It is quite possible that under the different conditions of pre-Civil War America, anti-Catholic or antiforeign prejudices were not located preponderantly among the lower strata. However, the hypothesis does suggest the need to investigate the relationship between class and prejudice during that period.

Another group of concepts which may be useful for historians is that subsumed in the terms "frame of reference" and "reference group." These concepts involve the assumption that, to understand the behavior of individuals or groups, it is necessary to locate the framework within which they evaluate or compare stimuli. Implicit here is the assumption that two events or measures which are objectively similar when judged against an absolute standard may have quite varying consequences when viewed from different frames of reference. Thus, an income or occupation which places a man close to the top of the stratification system in a small community may locate him in the lower-middle class in a large city or in the nation as a whole. To specify social location in relative rather than absolute terms may enhance explanatory analysis. To cite an example from my own work, a study of voting patterns in the elections of 1860 indicated that the extent of slavery in Southern counties correlated with the way in which they voted in the presidential race and the subsequent secession referenda. However, if counties are classified in terms of whether they ranked high or low in proportion of slaves in the South as a whole, the correlation is quite low. If the classification of high or low is made within state lines, then the correlation is much higher. High slave counties within state boundaries behaved similarly politically, even though the statistical meaning of high proportion of slaves varied greatly from states with many slaves to those with few.[8] Thus, it would appear that the relative position of areas within the frame of reference of state politics strongly affected their reaction to the secession question.

The concept of reference group has, of course, emerged largely within social psychology as a way of conceptualizing the group authorities from which individuals derive their standards of judgment. To understand the behavior of historically relevant actors, it may often be necessary to locate or impute their reference group, e.g., to determine whether a given political leader judges his actions by comparison with his estimate of those of his noteworthy predecessors, whether a man relates his present behavior to those standards held by his peers when he was young, and the like. Such guides to action may not be located by examining the immediate external pressures on a decision maker, but require detailed biographical knowledge which permits imputations concerning an individual's reference group. As Thomas Cochran, however, points out: "In many cases empirical evidence short of that from interviews by skilled psychologists will not suffice to establish a reference group. Occasionally such information is plausibly given in autobiographies."[9]

There are, of course, many examples of the fruitful use of sociological concepts and hypotheses by historians. Stanley Elkins and Eric McKitrick applied concepts developed in the context of a sociological study of political participation in a contemporary New Jersey housing project to an analysis of the nineteenth-century frontier. Robert Merton has demonstrated the way in which new communities with a homogeneous population faced with a period of problem solving involve a very large proportion of citizens in politically relevant community activities. And Elkins and McKitrick were able to locate comparable processes and factors in new prairie frontier settlements, thus using Merton's propositions to locate the processes underlying many of Turner's assumptions about frontier democracy.[10]

In his study of the formation of political parties in early American history, William Chambers used Max Weber's analysis of the role of charismatic leaders in postrevolutionary situations to interpret George Washington's role in encouraging the trend toward a rational legal basis of authority.[11] He also examined some of the sociological propositions that have been advanced in a comparative context concerning the social requisites for democracy, and related these to the social structure of the early United States. Thus, the explanation for the success of early American democracy is linked to generalizations about factors associated with democratic institutions on a world-wide scale.[12]

Robert Lamb's interest in explaining some of the factors involved in American economic development (particularly in the cotton textile industry) between 1787 and 1816 was explicitly premised on the application of systematic social science approaches to a particular set of events. As Lamb described his method:

[W]e need models descriptive of the structures and functions of national and international communities at moments of time, and of their changes through time. These models should be made by students of entrepreneurship, working with political, social and economic historians. To build such models we need, for example, to trace the pattern of a given social structure such as an extended-kinship system at a moment of time, study its connections with the surrounding community, and follow its changes over time."[13]

In addition, Lamb argued, the weakness of efforts to analyze early American economic development lay in large part in the lack of experience by entrepreneurial historians in dealing with such models. One needed a model with its subsumed hypotheses to indicate the kinds of data to collect, the relationships which needed tracing, and so on. He developed his own research within the context of a model of community decision making. His concern with the decision-making process led him to look for the effective basis of the influence by the successful entrepreneurs on their communities and regions, which he traced to the extended kinship system and family connections.

The efforts of sociologists to differentiate a number of stratification dimensions and to suggest that incongruent positions, high in one dimension, low in another, would affect behavior in determined ways have been applied in various analyses of different events in American history. Thus, the emergence of the temperance movement and the various stages it has taken since the early nineteenth century have been explained in terms of reactions of groups to the tensions inherent in conflicting stratification positions.[14] A number of writers have discussed status tensions as a source of support and leadership for the abolitionist movement.[15] Stanley Elkins applied the analysis of the French sociologist, Emile Durkheim, of the social conditions which result in *anomie*, a social state in which individuals feel disoriented, unrelated to strong norms—and hence more available for recruitment to new movements—to an understanding of the emergence of the abolitionist movement. He suggests the intense expansion of the 1830's resulted in a situation "in which limits were being broken everywhere, in which traditional expectations were disrupted profoundly."[16]

The study of ethnic prejudice and nativist social movements is clearly one in which the substantive interests of historians and sociologists overlap. And here again, propositions concerning status tensions have informed the analysis of historians. John Higham has pointed to status rivalries occasioned by upward mobility as the basic set processes which underlie the conflicts of different ethnic and religious groups. He has applied on the level of broad historical events the same sort of analysis of these tensions that one may find in the detailed community studies by sociologists of the frictions fostered by ethnic and religious status conflicts.[17]

A comprehensive discussion of the application of the concepts of social science to the work of the historian may be found in the report of the Committee on Historical Analysis of the Social Science Research Council. It is interesting to note that the one sociological concept discussed in any detail there is that of social role. The interest in this concept seems to reflect a concern with the need to specify clearly the expectations held by a group or society concerning behavior associated with a given status or position. As Thomas Cochran put it: "Much of the value of history, whether viewed aesthetically or scientifically, depends on assumptions or generalizations regarding anticipated uniformities in role-playing. . . . Knowledge of the intricacy of role analysis can also guard the historian against over-simplified views of the pattern of social interaction."[18]

Perhaps as significant as the interchange of concepts between sociology and history is the transference of methods. Lee Benson has pointed to the failings in much of American political history occasioned by the fact that many historians have attempted to explain political shifts without doing the necessary research on easily available voting statistics.[19] Much as the sociologist prefers to deal with quantitative data drawn from interviews, the historian seems to prefer qualitative materials drawn from printed matter, diaries and letters. The "reasons" often given by historians for the defeat of a particular party may be tested through a simple statistical analysis of voting returns. We can find out, for example, how many of the gains made by the Republicans between 1856 and 1860 occurred in areas which were sharply affected by the depression of the late 1850's, or were shifts to the Republicans of Know-Nothing votes, as contrasted with increases from districts which had shown concern with the slavery issue. Research on the election of 1860 in the South indicates that the division between Breckenridge and Bell, the two candidates who secured most of the vote in that region, correlated greatly with the lines of electoral division which formed around the Jacksonian Democrats three decades earlier. Specifically, Breckenridge, the secessionist Democrat, secured the bulk of his votes from the traditionally Democratic poor-white areas where there were relatively few slaves; while Bell, the antisecessionist Constitutional Union candidate, received most of his votes from areas characterized by plantation agriculture, a high ratio of slaves, and a past tradition of voting Whig. In subsequent referenda and convention delegate elections in late 1860 and early 1861—held not on party lines but on the issue of union or secession—the majority of the plantation areas, which voted for the Constitutional Unionists, opted for secession, while the majority of the low slavery counties, which had backed the secessionist Democrats in the presidential election, voted for the Union. Analysis of shifts of sentiments and behavior of this kind provides firm evidence regarding the trends and processes at work in the American population during the crucial years before the Civil War and raises questions concerning assumptions of a consistent relationship between party policies and opinions of party supporters.[20]

In his effort to spell out ways in which historians may verify generalizations about national character differences, Walter Metzger detailed the way in which sociologists handle multivariate analysis in survey research. As he points out, one of the major problems in drawing conclusions about national character is to distinguish among attributes of societies which are properly characteristic of the culture and those which result from the fact that societies vary in their internal composition, containing more of certain groups or strata than another. Thus, the question may arise as to whether society A differs from B because it is predominantly rural, or Catholic, or has a much higher level of education, rather than because basic values or "character" vary. To test out these possibilities he suggests a simple trick of the sociological trade (one familiar in this discipline but surprisingly little appreciated by historians), namely, to hold factors constant as is done in intranational opinion research. One may compare Catholic Canadians with Catholic Americans, or college-educated Canadians with Americans of comparable education.[21]

In yet another area of political history, the sociologist Sidney Aronson has tested the various assumptions made by historians concerning the supposed introduction of the spoils system by Andrew Jackson. Aronson carefully coded the social background characteristics of the higher civil servants in the administrations of John Adams and Thomas Jefferson, and of John Quincy Adams and Andrew Jackson, much as one does with interview data. He is able to show that the overwhelming majority in all four administrations came from the socioeconomic elite.[22] This study offers another example of the way in which contemporary observers may be deceived about what is happening around them, particularly when they are making statistical guesses about facts which actually are unavailable to them. The ideology of a group may lead it to claim to be doing things which in fact it is not doing. Thus, Jackson sought to appeal to a mass electorate, the claim that he was throwing old Federalists from office and replacing them by good plebeian Democrats may have been good politics. Both friend and foe alike may have agreed in print concerning his actions, and thus misled not only contemporaries but also future historians.

Paul Lazarsfeld has pointed out the utility for historical research of the opinion survey, a method long used by sociologists.[23] He has called the attention of historians to the enormous quantities of information on a multitude of issues which have been gathered by commercial and academic polling organizations over the past three decades. Unlike historians dealing with pre-New Deal events, contemporary historians of the New Deal period have available to them, as will historians in later decades or centuries who will study the twentieth century, fairly reliable data about the state of public opinion, voting behavior, and various other activities such as church attendance, membership in voluntary organizations, drinking and gambling habits, and much more. In evaluating Roosevelt's or Eisenhower's role in a foreign policy crisis, the historian will be able to know what the American people thought of the issues. He will be able to differentiate as to the characteristics of those who attended church regularly, as to shifts in sentiments toward McCarthy or racial integration, and so on.

To do this, however, the historian will have to take courses in survey analysis—he may want to learn certain statistical techniques so as to know how to make up various attitude scales, or to evaluate the validity and reliability of his results. And to maximize the use of survey data for future historians, those of the present may want to dictate some of the questions which are asked by contemporary pollsters. For the sake of future generations of historians, it may be useful to repeat the identical questions about certain attitudes and behaviors every few years so that a reliable estimate of changes may be made.

At the moment, however, few historians, including those dealing with the modern period of American history, seem to have been aware of the uses of survey data for their problems. One may point to books on the 1930's which make inferences concerning the social base of the Coughlin movement, isolationism, and popular attitudes toward the third term or toward Roosevelt's proposal to enlarge the Supreme Court, which were written in apparent ignorance of the body of opinion data dealing with these matters. And in a number of cases, historians relying on their interpretation of election results, or assuming that congressional or press reaction reflected predominant trends among the public, have been quite wrong in their conclusions. Such mistakes are not likely to recur since many younger historians have now begun to apply quantitative techniques to the study of political history.

While the sociologist believes that he might help the historian methodologically, he would like assistance from the historian to test some of his generalizations about changes in social structure. Many social scientists have presented hypotheses concerning the relationship of changes in the occupational and class structures to other institutions. It has been suggested, for example, that the development of a predominantly bureaucratic and tertiary economy, oriented around leisure and consumption, has led to a change in many fundamental patterns such as child-rearing practices, the content of American religion, or the modal personality structure. In *The First New Nation* I have questioned the validity of many of these propositions concerning fundamental changes in American values and behavior, but for the most part, I, too, relied heavily on extant reports of subjective observations.[24] The techniques of content analysis, which involve the coding of qualitative documents so as to permit quantification, have obvious applicability to efforts to verify assumptions concerning the direction and extent of such changes. Analyses of diaries and other autobiographical materials, coding of the themes of ministers' sermons, and examination of newspaper discussions of how to raise children could undoubtedly tell us a great deal about social changes.[25]

Some indication of the utility of content analysis applied to a historical issue may be found in a study dealing with the extend to which consciousness of being Americans rather than British colonials, overseas Englishmen, or residents of a particular colony, existed among the inhabitants of the colonies prior to the American Revolution. Richard Merritt analyzed the symbols in newspapers from Massachusetts, New York, Pennsylvania, and Virginia from 1735 to 1775. He found a sharp increase in reference to American rather than English events, and in the use of the term Americans.[26]

It is important to recognize that values expressed in the mass media at any given time may not be a good indicator of popular attitudes. Thus a recent analysis by Fred Greenstein, which compares a "forgotten body of survey data" from the late nineteenth and early twentieth centuries (questionnaire studies of school children's ideals and occupational aspirations) with comparable ones from recent years, reports little change over a 60-year period. His results contradict the assumption of writers such as David Riesman, William Whyte, Erich Fromm, and others, that the achievement goal or "Protestant ethic" has been declining in American life. The one major change which seems to have occurred is a decline in references to national heroes, particularly to George Washington. Since some studies of the themes of children's textbooks or popular fictional idols, these findings argue for the thesis that changes in social ideology, as expressed by popular or textbook writers, need have little relationship to variations in the underlying popular values. And latterday intellectuals who conclude that intellectual consensus equals popular agreement may be confounding "rationalization with reality."[27]

---

[1]See Handlin's reviews of two books of W. L. Warner and associates, "The Social Life of a Modern Community," New England Quarterly, XV (1942), 556, and "The Social System of the Modern Factory," Journal of Economic History, VII (1947), 277; and Stephan Thernstrom, Poverty and Progress: Social Mobility in a Nineteenth Century City (Cambridge: Harvard University Press, 1964), and his chapter in this book [Sociology and History: Methods, Vol. I, ed. Hofstadter and Lipset].

[2]See T. H. Marshall, Class, Citizenship, and Social Development (New York: Doubleday, 1964).

[3]Lewis Namier, "History and Political Culture," in Fritz Stern, ed., *The Varieties of History* (New York: Meridian Books, 1956), p. 372.

[4]See G. H. Smith, "Liberalism and Level of Information," *Journal of Educational Psychology*, XXXIX (1948), 65–81; and "The Relationship of 'Enlightenment' to Liberal-Conservative Opinions," *Journal of Social Psychology*, XXVIII (1948), 3–17. See also Herbert H. Hyman and Paul Sheatsley, "Trends in Public Opinion on Civil Liberties," *Journal of Social Issues*, IX (1953), No. 3, 6–17.

[5]See S. M. Lipset, *Political Man* (Garden City, N.Y.: Doubleday, 1960), pp. 96–130.

[6]Marvin Meyers, *The Jacksonian Persuasion; Politics and Belief* (Stanford, Calif.: Stanford University Press, 1957), pp. 189–190.

[7]S. M. Lipset, "Class, Politics, and Religion in Modern Society: The Dilemma of the Conservative," *Revolution and Counterrevolution: Change and Persistence in Social Structures* (New York: Basic Books, Inc., 1968), pp. 246–303.

[8]Lipset, *Political Man*, pp. 344–354. I did not report the methodological analysis in this discussion.

[9]Thomas C. Cochran, "The Historian's Use of Social Role," in Louis Gottschalk, ed., *Generalization in the Writing of History* (Chicago: University of Chicago Press, 1963), pp. 107–108.

[10]Stanley Elkins and Eric McKitrick, "A Meaning for Turner's Frontier," in Richard Hofstadter and S. M. Lipset, eds., *Turner and the Sociology of the Frontier* (New York: Basic Books, Inc., 1968), pp. 120–151.

[11]William Nisbet Chambers, *Political Parties in a New Nation* (New York: Oxford University Press, 1963), pp. 36, 42, 95.

[12]*Ibid.*, pp. 99–101.

[13]Robert K. Lamb, "The Entrepreneur and the Community," in William Miller, ed., *Men in Business* (Cambridge: Harvard University Press, 1952), p. 93.

[14]Joseph Gusfield, *Symbolic Crusade: Status Politics and the American Temperance Movement* (Urbana, Ill.: University of Illinois Press, 1963).

[15]David Donald, *Lincoln Reconsidered* (New York: Vintage Books, 1961), pp. 19–36; Stanley Elkins, *Slavery* (Chicago: University of Chicago Press, 1959), pp. 165–167.

[16]*Ibid.*, pp. 165–166.

[17]John Higham, "Another Look at Nativism," *Catholic Historical Review*, XLIV (1958), 148–158.

[18]See Cochran, *op. cit.;* see also Walter Metzger, "Generalizations about National Character: An Analytical Essay," in Gottschalk, *Generalization in the Writing of History*, pp. 90–94.

[19]Lee Benson, "Research Problems in American Political Historiography," in Mirra Komarovsky, ed., *Common Frontiers of the Social Sciences* (Glencoe, Ill.: The Free Press, 1957). esp. pp. 114–115.

[20]Lipset, *Political Man*, pp. 344–354.

[21]Metzger, *op. cit.*, pp. 99–100.

[22]Sidney Aronson, *Status and Kinship in the Higher Civil Service* (Cambridge, Mass.: Harvard University Press, 1964).

[23]See Paul Lazarfeld's article in this volume [*Sociology and History: Methods, Vol., I*, ed. Hofstadter and Lipset].

[24]S. M. Lipset, *The First New Nation* (New York: Basic Books, Inc., 1963).

[25]An example of such research may be found in Clark E. Vincent, "Trends in Infant Care Ideas," *Child Development*, XXII (September 1951), 199–209. In this

study Vincent analyzed the literature of infant care from 1890 to 1949 dealing with "breast versus artifical feeding," and tight versus loose feeding schedules.

[26]See the chapter by Richard Merritt in this volume [*Sociology and History: Methods, Vol. I*, ed. Hofstadter and Lipset].

[27]See Fred I. Greenstein, "New Light on Changing American Values: A Forgotten Body of Survey Data," *Social Forces*, XLII (1964), 441–450. Greenstein cites a number of studies of changes in values as measured by content analyses, and also many studies of children's beliefs and values made since the 1890's.

THE HERO AS EVENT
AND PROBLEM

Hook's essay was written in 1943, but it is dated only with respect to its emphasis on dictators. Hitler, Mussolini, and Stalin have passed from the scene, leaving only minor dictators such as Franco in Spain as a remnant of the past. But social movements still provide an arena for would-be dictators who rule the lives of their members as Hitler, Mussolini, and Stalin once dominated the lives of their societies. Historically, dictators rode to power on social movements. Mussolini was the leader of a ragtag group of Brown Shirts before he became ruler of Italy. Hitler was not taken seriously until the Nazis took power after the 1932 election, in which they won only 37.4 percent of the vote.

Although the conversion of ideological leadership into political power is a long shot in today's cynical political world, the possibilities cannot be overlooked. Hook's essay emphasizes the factor of leadership in mobilizing the masses at turning points in history. He discusses the symbolism of heroes and leaders, suggesting that myths and legends play a significant role in social movements. This suggestion will be explored further in Parts Three and Four. Hook also discusses the tendency of the mass media to create "synthetic" heroes. Today the mass media are much more influential than when Hook wrote his essay, and many leaders of social movements, especially the new radical leaders, are experts at using the media for their own purposes. Thus Hook may have anticipated developments in social movements today.

SIDNEY HOOK

SOURCE: From The Hero in History by Sidney Hook. New York: Humanities Press, Inc., 1943.

There is a perennial interest in heroes even when we outgrow the hero worship of youth. The sources of this interest are many and deep. But they vary in intensity and character from one historic period to another. In our own time interest in the words and acts of outstanding individuals has flared up to a point never reached before. The special reasons for this passionate concern in the ideas and deeds of the uncrowned heroes of our age are quite apparent. During a period of wars and revolutions, the fate of peoples seems to hang visibly on what one person, perhaps a few, decide. It is true that these special reasons reflect the dramatic immediacy of issues joined in battle, but there are other sources of interest which operate in less agonized times. We shall discuss both.

1. The basic fact that provides the material for interest in heroes is the indispensability of *leadership* in all social life, and in every major form of social organization. The controls over leadership, whether open or hidden, differ from society to society, but leaders are always at hand—not merely as conspicuous symbols of state, but as centers of responsibility, decision, and action. There is a natural tendency to associate the leader with the results achieved under his leadership even when these achievements, good or bad, have resulted despite his leadership rather than because of it. Where many factors are at work, the fallacy of *post hoc, ergo propter hoc* has a fateful plausibility to the simple mental economy of the uncritical multitude as well as to impatient men of action. A Hoover will be held accountable for a depression whose seeds were planted long before his advent. A Baldwin will be considered safe and sane if no social catastrophe breaks out during his ministry, even if he has lit a slow-burning fuse to the European powder magazine.

In our own day, the pervasive influence of leadership on the daily life of entire populations need no longer be imputed. For good or evil, it is openly proclaimed, centrally organized, and continuously growing. The development of corporate economies under centralized governments in the major countries of the world is such that we may say, without exaggeration, that never before have so few men affected so many different fields at once. The key decisions in politics, economics, foreign relations, military and naval affairs, education, housing, public works, and relief, and—save in Anglo-America—in religion, art, literature, music, architecture, and science are made by a handful of national leaders, and frequently by one figure whose judgment and taste become the absolute laws of the land. The tremendous development of means of communication, which makes it possible to transmit decisions with the speed of light to every nook and corner, ensures an effectiveness of control never known before.

A Caesar, a Cromwell, a Napoleon could and did issue decrees in many fields. But these fields, administratively and functionally, were not knotted together so tightly as they are today. They could not exact universal obedience to their decrees, or even suppress criticism. Some avenues of escape could never be closed. Some asylums of the spirit remained inaccessible to their law-enforcement agencies. The active presence of conflicting tendencies not only in politics but in religion and philosophy, during the reign of absolute rulers of the past, showed that they could not box culture within the confines of their dogmas and edicts. Their failure was not for want of trying.

How different is the picture in much of the world today! A Hitler, a Stalin, a Mussolini not only can and does issue decrees in every field, from military organization to abstract art and music; such dictators enforce them one hundred percent. Their decisions affect not only the possibilities of earning a livelihood—something not unique to totalitarian countries—but all education of children and adults, and both the direction and content of their nations' literature, art, and philosophy. They cannot, of course, command geniuses to rise in the fields they control but they can utterly destroy all nonconforming genius and talent. Through schools on every level, since literacy is a weapon; through the radio, which no one can escape if it is loud enough; through the press and cinema, to which men naturally turn for information and relaxation—they carry their education to the very "subconscious" of their people.

Silence and anonymity are no longer safeguards. All asylums of the spirit have been destroyed. The counsel of prudent withdrawal and disinterested curiosity from afar that Montaigne offered to those who would escape the political storms of their time—a counsel echoed by Saint-Beuve a century ago—would today almost certainly arouse the suspicions of the secret police. This not only marks the distance which Europe has come from the absolutisms of yesterday; it is a sign that, except for the leader and his entourage, everyone has lost his private life without acquiring a public one.

. . .

2. Another source of interest in the hero is to be found in the attitudes developed in the course of educating the young. The history of every nation is represented to its youth in terms of the exploits of great individuals—mythical or real. In some ancient cultures the hero was glorified as the father of a nation, like Abraham by the Israelites, or as the founder of a state, like Romulus by the Romans. Among modern cultures the heroic content of historical education in the early years has remained comparatively unaffected by changing pedagogical fashions. This may be due to the dramatic effect of the story form that naturally grows up when history is treated as a succession of personal adventures. Or perhaps it reflects the simplest approach to the moralistic understanding of the child. Reinforced by folklore and legend, this variety of early education leaves a permanent impress upon the plastic minds of the young. To ascend from the individual to social institutions and relations between individuals is to go from the picturesque and concrete to an abstraction. Without adequate training the transition is not always easy. This undoubtedly accounts for the tendency of many people to personify "social forces," "economic laws," and "styles of culture." These abstractions compel and decree and rule, face and conquer obstacles almost like the heroes of old. Behind the metaphor in much orthodox Marxist writing one can almost see "the forces of production" straining at the shackles with which Capital and Profit have fettered them, while human beings, when they are not tugging on one side or another, watch with bated breath for the outcome.

Even on higher levels of instruction the "heroic" approach to history has not been abandoned. The school of American historians who clustered around James Harvey Robinson and the "New History" has given an impressively realistic account of the American past. But in imagining that they were dispensing with heroes and great men to follow the sober course of economic and social "forces," they were deceiving themselves. They removed the kings, statesmen, and generals from their niches and then set up in their places the great captains of industry and finance, and the great thinkers in philosophy and science. The substitution is undoubtedly an improvement but its implication is difficult to square with their theory of the historical process which systematically underplays the significance of the individual. The intelligent student often gets the impression from their work that, for example, "Rockefeller, Gould

and Morgan were the truly great men of the era; if they had only
been utilized in the political field *how different things would have
been!"* [1]

In our own day, this attitude toward the hero and leader is not
merely the unintended by-product of historical education. In most
countries, particularly totalitarian countries, the cult of the hero
and leader is sedulously developed for adults as well as for children
and students. Here again technical advances in communication,
together with the new psychological methods of inducing belief,
make it possible to create mass enthusiasm and worship of leaders
which surpass anything evolved in Byzantium. Where a Roman em-
peror was able to erect a statue of himself, modern dictators can
post a million lithographs. Every medium is exploited by them to
contribute to their build-up. History is rewritten so as to leave no
doubt that it was either the work of heroes, predecessors of the
leader, or the work of villains, prototypes of the leader's enemies.
From the moment the leader comes to power, his activity is publicly trumpeted as the proximate cause of every positive achievement. If crops are good, he receives more credit for them than does
the weather. Similarly, the historical situation which preceded his
advent to power is presented as a consequence not of social and
economic causes but of a conspiracy and betrayal by the wicked.

Today, more than ever before, *belief* in "the hero" is a synthetic
product. Whoever controls the microphones and printing presses
can make or unmake belief overnight. If greatness be defined in
terms of popular acclaim, as some hasty writers have suggested,
then it may be thrust upon the modern dictator. But if it is not
thrust upon him, he can easily arrange for it. It would, however,
be a serious error to assume that the individual who affects history—
that is, who helps redetermine the direction of historical events—
must get himself believed in or acclaimed, as a condition of his
historical effectiveness. Neither Peter the Great nor Frederick II
had a mass following. It is only in modern times, where populations are literate, and lip allegiance to the democratic ethos pre-
vails even in countries where its political forms are flouted, that
the leader must get himself believed in to enhance his effectiveness. It should also be noted that the modern leader or dictator
has emerged in a period of mass movements. In consequence he
must have a mass base of support and belief as a counterweight to
other mass movements. Mass belief in him before he reaches power

is born of despair out of need, and nurtured by unlimited promises. Once he takes the reins, the dictator needs some mass support to consolidate his power. After that he can manufacture popular belief in his divinely ordained or historically determined mission almost at will.

Mass acclaim, which was not a necessary condition of the leader's effectiveness in past eras, is not a sufficient condition of historical effectiveness in the present. A figurehead like the King of Italy or a royal romantic like Edward VIII may be very popular, but he decides nothing. For our purpose the apotheosis of an historical figure is relevant only when it permits him to do historically significant things which he would have been unable to accomplish were he unpopular or without a mass following.

3. Whoever saves us is a hero; and in the exigencies of political action men are always looking for someone to save them. A sharp crisis in social and political affairs—when something must be done and done quickly—naturally intensifies interest in the hero. No matter what one's political complexion, hope for the resolution of a crisis is always bound up with hope for the appearance of strong or intelligent leadership to cope with difficulties and perils. The more urgent the crisis, the more intense is the longing, whether it be a silent prayer or public exhortation, for the proper man to master it. He may be called "savior," "man on horseback," "prophet," "social engineer," "beloved disciple," "scientific revolutionist," depending upon the vocabulary of the creed or party. Programs are important, but they are apt to be forgotten in periods of heightened tension, when want or danger is so palpable that it sits on everybody's doorstep. Besides, programs are only declarations of intent and promise. As declarations, they remain in the limbo of the possible until they are realized, and for this competent leadership is required. As promises, they can be betrayed or broken, depending upon who makes them and who carries them out.

Despite their theoretical pronouncements, according to which every individual, no matter what his status, is a chip on a historical wave, social determinists of all hues cannot write history without recognizing that at least *some* individuals, at *some* critical moments, play a decisive role in redirecting the historical wave. Engels speaks of Marx, Trotsky of Lenin, Russian officialdom of Stalin in a manner completely at variance with their professed ideology. Even theological determinists like the Popes, who believe we can trace the finger of God in all historical events, speak of western culture since the Reformation as if it had been created by Luther and Calvin behind God's back. The twists and turns by which these contradictions are extenuated we shall examine later. The fact remains that, for all their talk of the inevitable, the determinists never resign themselves to the inevitable when it is not to their liking. Their words, however, confuse their actions both to themselves and to others. In the end we understand them truly by watching their hands, not their lips.

Crises in human affairs differ in magnitude and intensity. But, judging by the history of peoples of whom we have more than fragmentary records, there has never been a period which has not been regarded by some of its contemporaries as critical. History itself may not inappropriately be described as one crisis after another. Whatever the social forces and conditions at work, and they always are at work—*insofar as alternatives of action are open, or even conceived to be open*—a need will be felt for a hero to initiate, organize, and lead. The need is more often felt than clearly articulated, and more often articulated than gratified. Indeed, the more frequent the cries, and the higher their pitch mounts for an historical savior or for intelligent leadership, the more *prima facie* evidence accumulates that the candidates for this exalted office are unsatisfactory.

A democratic society has its "heroes" and "great men," too. It is no more exempt from sharp political crisis than other societies, and rarely lacks candidates for the heroic role. It selects them, however, on the basis of its own criteria. Where a democracy is wise, it will wholeheartedly cooperate with its leaders and at the same time be suspicious of the powers delegated to them—a difficult task but one which must be solved if democracy is not to become, as often in the past, a school for tyrants.

4. The role of the great man in history is not only a practical problem but one of the most fascinating theoretical questions of historical analysis. Ever since Carlyle, a century ago, proclaimed in his *Heroes and Hero-Worship* that, "Universal History, the history of what man has accomplished in this world, is at bottom the History of the Great Men who have worked here," the problem has intrigued historians, social theorists, and philosophers. Unfortunately, Carlyle's book was not taken for what it is—a tract for the times, full of damply explosive moral fervor, lit up here and there with a flash

of insight, but contradictory, exaggerated, and impressionistic. Instead it was taken as a seriously reasoned defense of the thesis *that all factors in history, save great men, were inconsequential.* Literally construed, Carlyle's notions of historical causation are clearly false, and where not false, opaque and mystical. Some of his apostrophes to the great man and what is permitted him apologists could use for any totalitarian leader to throw a mantle of divine sanction around his despotic acts—if only they are sufficiently ruthless and successful. On the other hand, Carlyle's paens to revolution could be cited in justification by any man who fires at a king or dictator—and doesn't miss.

The Spencerians, the Hegelians, and the Marxists of every political persuasion—to mention only the most important schools of thought that have considered the problem—had a field day with Carlylean formulations. But in repudiating his extravagance, these critics substituted another doctrine which was just as extravagant although stated in language more prosaic and dull. Great men were interpreted as colorful nodes and points on the curve of social evolution to which no tangents could be drawn. What is more significant, they overlooked a possible position which was not merely an intermediate one between two oversimplified contraries, but which sought to apply one of Darwin's key concepts to the problem; namely, *variation*. According to this view, the great men were thrown up by "chance" in the processes of natural variation while the social environment served as a selective agency in providing them with the opportunities to get their work done.

It was William James, the American pragmatist, who took up the cudgels for a position which had been rendered unpopular among historians and the reading public by the scientific high priests of social evolution. Controversial zest together with a lack of interest in specific problems of economic and historical causation led him to a disproportionate emphasis on the role of the individual. But he formulated his position in such a way that it was free from the Carlylean fantasy that the great man was responsible for the very conditions of his emergence and effectiveness. James's thesis sounds extreme enough; yet in stressing "the receptivities of the moment" which must be met before greatness becomes actual—receptivities that leave a Leonard Nelson in obscurity but carry a Hitler to the summits of power—he goes far in mitigating its severity. His recognition of the relative autonomy of the realms of nature, society, and individual personality, combined with his belief in the plurality of historical causes, carries to the heart of the problem. And this despite the fact that these views were derived from a larger philosophical attitude about the place of man in the world and not from a study of specific historical issues.

Nonetheless, James's thesis as he left it is oversimplified and invalid. "The mutations of societies from generation to generation," he tells us, "are in the main due directly or indirectly to the acts or examples of individuals whose genius was so adapted to the receptivities of the moment, or whose accidental position of authority was so critical that they became ferments, initiators of movement, setters of precedent or fashion, centers of corruption, or destroyers of other persons whose gifts, had they had free play, would have led society in another direction."[2]

What William James is saying is that no significant social change has ever come about which is not the work of great men, and that the "receptivities" of today which make that work possible are the result of the acts or examples of the outstanding individuals of yesterday. This may seem to cover adequately the vast changes that have unrolled before our eyes as a result of Lenin's effort to reorganize the world along new social lines. It may, perhaps, throw some light from a new direction on the efforts of Hitler and Mussolini to conquer and enslave Europe in order to prevent not only Lenin's plan from being realized but any democratic transformation of European society. Yet the First World War, and the breakdown of Russian economy which gave Lenin his chance, were certainly not the result of the act or example of any great individual. Nor were most of the antecedent conditions of social conflict—political, economic, ethnical—that were set off in 1914 attributable to the acts or examples of an individual.

The rise of capitalism, the industrial revolution, the march of the barbarians from the east, the Renaissance—none, of course, would have been possible without the acts or examples of individuals. But no matter what *particular* individuals are named in connection with these movements, there is no evidence that the individuals were indispensable in the sense that without them these movements would not have got under way.

The easy contention that, had a "great man" been present, the First World War, say, would never have taken place cannot be upheld by any empirical evidence so far known. He would have had to be a very special sort of "great man"—that is, of a sort that has never appeared in comparable situations. Not infrequently contentions that make much of the decisive influence a great man would exercise if only he had been there are in principle not verifiable. This is the case when the hypothetical great man who would have prevented the First World War is identified not in virtue of independent traits but in terms of his hypothetical success. This is tantamount to offering a definition of what would constitute a great man in these circumstances. Our point here is not that the First World War was inevitable, but that the presence of a "great man" on the order of the great men of the past would probably not have altered matters much. Some other events could have altered things to a point of preventing the occurrence of the war, nor do we have to go to the realm of natural catastrophes to find them. For example, had the international socialist movement lived up to its pledges made at the Basle Congress, war might have been declared but it could not have been fought. But as far as the particular problem is concerned, no matter what *individuals* had occupied the chancellories of Europe in 1914, the historical upshot of commercial rivalries, Germany's challenge to British sea power, chauvinist resentments in western Europe, the seething kettle of Balkan intrigue, would very probably have been much the same.

Fashions of interpretation have shuttled back and forth between historians and philosophers of history during the last hundred years. On the one hand we have sweeping forms of social determinism according to which the great man is a symbol, an index, an expression, an instrument or a consequence of historical laws. To be sure, distinguishing traits between a great man and other men are recognized. But as a forceful writer of this school has put it, "The 'distinguishing traits' of a person are merely individual scratches made by a higher law of (social) development." On the other hand, we have the conception of the possibility of perpetual transformation of history by innovators whose existence, strategic position, and shattering effect upon their fellow men cannot ever be derived from the constellation of social forces of their day. Intermediate views have not been wanting. They have expressed little more than the eclectic belief that sometimes the great man and sometimes the weight of environment controls the direction of historical change. But they have not specified the general conditions under which these factors acquire determining significance.

Once the theoretical question is firmly grasped, no one interested in understanding history can escape formulating some answer to it. There has hardly been a great period or outstanding individual in history that has not been handled differently by historians with varying attitudes toward the question. During the twentieth century the overwhelming majority of historians have been in unconscious thralldom to one or another variety of social determinism. This has not prevented them from conducting fruitful investigation. Much light has been thrown on the fabric of social life of past times and on the slow accumulation of social tensions which discharge themselves with volcanic fury during periods of revolution. Without impugning the validity of their findings, one wonders whether they have done as much justice to the activity of the leading personalities during the critical periods of world history whose roots they have uncovered so well. Too many figures of history have been surrendered for exploitation to *belle-lettrists* and professional biographers who draw their subjects with one literal eye on earlier portraits and one imaginative eye on Hollywood.

5. The psychological sources of interest in great men may, with as much justification, be regarded as means by which great men exert influence on their followers. These sources are, briefly, (a) the need for psychological security, (b) the tendency to seek compensation for personal and material limitations, and (c) the flight from responsibility which expresses itself sometimes in a grasping for simple solutions and sometimes in a surrender of political interest to professional politicians. These sources are obviously interrelated, but for purposes of analysis we shall treat them separately.

a. The fact that the great man or leader often thinks of himself as the "father" of his country, party, or cause, and is even more often regarded by his following as their "father," may seem to lend color to the Freudian view that most individuals are in perpetual quest of the father (or mother) who supplied the axis of security and emotional stability in their early youth. There is a certain insight expressed here which, as is the case with whatever of value has emanated from Freud and his school, is completely independent of the mythological underpinnings of the Freudian system. Many people never outgrow their dependence on their parents, teachers, or whoever it is that plays the dominant role in supplying their wants, quieting their fears, and answering their questions as they grow up. Consequently, there is always ready a pattern of belief and acceptance, of incipient behavioral adjustment, that may be filled by a leader who talks and acts with the assurance of a parent and makes claims to a role in the community analagous to the role of the father in the family.

The more troubled the times and the more conventional the education, the stronger are the vestigial patterns of dependence, and the easier it is for the leader to slip into its frame. Whether or not the latter proves himself by works is a minor matter at first. To adapt a remark of Santayana: for those who believe, the substance of things hoped for becomes the evidence of things not seen. The leader cannot, of course, survive irresistible evidence of catastrophe, but he is under no necessity to enhance the material security of those who believe in him because the belief itself, at the beginning, eases their fears and increases their confidence.

It must not be overlooked that the psychological need for security is inconstant both in existence and intensity. When the need is present, social contexts and pressures rather than raw, instinctive impulse determine what emotional shelters are sought. During times that are relatively untroubled, and particularly where education makes for critical maturity instead of fixing the infantile response of unquestioning obedience, the need for a father-substitute is correspondingly weakened. Under other historic circumstances where great leaders and individuals do not appear, an institution like the Church or *the* Party will assume the primary role of authority.

b. Perhaps a more important source of appeal made by the leader to his following lies in the vicarious gratification of their yearnings through his presumed traits and achievements. The splendor, the power, the flame of the leader are shared imaginatively. New elements of meaning enter the lives of those who are emotionally impoverished. The everyday disparities and injustices of social life, and sometimes the lacks and incapacities of personal life, fade out of the center of concern. The ego is enlarged without effort and without cost. The skillful leader makes effective use of this, especially in the modern era of nationalism when fetishistic attitudes toward abstractions like the state and nation have been developed. By identifying his struggle for power with these abstractions, the leader effects a transference to himself of emotions previously directed to historic traditions, institutions, symbols, and ideologies.

He is then able to change the old and established in the name of the old and established.

The tendency to compensate for one's deficiencies by sinking them in the glorious achievements of more fortunate mortals may be an ever-present feature of social life. It may even explain, as Ludwig Feuerbach persuasively argued, the character of the gods men worship. But it should not be lost sight of that the persons and traits chosen for identification are historically variable. There usually are at least two possible ideals into which a need may be projected. A poor man may worship a rich god or an austere one; a people suffering from injustice may exalt a just ruler but they may also take pride in the fact that their tyrant is greater than all other tyrants. Why individuals should feel glorified in the exploits of a Hitler rather than in the wisdom of a Goethe, in the ruthlessness of a Stalin rather than the saintliness of a Tolstoy, cannot be explained simply in terms of the tendency to seek vicarious satisfaction for their limitations. The type of satisfaction sought is derived from the values of their culture.

c. If everyone, or even many, were candidates for political leadership, social life would be far more disturbed than it is. We would not need to be fearful of this disturbance if mechanisms of selection were evolved that would give us highly qualified leaders responsive to the needs and wishes of an informed and politically active electorate. But this is a long way off, and we are discussing what has been and is. A survey of political history shows that aspirants for leadership constitute, comparatively speaking, a mere handful in every community. The truth seems to be that the overwhelming majority of people have little desire to assume positions of power and responsibility.[3]

Conditions of political leadership, of course, change, but politics pursued as a professional career has been and always will be a risky game. Sometimes reluctance to serve as political leader has been so strong that elections have been conducted by lot as in the Greek cities. Even in modern times individuals have often been "drafted" from plow or workshop or office to fill offices. The point is, not that there is ever really lacking a sufficient number of persons willing, and even eager, to assume leadership, but rather that the ease with which such persons usually acquire and keep power, and the manifold ways by which they expand the authority originally delegated to them, would be impossible unless there were comparatively so few others interested in competing for the posts of leadership. So long as they are permitted to grumble, most people are gratefully relieved to find someone to do their chores, whether they are household chores or political chores. Politics is a messy business, and life is short. We put up with a great many evils in order to avoid the trouble of abolishing them.

This feeling is natural even if it is not wise. Political leadership is a full-time career with little opportunity for relaxation or cultivation of other interests. In retrospect few intelligent men who have enjoyed power have felt that its rewards were commensurate with the personal sacrifices it entailed. According to one of Plato's myths, Odysseus, the crafty politician, chooses as his lot in his next reincarnation on earth a humble life in a forgotten corner far from the alarms of politics. What is true for the successful politician is also true for his rival. Serious political *opposition* is likewise a full-time activity. In political struggle, therefore, the integrated individual who has a plurality of interests, which he is loath to sacrifice on the sullied altars of politics, is always at a disadvantage. So is the sensitive and high-minded idealist who shrinks from the awful responsibility of deciding, quite literally, other people's lives, and from the moral compromises and occasional ruthlessness required even by statemanship of a high order. Further, political questions are difficult. We accept a great many decisions because we have not the dogmatic certitude that we know what decision is the right one, although we do know that some decision is necessary.

Yet it is an old story that when we refuse to upset our "normal life" by plunging into the political maelstrom, and entrust power to others, we awake someday to find that those to whom we entrusted it are well on their way to destroying "the normal life" we feared to interrupt. This is not only an old story but an ever-recurrent one. It will repeat itself until it is widely realized that political decisions must be made in any event; that responsibilities cannot be avoided by inaction or escape, for these have consequences; and that, considered even in its lowest terms, political effort and its attendant risks and troubles are a form of social insurance.

To the extent that knowledge of these elementary truths spreads and is acted upon, interest in political leadership becomes critical. Identification with it is then a conscious process, not a quest for a father-substitute. We may legitimately take credit for its achievements to which we would not be entitled if it were the work of our fathers, for whom we are in no way responsible. To the extent that these elementary truths are disregarded, every aspirant to leadership—even to dictatorship—can count to an appreciable degree upon the indifference of the population. They will yield him homage after he has succeeded. Whether they do or don't, if *he* cares enough about it, he has the means today to make them pay homage to him.

---

¹This quotation is from a student's paper.

²"Great Men and Their Environment," in *Selected Papers on Philosophy*, p. 174, Everyman Edition.

³*Cf.* the remarks of Robert Michels in *Political Parties*, Eng. trans., pp. 49*ff* New York, 1915.

PART II

RADICALISM
AND
FUNDAMENTALISM

OLD RADICALISM

Radicalism has a long history in America. As an ideology, the roots of radicalism can be traced back to the American Revolution.* As an organized movement, socialism originated in the political parties and labor unions supported by German immigrants who fled the homeland after the 1848 revolution.† The first significant socialist organization in the United States was the Socialist Labor Party, founded in 1877. During the next fifty years, the socialist movement was to undergo numerous splits, including the breakaway of "reformist" elements in 1886 to help found the American Federation of Labor; the decimation of the leadership ranks in 1901 when the Socialist Party was formed; the schism between the left-wing and right-wing socialists which led to the formation of the Communist Party in 1919–21; and the defection of the Trotskyists in 1928. These schisms can be partly attributed to the fact that the socialist movement never produced a major political party. The Socialist Party, founded in 1901, was a large third-party movement during its first decade of life; in 1912 the largest vote for any socialist presidential candidate before or since (6 percent of the electorate) was attained by Eugene V. Debs, but the party never had a real chance to control the Presidency or Congress. Therefore, the socialist movement suffered the fate of other third-party movements which, with the exception of the Republican Party in 1860, were unable to attain the status of major parties in the American political system.

The "outsider" status of the socialist movement in the American political system has been reinforced by its constituency. Most of the members of the various socialist parties in the 1800's were immigrants; many of the members of the radical groups in the 1900's were middle-class alienated intellectuals.* Neither of these

---

*Seymour Martin Lipset, *First New Nation* (New York: Basic Books, 1963).

†Theodore Draper, *The Roots of American Communism* (New York: Viking Press, 1957), pp. 11–12.

*Nathan Glazer, *The Social Basis of American Communism* (New York: Harcourt, Brace & World, 1961).

groups supported a major political party of the working class; the immigrants were not eligible to vote until naturalized, a difficult process for a working-class immigrant; and the middle-class intellectuals of twentieth-century American radicalism lacked rapport and access to the potential working-class base of socialism. This, plus the territorial structure of American politics, precluded the development of an American Socialist Party comparable to those in Europe. This does not mean that socialist groups have refrained from participation in electoral politics; three radical parties—the Communist Party, U.S.A., the Socialist Workers Party, and the Socialist Labor Party—have nominated candidates for President and Vice-President in recent elections. Rather, it means that the candidates have had no realistic chance for election and that they have recognized this fact. The campaigns are used as sounding boards for radical rhetoric, and to recruit new members.

Factional disputes and splits in the socialist movement demonstrate the ambivalence of old radicalism vis-à-vis the American political system. If successful participation in electoral politics is precluded by the structure of the political system, the rationale of the movement must be shifted toward ideology. Yet the ideology has stressed change of the society, and often the only effective avenue of change is the political system. Each time a split has occurred in the socialist movement, the issue has been whether to work within the American political system or to promote the overthrow of that system. In the selections that follow, several historians examine the reasons why the old radical movements never resolved the dilemma of political participation. Although the old radical groups made numerous attempts to elect candidates to office, they were always forced by historical and political conditions to remain social movements. Their most successful endeavors were ideological, not political.

In the first selection, Daniel Bell describes the dilemma in terms of the irreconcilable differences between the dreams of socialism and the realities of American life: socialism was based on a utopian ethic, American life on a pragmatic ethic, and they were destined to clash over the issue of political compromise.

DANIEL BELL

SOURCE: From Daniel Bell, "The Background and Development of Marxian Socialism in the United States," in Donald Drew Egbert and Stow Persons, Socialism and American Life, Vol. I (copyright 1952 by Princeton University Press). Reprinted by permission of Princeton University Press.

Socialism was an unbounded dream. Fourier promised that under socialism people would be at least "ten feet tall." Karl Kautsky, the embodiment of didacticism, proclaimed that the average citizen of a socialist society would be a superman. The flamboyant Antonio Labriola told his Italian followers that their socialist-bred children would each be Galileos and Giordano Brunos. And the high-flown, grandiloquent Trotsky described the socialist millennium as one in which "man would become immeasurably stronger, wiser, freer, his body more harmoniously proportioned, his movements more rhythmic, his voice more musical, and the forms of his existence permeated with dramatic dynamism."[1]

America, too, was an unbounded dream. The utopians gamboled in its virgin wilderness. Some immigrants called it the *Goldene Medinah*, the golden land. Here it seemed as if socialism would have its finest hour. Both Marx and Engels felt a boundless optimism. In 1879 Marx wrote, ". . . the United States have at present overtaken England in the rapidity of economical progress, though they lag still behind in the extent of acquired wealth; but at the same time, the masses are quicker, and have greater political means in their hands, to resent the form of a progress accomplished at their expense."[2] Engels, who wrote a score of letters on American scene in the late 1880's and early '90's, repeated this prediction time and again. In his introduction to the American edition of *The Conditions of the Working Class in England*, written at the height of enthusiasm over the events of 1886—notably the spectacular rise of the Knights of Labor and the Henry-George campaign— he exulted: "On the more favored soil of America, where no medieval ruins bar the way, where history begins with the elements of modern bourgeois society, as evolved in the seventeenth century, the working class passed through these two stages of its development [i.e., a national trade-union movement and an independent labor party] within ten months." And five years later, his optimism undiminished by the sorry turn of events, Engels wrote to Schlüter: ". . . continually renewed waves of advance, followed by equally certain set-backs, are inevitable. Only the advancing waves are becoming more powerful, the set-backs less paralyzing. . . . Once the Americans get started it will be with an energy and violence compared with which we in Europe shall be mere children."[3]

But there still hovers the melancholy question, posed by Werner Sombart at the turn of the century in the title of a book, *Why Is*

There No Socialism in the United States? To this Sombart supplied one set of answers. He pointed to the open frontiers, the many opportunities for social ascent through individual effort, and the rising standard of living of the country as factors. Other writers have expanded these considerations. Selig Perlman, in his *Theory of the Labor Movement*, advanced three reasons for lack of class consciousness in the United States: the absence of a "settled" wage-earner class; the "free gift" of the ballot (workers in other countries, denied such rights—for example, the Chartists—developed political rather than economic motivations); and third, the impact of succeeding waves of immigration. It was immigration, said Perlman, which gave rise to the ethnic, linguistic, religious, and cultural heterogeneity of American labor, and to the heightened ambitions of immigrants' sons to escape their inferior status.

In the end, all such explanations fall back on the naturally-endowed resources and material vastness of America. In awe of the fact that the Yankee worker consumed almost three times as much bread and meat and four times as much sugar as his German counterpart, Sombart finally exclaimed: "On the reefs of roast beef and apple pie socialistic Utopias of every sort are sent to their doom."[4]

Other explanations have indicated equally general, and relevant, facts. Some have stressed the agrarian basis of American life, with the farmer seesawing to radicalism and conservatism in tune to the business cycle. Others have pointed to the basically geographic, rather than functional, organization of the two-party system, with its emphasis on opportunism, vacuity of rhetoric, and patronage as the mode of political discourse; hence, compromise, rather than rigid principle, becomes the prime concern of the interest-seeking political bloc.

Implicit in many of these analyses, however, was the notion that such conditions were but temporary. Capitalism as an evolving social system would of necessity "mature." Crises would follow, and at that time a large, self-conscious wage-earner class and a socialist movement, perhaps on the European pattern, would probably emerge. The great depression was such a crisis—an emotional shock which shook the self-confidence of the entire society. If left permanent scar tissue in the minds of the American workers. It spurred the organization of a giant trade-union movement which in ten years grew from less than three million to over fifteen million workers, or one-fourth of the total labor force of the country.[5] It brought in its train the smoking-hot organizing drives and sit-downs in the Ohio industrial valley which gave the country a whiff of class warfare. In the 1940's labor entered national politics with a vigor—in order to safeguard its economic gains. Here at last was the fertile soil which socialist theorists had long awaited. Yet no socialist movement emerged, nor has a coherent socialist ideology taken seed either in the labor movement or in government. So Sombart's question still remains unanswered.

Most of the attempted answers have discussed not *causes* but *conditions*, and these in but general terms. An inquiry into the fate of a social movement has to be pinned in the specific questions of time, place, and opportunity, and framed within a general hypothesis regarding the "why" of its success or failure. The "why" which this eassay proposes (with the usual genuflections to *certeris paribus*), is that the failure of the socialist movement in the United States is rooted in its inability to resolve a basic dilemma of ethics and politics. The socialist movement, by its very statement of goal and in its rejection of the capitalist order as a whole, could not relate itself to the specific problems of social action in the here-and-now, give-and-take political world. It was trapped by the unhappy problem of living "*in* but not *of* the world," so it could only act, and then inadequately, as the moral, but not political, man in immoral society. It could never resolve but only straddle the basic issue of either accepting capitalist society, and seeking to transform it from within as the labor movement did, or becoming the sworn enemy of the society, like the communists. A religious movement can split its allegiances and live *in* but not *of* the world (like Lutheranism); a political movement can not.

Bell's essay dealt with the more general questions of American culture and socialist ethics. In the next selection, David Shannon discusses the specific mechanical problems of politics which the Socialist Party was unable to overcome. He concludes by noting that the Socialist Party failed to win organized labor, potentially its strongest constituency.

DAVID SHANNON

SOURCE: *Reprinted with permission of The Macmillan Company from* The Socialist Party of America *by David Shannon.* © *1955 by David A. Shannon.*

There are two categories of factors to be considered in dealing with the question of why the American Socialist Party died. There are, first, weaknesses, inadequacies, failures, errors of commission and omission on the part of the Socialist Party. Besides these internal factors there are external factors, basic conditions in American society that militated against Socialist success and were largely beyond the power of the Socialists to change. This book, concerned primarily as it is with the Socialist Party's internal history, comes nearer offering insights into the internal factors than into the external ones. The external factors of Socialist failure, however, are probably the more important. A full investigation of these external factors requires much more than a history of the Socialist Party; it requires an investigation into all of American history.

One of the most serious errors of the Socialist Party was its failure to behave the way political parties in the United States must in order to be successful. The Socialist Party never fully decided whether it was a political party, a political pressure group, a revolutionary sect, or a political forum. It tried to play all these roles at the same time. One of the first rules of American politics is to build strong local and state organizations. Outside a few places, notably Milwaukee and Oklahoma, the Socialists failed to establish political machines. Indeed, they usually did not even try to build them. The Socialist Party time and again committed itself to political action, rejecting first the "direct action" of the syndicalists and later the revolution of the Communists, but it usually made little attempt to organize political machines at the local level. And it is at the local level, of course, that voting is done. Only in Milwaukee and Oklahoma and a few small cities did the Socialists have an organization in each precinct to distribute literature, get voters registered, get voters to the polls, watch the count of the vote, and all the other routine tasks of political party workers. Watching the count of the vote is a critical activity, especially critical for minor parties. After the election of 1932 it was estimated that only about half the Socialist vote was counted. Socialists cried fraud when Debs was defeated in his race for Congress in 1916.

They claimed that at least 70 percent of the voters of Terre Haute, Debs's home town, had promised their votes to Debs, but that Debs had been "counted out." If the charge were valid—and considering the aroma of Indiana politics of that era it was not beyond the realm of possibility—the Socialists had no one to blame but themselves. Watchers would have assured Debs a fair count.

But most Socialists never saw the value of political organization. They regarded the building of local machines as "ward heeling," sordid truckling for votes beneath the ideals of Socialism. Debs wrote during his 1916 campaign: "Let it not be supposed for a moment that on the part of the Socialists this is going to be a vote-chasing campaign. . . . We shall explain socialism and make our appeal to the intelligence, the manhood and womanhood of the people, and upon that . . . high plane, whatever the outcome, we are bound to win." With such an approach he had no grounds for optimism.

Nor did Socialists generally concern themselves with local issues. Their interests were nearly altogether in national and international matters. This lack of interest in local matters was a disregard of one of the basic features of American politics. The positions of the major parties on regional and local problems command political loyalties perhaps as much as their positions on national affairs. But usually the Socialists ignored local affairs, and rarely did the Socialists run a full slate of local and state candidates. Evidence of what success the party might have enjoyed from a more intensive concern with local problems can be seen in the experience of those parts of the party that did so concern themselves. The Milwaukee Socialists offered the voters a local program, and they became the city's dominant party. Indeed, Milwaukee voters supported the Socialists because of their local program and record and in spite of their national affiliation. Oklahoma Socialists became strong because of good organization and their concern with local matters. Lacking the money to finance a state Socialist newspaper, Oklahoma Socialists did the next best thing in arranging with the publisher of the *Appeal to Reason*, which circulated very widely in the state, to have inserted a special "Oklahoma page" in each copy mailed to Oklahoma. The "Oklahoma page," edited for many years by J. O. Welday, a highschool principal of Oklahoma City, was concerned almost altogether with state and local matters. The results in the membership rolls and at the polls were gratifying.

When the Socialist Party occasionally strove to become homogeneous, to cast all members in the same mold, it violated one of the basic principles of American political parties. The major American political parties are anything but homogeneous. They are coalitions, and their platforms are compromises, the result of bargaining among the various interests in the parties. In its early days the Socialists were as diverse, regionally and ideologically, as their major-party opponents, and they were a force that caused the major parties some unrest. But over the years the Socialist Party became increasingly homogeneous. By the time the United States entered World War II the Socialist membership was pretty much of the same mold, all social democratic pacifists, and they were very few in number. It is almost a political axiom that any party that is "pure," whose members are unanimous in their opinions, is a weak party. A homogeneous party of Socialists may work in European politics, under a cabinet system with several political parties, where the compromises come *after* the election in the formation of a government, but such a party is not suited to American conditions.

In some of the party's splits, of course, the disagreement among factions was too wide to compromise. In 1912–1913 the differences between the syndicalists and the political actionists were too great to be reconciled. In 1919 the Communist split could not have been avoided. The Left Wing Section had determined that it would either capture the Socialist Party or secede from it. Again in the 1930's there was no hope of party harmony with the Trotskyites. Wide disagreement over basic principles will plague any party of the Left, and splits are likely in parties without the political paste of patronage, or real promise of patronage.

Another of the weaknesses of the Socialist Party was its failure to win organized labor to its cause. This failure was by no means exclusively the fault of the Socialists. There were and are important reasons for labor's shunning the Socialists beyond the power of the Socialists to alter. But, even so, the Socialist wooing of labor's hand was a blundering affair.

In the following excerpt, H. Wayne Morgan joins with Daniel Bell and David Shannon in discussing the reasons the socialist movement was destined to fail as a political party. But he continues with some suggestions about its potential success as a social movement. Morgan notes that Eugene Debs, who was the presidential candidate of the Socialists during the "golden decade" ending in 1912, was able to attract support for the movement through sheer idealism. This demonstrates the significance of leadership and "heroism" in social movements.

H. WAYNE MORGAN

SOURCE: H. Wayne Morgan, Eugene V. Debs: Socialist for President. Copyright © 1962 by Syracuse University Press. Reprinted by permission of the publisher.

In the last analysis, the American socialist movement failed to conquer capitalism and its society for deeper reasons than internal strife. The unexpected vitality of capitalism, the immovable middle-class psychology of the workers, the truly basic American belief in individual rather than cooperative effort, the conservative constitutional features of the political system, and the anti-socialism of organized labor which prevented a broadly-based coalition party—these deeply woven threads in the fabric of American life prevented socialism's triumph.

Yet American socialism's ultimate failure is not so impressive as its temporary success. The people who voted for Debs five times apparently believed in many of his ideals; the party elevated several hundred of its members to office; undeniably socialism influenced the older parties in their search for reform measures. The mere fact that socialism flourished indicated to Republicans and Democrats that reform was necessary. Thus the party fulfilled the historic role of third parties in the American system—it attained enough success with the people to force older parties to steal its thunder. Despite its idealism and seemingly un-American approach to the problems of the day, the Socialist Party gained more success with the voters than any other recent third party except the Populists.

Many condemned socialism's idealism, pointing out that the American electorate traditionally opposed impractical solutions. But in the end, American socialism suffered not so much from its ideals as from its illusions. The idea that capitalism was not flexible enough to adapt to the demands for reform and change, that Americans were deeply dissatisfied with their political system, that man was basically logical rather than emotional, that industry would never cooperate with organized labor, that the older parties would never reform—these were the illusions which, together with the passing of the public demand for reform, the World War, and the final onrush of party factionalism, ended the socialist dream of triumph in America.

Yet the solid body of past achievement remains an instructive lesson in the degree and manner of socialist success. However limited it was, it was nonetheless a monument to the best efforts of men like Eugene Debs during the age when America boasted a powerful socialist movement.

None gave more to that movement than Eugene Victor Debs. If he was often beset by doubts, if he often vacillated on momentous issues, if he partially failed in his role as a leader within the Socialist Party, and if his thinking was indeed shallow, he was no less effective. He appealed frankly to the people whom he understood in terms they understood and let others in the movement explain the fine points. Though he wore his romantic idealism like a crusading knight capitalizing on every gain to be made from the dramatic role, his sincerity was above question. He did in truth believe that socialism was inevitable, and that its inauguration would mean the rule of reason and love on earth. He suffered for his beliefs, yet did not abandon them. Twice imprisoned, once as an old man, he nonetheless clung to his ideals. "I do not consider that I have made any sacrifice whatever," he said early in his career, "no man does, unless he violates his conscience." At the end of the road he might well have repeated that phrase, for indeed he had not violated his own.

Despite his successes, Debs was unable to maintain the unity of the old radical movement. He had sympathies for the 'left wing' of the Socialist Party, especially the "Wobblies" (Industrial Workers of the World), but he could not bring himself to join or support the fledgling Communist Party which broke off from the Socialist Party in 1919. Until his death in 1926, Debs remained a faithful member of the Socialist Party; he ran for President for the last time in 1920. After his death, Debs was succeeded by Norman Thomas, whose ethical orientation as a former minister— his pacifism and idealism—was well suited to the needs of the increasingly ideological socialist movement. Norman Thomas also ran for President many times, but after his last attempt in 1948 he decided that it was futile to regard the Socialist Party as a political party and urged that it become a "pressure group." This was to be the eventual fate of the Socialist Party; in the following selection H. Wayne Morgan suggests that it would have been the best strategy of the party under Debs.

H. WAYNE MORGAN

SOURCE: *H. Wayne Morgan,* Eugene V. Debs: Socialist for President *Copyright © 1962 by Syracuse University Press. Reprinted by permission of the publisher.*

Debs came to American socialism at a time when it needed his qualities most. He gave to it his color, enthusiasm, boundless energy, and American ideals. He became a figure around whom socialists of every stripe could rally in time of crisis. He brought a national reputation and important connections with the labor movement and the common people. The socialists could indeed be proud of having captured his allegiance. He was one with his new comrades in the belief that the future belonged to socialism. The year 1900 saw the birth of a new century and a new force in American politics and it marked the rise of Eugene Debs as a political leader. In more ways than one this was a new century. Underneath the seeming content of America, ferment was at work. Eugene Debs was to have a leading role against the backdrop of the new century and the restless men it produced.

. . .

Yet, because they recognized his basic Americanism and because he was at such pains to disavow the more extreme socialist tendencies even if it displeased his comrades, the Americans who voted for him did not fear him. His belief in the goodness of man, and his personal sentimentality tempered whatever edge of violence remained on the doctrines he spoke. Knowing little of formal socialist logic he was indebted to no theorizer or dogmatist for his doctrines.

This in part explains his remarkable effectiveness with the voting public of his day, for he cast doctrine and theory aside, like most good politicians, and fitted his remarks and his program into the mainstream of the time. He appealed to many different groups successfully because he realized that to be effective any political doctrine, even idealistic socialism, must be understood by its audience. Thus he avoided extended philosophical discussions, preferring the concrete realities of the life around him to sophistry.

However wise this may have been in terms of gathering votes and followers, it is one measure of Debs' weakness as a leader that he did not fully grasp the elements of socialist theory and use them in his leadership. He was not, strictly speaking, a socialist party leader yet he was the most famous socialist of his day. Characteristically, he preferred to leave control of the party, with all its bitter dissension and routine labor, to others while he himself used his talents to rally popular opinion for what he considered the party program. From his point of view it was wise to remain above faction that he might be a true leader above the battle to whom all socialists could look for leadership. Yet in doing so he permitted the party organization to drift into the firm control of men with whom he disagreed, while he could not wholeheartedly join the men with whom he agreed. Thus, like many radical leaders, he was perpetually between two fires, radical socialism and evolutionary socialism. Had he chosen to exercise the power represented by his following he no doubt could have dominated the party; yet by doing so he would have risked his neutral position and the formation of yet another faction. The loosely organized party, composed of varied elements prone to disagreement, was hard to govern at best and Debs disliked the formality and procedures of such rule as much as the methods of obtaining them.

If he did not fully exercise his talents for leadership within the party he did so outside the party organization. As the best-known socialist of his day, and recognizing his role as the prophet and evangelizer of socialism, he lent his talents to spreading the meaning if not the formal doctrines of American socialism. His career was varied, though it flowed from the same central source; he worked as a labor organizer, protest leader, socialist propagandizer, and as a symbol of freedom in a time of oppression. In his role as a presidential candidate he brought to bear all his understanding of the temper of the times, of human nature, and of the political system in which he worked. His idealism did not prevent him from being a shrewd judge of character and men, and he understood mass psychology as well as or better than any other political leader of his day. Debs' political career illustrates the curious blending of intellectual and emotional idealism and practical realism so common to liberal politics in America. On the one hand he sincerely believed in the utopian idealism he preached; on the other hand he knew full well that his new order could be attained only by working within the existing system. This was a wise and profound understanding on his part, and it is the measure of his familiarity with the political habits of his countrymen. Thus he eschewed violence not only because he himself could not justify it but because he knew it would ruin his chances of success with the American people.

Debs' presidential campaigns were important to the Socialist Party for they focused the strength of socialism every four years. Furthermore, Debs' evangelizing and his popularity with the sympathetic masses to whom he appealed added new members to the rolls, stimulated the party press, brought others to work for socialism and illustrated to those in doubt the vigor of the movement. Debs, acutely aware of this, missed no chance to add to the party strength by appealing to labor, seeking members, and doing organizational work.

The factionalism which rent the Socialist Party before 1919, when the Communist Party split off, continued to plague the new communist movement. At first, there were two communist groups, the Communist Labor Party and the Communist Party. Under orders from Lenin they merged, but factions continued to go their separate ways throughout the following decade. One of the many factional fights involved the party's tactics in dealing with suppression from governmental authorities. The party had formed a front group called the Workers Party to run local candidates for office and to publish a newspaper. In the following selection, Irving Howe and Lewis Coser describe the conflicting attitudes toward the Workers Party and the conflicts of principles which were involved in the factional fight.

IRVING HOWE AND LEWIS COSER

SOURCE: From Irving Howe and Lewis Coser, The American Communist Party (New York: Frederick A. Praeger, Inc., 1962).

A majority of the American Communists—led by Israel Amter, Abraham Jakira, L. E. Katterfeld, and, upon his first release from prison, Benjamin Gitlow—held in effect that the Workers Party was a mere necessary nuisance, a concession to the Comintern. The legal party, they felt, could be used for recruiting members to the pure underground party, but it would be an error to allow legal work to monopolize the primary loyalties or energies of the true believers. This sectarian wing of the party came to be known— it is one of the few flashes of poetry in the history of American Communism—as the Goose faction.[5]

On the other side of the party's barricades were the Liquidators, led by Ruthenberg, Lovestone, Max Bedacht, and James P. Cannon, who paid lip service to the idea of an underground apparatus (as distinct from an underground party) but were really intent upon making the Workers Party the essential arm of American Communism. The term "Liquidators" had been Lenin's contemptuous label for those Russian Marxists who in 1905 had wanted to set up a politically diffuse organization that would conform to the legal requirements of Czarism—a situation that had of course nothing to do with the one in the United States, though mimicking it gave the forlorn demons of American Communism the pleasure of reenacting the drama of the Bolshevik past.

The primary difference between the two factions—it was an archetypal difference that would reappear again and again in radical history—was that between a group infatuated with its ideological sanctity and a group that wanted to participate in the life of the labor movement even if that meant collaboration with "centrists" and other uncertified American radicals. At first the Comintern, which certainly did not want its American supporters to commit themselves in principle to parliamentary politics, was rather cool toward the Liquidators, warning against "the tendency to become legal in fact as well as in outward appearance." But Ruthenberg, who was shrewd enough to realize that without legality American Communism would simply succumb to its inner cannibalism, kept insisting that there was no inherent political virtue in being underground. A simple enough idea, but hard for all the communists to learn.

Even as this battle was being fought out in the party halls, the political factors that had helped drive the Communists underground were rapidly disappearing. The postwar hysteria, which had reached a climax during the Palmer raids, began to abate by the beginning of 1921. A year or so later the atmosphere in the country was both calmer and more rational than during the fiercely illiberal months

that concluded Woodrow Wilson's administration. It was sympto-
matic that when William Z. Foster was deported from Colorado in
1922, only to be refused the right to detrain upon the sacred soil of
Wyoming, the politicians and state troopers who had carried out this
coup were not hailed as saviors of the republic. Quite the contrary;
the treatment of Foster became a political issue in the 1922 Colorado election that contributed to the victory of a somewhat liberal
administration.

The factional fights of the 1920's were finally resolved when the Trotskyists, under James B. Cannon, left the Communist Party in 1928. One consequence of the resolution of the factional struggles was the transformation of the party from a relatively open, democratic movement into a highly disciplined cadre organization, a process which has been called "bolshevization" and "Stalinization."* This process insured that the American Communist Party would always be alienated from American politics and that pragmatic political activity would be subordinate to ideological issues of loyalty.

The aftermath of the 1920's was the "Third Period," characterized by the "ultra-leftism" in the early 1930's. By this time, alienation had become institutionalized and isolation from American life had become almost a fetish to the party members, as described in the following selection.

*Theodore Draper, *American Communism and Soviet Russia* (New York: Viking Press, 1960).

IRVING HOWE AND LEWIS COSER

SOURCE: From Irving Howe and Lewis Coser, The American Communist Party *(New York: Frederick A. Praeger, Inc., 1962).*

The Third Period was not merely a time of political adventurism
and extreme leftism; it soon came to indicate a unique style of life.
This was a style of life in which Bohemianism combined with
quasi-military discipline; a righteous estrangement from the mores
of American society with a grotesque mimicry of Bolshevik tough-
ness; a furious effort to break past the barriers of hostility en-
countered by Communism at almost every point in American life
with a solemn and consoling absorption in the rituals of the move-

ment. Throughout these years the party remained a sect, that is, a compact assembly of the chosen, bound together by the faith that in their ideology alone resided Historical Truth; that all those who deviated from their path would soon be tumbling greedily into the arms of the Devil; that the test of their behavior lay in the growth of their power; that the freedom of the follower blossomed in his obedience to the apparatus; that the member had to yield the "whole of his life" if he were to be deemed worthy of membership at all. The style of the Stalinist sect regulated everything from belief to dress, from the ineluctable correctness of "socialism in one country" to the preference for caps and leather jackets in Union Square.

Furiously energetic, driving its members to both ecstasy and exhaustion, the party suffered from a hopeless contradiction during the early thirties. It repeatedly proclaimed that its goal was to break out of its isolation and become a rooted part of American life; it strained every nerve and muscle to achieve that end; but its ideology and ingrained habits of life were insuperable handicaps. Because the true nature of this contradiction could not be acknowledged—it would involve criticizing some fundamental assumptions of Stalinism—the party had to improvise a variety of bureaucratic deceits. Such as: the line is correct, always has been correct, but (somehow) is never properly carried out. Or: if the members drove themselves just a little harder, the magical union with the masses might be achieved and then the party, today so unloved and disheveled, would become the radiant bridegroom of history. The characteristic tone of party life during these years was a feverish straining, a willful sacrifice of human resources: revolution, revolution everywhere (cried the Comintern, the Theses, the Leaders) but in America hardly a revolt in sight.

Fortunately for the Communist Party, its isolation was temporarily halted in 1935 by an edict of the Comintern (Communist International) ordering the Communist Parties of the world to seek unity with other radical groups in Popular Fronts. This tactic enabled the European parties, especially the French party, to flourish for a short time. The American Communist Party was unable to resolve its differences with the Socialist Party and the two remained divided, but it did adopt a different strategy under the leadership of Earl Browder. It became the "Communist Political Association" and supported the war effort after the German invasion of the Soviet Union; thus the wartime alliance of the U.S. and the U.S.S.R. did permit the Communist Party to support American policies for a few years. More important for the internal strength of the Communist Party, the alliance made the party more attractive to American radicals and party membership reached a peak of 100,000 in 1945. But this membership was highly unstable; it underwent an estimated *annual* turnover of 90 percent, a sure indication of internal difficulties. These difficulties have been attributed to the discrepancies between the external or "exoteric" doctrines of the party, which capitalized on popular issues such as anti-fascism, civil rights, and economic justice, and the internal or "esoteric" doctrines, which stressed organizational survival at any cost.* Those members who were unable to tolerate the twists and turns of the party line tended to abandon their membership commitment soon after joining.

Unfortunately for the party, the Popular Front tactics did not long survive the war. The onset of the Cold War after 1945 led to a gradual isolation of the party which culminated in the McCarthyist persecutions of the early 1950's. These persecutions were primarily an expression of the intolerance of American society for radical movements. But as David Shannon indicates, they were not entirely a result of one-sided intolerance. The Communist Party throughout its history has been intolerant of American politics, and this intolerance tended to isolate it from the host society.

*Gabriel Almond, *The Appeals of Communism* (Princeton: Princeton University Press, 1965).

DAVID SHANNON

SOURCE: From The Decline of American Communism *by David Shannon. Reprinted by permission of Harcourt, Brace, Jovanovich, Inc.*

This, then, was the outward face of the Communist Party in the late 1940's and early 1950's. It clearly was in retreat. American public opinion had reached an unprecedented pitch of opposition to Communists and their ideas. The government's prosecution of Communist Party leaders and the kind of defense that the party elected to make against the prosecution had resulted in an important handicap to the party's efficiency. The manner in which the party conducted its "peace" campaign had further isolated it from the non-Communist Left and from the movement for Negro equality, and the Communists "hard" line had contributed to the decline of the Progressive Party and the elimination of Communist influence in the decisions of the C.I.O.

Facing attack from government, from the trade unions, and from the public in general, the Communists endeavored to appear as militant advocates of freedom and justice, as defenders of the Jeffersonian tradition of civil liberty. They sought to be regarded as the innocent victims of a society that had lost its restraint and that had forgotten a noble tradition of due legal process and fair play toward dissenters from majority attitudes. The Communists and their organizations obviously were the victims of a reaction that was sometimes disrespectful of the highest traditions of law and justice, but they were hardly innocent victims.

In the 1960's the Communist Party enjoyed a brief respite from its isolation from American politics when the new radical movements adopted a policy of "nonexclusion." This meant that conventions and demonstrations organized by new left groups were open to participation by Communist Party members. Michael Miles describes one such convention in his article on the National Conference for a New Politics in 1967. In many ways this was the peak of the new left movement in America: the height of its influence and the beginning of the breakup of new left movements such as the Students for a Democratic Society. The conference broke apart into white and black caucuses, and new left groups began to imitate the factionalism of the old radicals.

In the second selection, Peter Stuart describes some of the factionalism still endemic in the Communist Party. He also investigates some of the other reasons for its decline, and mentions the ultimate insult to the party: the FBI is no longer paying much attention to it.

MICHAEL MILES

SOURCE: From Michael Miles, "The Communist Party Today." *Reprinted by Permission of The New Republic,* © *1968, Harrison-Blaine of New Jersey, Inc.*

In the last year especially, the party has come a long way in its quest for respect on the left and respectability elsewhere. The major breakthrough has been the left's acceptance of the "principle of nonexclusion"—nonexclusion of communists in coalitions organizing in the peace, anti-draft and black freedom movements. The CP participated, for instance, in the planning and organization of last April 15's Spring Mobilization against the war. A party leader recounts that "at the planning meeting in Cleveland people were at the point of dropping the whole idea as a waste of time. Then Arnold Johnson [a communist] stood up. He swung the meeting. That was the first time that anything like that had happened in a long, long time."

But the "coming-out of the party" was last summer's National Conference for a New Politics. Not necessarily held in high esteem previously by young white or black militants, the party demonstrated an impressive capacity to function coherently amidst the random motion of the NCNP cloud chamber. As the only political organization represented in both the Black Caucus and the predominantly white convention, the party was able to apply vectors to both in an attempt to effect the eventual convergence of blacks and whites in support of a third-party presidential ticket. While black communists were influential in the Black Caucus in preventing it from walking out on the convention altogether, white communists pressed for acceptance of the caucus' thirteen demands, which included 50 percent representation in convention voting and condemnation of Israel's role in the Middle East war. The Black Caucus did not leave the convention and the whites accepted the demands. In the end, however, the blacks united with a white minority caucus of New Left organizers to defeat the third party proposal on the grounds that radical politics are really about local organizing and electoral politics are premature, if not intrinsically repulsive.

More recent evidence of the party's new prestige and activity on the left was its participation in last October's Stop the Draft Week. Curiously, although the party was represented on the anti-draft steering committee in New York, Bay Area communists refused to endorse the Oakland, Calif., draft demonstrations which during the week variously mobilized from 5,000 to 10,000 people. This says something for the legend of the devilish efficiency of the party monolith: the order goes out from New York and the Local party group immediately does the opposite. Young Communists say that the party is not only capable of inefficiency, the inefficiency is often a result of party democracy. Although some hear tell of undemocratic practices in the forties and fifties, few admit to any similar experiences in the sixties. The independence of some of the party districts is said to verge on rivalry. At the left-liberal "Power and Politics" conference in California before the Reagan-Brown election, the districts of Northern and Southern California had literally to negotiate their differences. In the end, they issued pamphlets urging contradictory actions.

Older-generation communists have special problems understanding their young, because McCarthyism effectively foreclosed the recruitment of a middle generation which might have mediated between the two groups. Although there are militants and iconoclasts in the older-generation leadership, and a fair share of party hacks among the younger, party dynamics tend to be generated among young communists who are just beginning to move into positions of party leadership (two members of the secretariat, almost 40 percent of the national committee, approximately half the staff of *The Worker*). Their criticisms of the party tend to parallel at certain points the critics from the New Left who say the CP is "too conservative."

PETER C. STUART

SOURCE: From Peter C. Stuart, "Communist Party, U.S.A.: Revolution Turned Middle-aged." *Reprinted by permission from The Christian Science Monitor.* © 1969 *The Christian Science Publishing Society. All rights reserved.*

The influence of Communist Party, U.S.A., may have declined even more than the drop in membership would suggest. In its heyday, the Party was closely associated with many labor unions, black organizations, and nationality groups. "We used to be able to multiply the number of members by 10 to measure how many people we directly influenced," Mr. Gates said. Today such roots have withered.

The austere appearance of its headquarters suggests that the party is hardly affluent. Recent party dropouts confirm the suspicion.

The party regularly used to raise $750,000 a year, as well as $200,000 a year to subsidize the newspaper. Originally some of the money came from abroad, but this aid eventually ceased, partly because of the relative wealth of American Communists. The party even donated $20,000 to the Italian party in 1948.

Today the party may be relying heavily on money—some of it invested profitably—accumulated in the prosperous years of the past, Mr. Gates said.

The ills of Communist Party, U.S.A., seem traceable to several conditions:

1. Soviet ties. Over the years the American party has been an unswerving supporter of the Soviet Union (except during the brief liberalization when it condemned Soviet intervention in Hungary).

"The young, particularly, are critical of the Soviet Union's history of repression—of Stalin, Hungary, Czechoslovakia," said George Charney, a former general secretary of the New York State Communist Party (largest unit in the national party) who left the party in 1958.

Furthermore, the needs of Soviet Communists didn't always jibe with the needs of American Communists. American Communists, for example, lost important support among unionists and black persons when they suspended the "class struggle" after the Soviet Union was invaded in World War II, lest the United States be weakened in the battle against the Soviet enemy, Nazi Germany.

2. Ideological competition. The doctrinaire Marxism of the American Communist Party faces stiff competition from more fiery ideologies, notably among the young. "The Communist Party," commented an organizer of the radical New York High School Student Union, "is too conservative for us."

Competitors include the New Left teachings of American Prof. Herbert Marcuse and French intellectual Jules Regis Debray. But perhaps the sternest ideological challenge comes from the Maoist-oriented Progressive Labor Party, itself an offshoot of the Communist Party. Progressive Laborites now make up a major faction within SDS, the faction which recently split with the rest of SDS at their Chicago convention.

"Maoist ideology has a bloodcurdling sound," said Mr. Jackson, Communist international secretary. "This gives it a momentary shock appeal. But later it becomes absurd." He likened the Progressive Labor movement to Trotskyism, which had appealed to him as a youth.

3. Internal problems. Sometimes the Communist Party erects its own barriers.

After a fling at "participatory democracy" at its 18th convention three years ago, in an open appeal to youth, the party returned to the old tight discipline for its 19th convention last month. "There was an influx of youth, but also confusion and anarchism," Mr. Jackson explained. The prevailing decision making process is "democratic centralism," under which decisions, once discussion is closed, become binding on all.

The party has been embarrassingly unable to throw itself wholeheartedly behind the burgeoning black liberation movement. While approving cooperation with the Black Panthers, party members at the convention last month voted down a resolution supporting the "struggle for complete liberation" by black communities.

American Communists continue to indulge in bitter internal squabbles, sometimes followed by defections or expulsions—a luxury that a small party can ill afford. Soon after the disastrous exodus of 1956-58 came the expulsion of a group which wanted the party to go underground. This group then formed the Progressive Labor Party.

After the invasion of Czechoslovakia, about 11 of the 90 national committeemen openly objected to the party's support of the Soviet role. One, Gilbert Green, head of theNew York State Party, was reprimanded but remains on the committee.

"It seems to be a law that every 10 years or so there is a challenge to the general line," Mr. Jackson observed. "In the long run it keeps the organization on its toes, but at the time it's painful and wasteful in personnel."

Perhaps the most telling measure of the Communist Party's declining fortunes is the change in watchdogging by police and the Federal Bureau of Investigation. Policemen and FBI agents, who used to interrogate party leaders regularly, gradually relaxed their tactics in the late 1950's and now pay Communists little heed.

William Z. Foster dominated the leadership of the American Communist Party from 1928 until his death in 1961, except for periods in the early 1940's when Earl Browder was ascendant and in the late 1950's when Gus Hall began to take over from the aging Foster. Foster came to communism from the trade-union movement, where he was a successful organizer and a popular leader. Ironically, he was never to have much influence in labor again because of the failure of the communists to maintain control in the unions they helped to organize.

The following biographical selections by Paul Franklin Douglass chronicle Foster's life—his childhood, his successes in organizing the meat-packing industry, his leadership of the Communist Party, and his part in bringing about the postwar isolation of the party.

PAUL FRANKLIN DOUGLASS

SOURCE: *From Paul Franklin Douglass,* Six Upon The World *(Boston: Little, Brown and Co., Inc., 1954). Reprinted by permission of the author.*

The birth year of 1881 stands likewise as a date of significant co-incidence; Foster was born in the same year that the American Federation of Labor was nationally organized in Pittsburgh. In this Pennsylvania city thirty-eight years later, Foster was to lead the bitter steel strike—directed, as he says, against the "shocking conditions," such as "the twelve-hour day, the seven-day week, company unionism, boss tyranny, and company domination in the steel towns."

. . .

Bill Foster's "kindergarten" schooling began in the neighborhood gangs of Philadelphia. Poor but big families supplied the membership for these roving bands which, when mobilized to full power, sometimes reached the formidable strength of five hundred. The virile aggregations of roving boys named themselves after animals, rivers, streets, districts, and parks. There were "Lions," "Parksparrows," "Reedies," and "Schuylkill Rangers." Whatever youthful social cohesion existed in the neighborhoods came from these organizations, which gave the lads a role to play in life. Experience in the gangs constituted a good part of a boy's fundamental education. Foster belonged to the "Bulldogs," a gang which controlled a sovereign territory running from Sixteenth to Seventeenth Streets and from South to Fitzwater. The Bulldogs, like the other bands which wandered the Philadelphia streets, constantly waged "war." Any boy away from his "corners" could expect to "shell out"—that is, to be robbed of his skates, cap, swimming tights, or pocket knife. Battles of rival gangs were pitched with fists, sticks, stones, and knives. The Bulldogs, operating in an especially tough neighborhood, boasted that no gang had ever licked them.

. . .

By the age of twenty-eight Foster was exploring the theory, plans, and practices of militant trade-unionism, which aimed by general strike and direct action to establish control over production through the collective force of organized workers.

By this time Foster had educated himself in the economic foundations of society to a degree sufficient for his subsequent political career. He had learned economic geography by travel, studied sociology as a hobo. He had taken his introduction to rail-and-water transportation by stepping the mast and riding the rods. He had learned public speaking through agitation, and group methods by means of organizing work. He had mastered crafts by working at them. He had become acquainted with books in the public library, in the secondhand stores, on board ship, and from the reading of socialist literature. He had become an omnivorous reader. His fingers itched for books. His mind was restless to encounter ideas. Foster's was a practical education—but make no mistake about it, his kind of preparation was as thorough and complete as it was informal.

At the age of sixty-eight, looking back on his labor experience, Foster once commented that he "was an efficient worker but always a rebellious one. I was a natural for the revolutionary movement." At heart he was concerned with people and ideas and the direct methods by which people are persuaded to act upon those ideas. He was presently to find a pattern of thought and action which accepted a thoroughgoing revolutionary doctrine.

. . .

While the Syndicalist League of North America lived only two years, it encouraged the idea of direct action among revolutionary workers. Upon the collapse of the Syndicalist movement, Foster in January 1915 set up a new labor organization—the International Trade Union Educational League. He chose Chicago as its headquarters city and selected himself as secretary. Promptly he set out on a seven-thousand-mile agitation tour, through the West. Despite his strenuous efforts, however, he failed to organize this program on a national scale.

For ten years Foster had worked in various capacities as a railroader. He liked railroads and railway men. There was something about the sense of power of control over long trains that appealed to him; something about the awareness that he occupied a strategic position in industry that gave him satisfaction; something in the opportunity to meet new people daily and to view new scenes that impressed him; something in the realization of the fact that he was a member of a strong labor union that gave him a sense of independence.

. . .

With the advent of World War I Foster was to find his real opportunity to advance the welfare of workers—by using the strike as a bargaining weapon in two key industries: in steel, the heart of munitions supply, and in meat-packing, where the slogan was being proclaimed that *Food Will Win the War.*

When the United States entered the conflict, Foster entertained some definite ideas about the meaning of American participation to revolutionary Socialists like himself. "Communists and other left-wingers," he explained, "do not support wars just because the capitalist clique controlling the government at the given time sees fit to plunge the country into war to further its class interests." To him, World War I was obviously an imperialist war—a struggle carried on for the division of the world among the "great imperialist powers." The workers had no interest in it, he said, except to bring combat to a conclusion as quickly as possible and upon the most advanced democratic terms that could be found. His position on the war directed the course of his actions. He felt no patriotic urge to support the American course, which he judged to be contrary to the democratic interests of workers and to their economic welfare. Strikes which presently occurred in the meat-packing and steel industry owed much to Foster's inspiration and organizing experience.

. . .

Foster had achieved his objective. Within a year after the idea popped into his head, the packing-house industry was organized throughout the country. More than two hundred thousand workers had come into the dozen federated unions. They included unskilled as well as skilled workers, immigrants and native-born alike, and fully twenty-five thousand new Negro members.

The meat-packing victory had been won in a struggle in the first mass production industry ever to be organized by trade-unions. It was accomplished by militant policies and by the application of the industrial union principle. To Foster and his militants of the old International Trade Union Educational League, the victory was a "glowing justification" of their policy of working inside the old trade-unions. It showed what could be done "on our theory of organizing the unorganized millions by militantly taking advantage of the war situation."

With the organization of the Communist Party in the United States in 1919, revolutionary elements rallied from the Socialist Party, the Socialist Labor Party, the I.W.W., and the Syndicalist League of North America. Eighteen months after it was organized, Foster himself, at the age of forty, joined the Communist Party and became a member of its Political Committee. He had arrived at what he calls "his political destination." For the remainder of his life he found within the party, as he says, the satisfaction at last of being at home among compatriots who shared a matured conception of economics and politics and knew how to use the state as a vehicle of revolution to establish a genuine socialist society. "Becoming a Communist," he says, "meant for me to put the logical capstone upon my whole previous life experience. Since joining the Communist Party it has been a never-ending effort on my part, with such diligence and self-criticism as I can command, to master the revolutionary principles of Marx, Engels, Lenin, and Stalin, and to apply them effectively in the American class struggle." From this position he never deviated. Thirty years later he said that "if I were starting out my life all over again, I would take the same course I have done. One thing I would surely do, despite the press of practical work, would be better to organize my time so as to enable me to indulge more than I have in reading of the science and history I love so much. This is one thing that the youth in the labor and Communist movement should most resolutely strive to accomplish —to combine the theoretical with the practical, to find time for lots of solid reading, notwithstanding the most urgent demands of the day-to-day struggle." To this point Foster had given himself an education tailor-fashioned for the purposes of revolutionary leadership. In the process, he had served as an industrial worker for twenty-three years.

In 1919 Lenin referred to the organization of the Communist International as the "general staff of the world revolution." Foster soon became a partner in the general staff work. With the steel strike over, he sailed the Atlantic—destination Russia. From New York he went by way of London, Liban, Riga, and Reval to Leningrad. In 1921, while attending the Communist International, he first saw Lenin at the Czar's Palace in Moscow. The sight, he says, "was one of the most inspiring moments of my life. There indeed was the great leader of the world's oppressed millions in every corner of the earth. I regarded him so intently as he went about the Congress that his whole makeup and characteristics literally burned themselves into my memory."

Lenin's influence moved Foster farther to the left, "exercising," as Foster says, "a most profound effect upon my ideology and my life work. After more than twenty years of intellectual groping about, I was at last, thanks to Lenin, getting my feet on firm revolutionary ground."

Foster thus became a full-fledged part of the world Communist movement. He attended world congresses, sat in executive meetings of the Comintern, and served in executive sessions of the Red International of Labor Unions. In these congresses and plenums he met, as he says, "the best Marxians in the world, militant revolutionary fighters who, for the past generation, have been in the heart of every great strike movement and revolutionary struggle from London to Shanghai and from Toronto to Buenos Aires." These international meetings, he pointed out, constituted the most interesting and instructive experiences of his political life.

In various congresses and central committee meetings of the Communist Party in the Soviet Union he also watched the triumph of Stalin over Trotsky and Zinoviev. He knew what intra-party struggle meant. He had feverishly read the writings of Lenin, mastered the literature of the party, and found it "spiritually satisfying"—its revolutionary doctrine as well as its atheism. When in the summer of 1935 he saw the vast Soviet Arctic development—on a trip from Moscow to Murmansk *via* the new Stalin Baltic–White Sea Canal—he held in his hand the first watermelon ever grown north of the Arctic Circle. He rejoiced in the fact that there were no churches in the new Socialist city of Murmansk, and he felt a sense of pride that the great canal, built by prison labor under the direction of the O.G.P.U., had offered "opportunity to regenerate the prisoners."

Foster was now ready to run as the Communist Party candidate for President of the United States. He entered the national elections of 1924, 1928, and 1932. In these campaigns he spoke to what he estimates to have been five hundred thousand people in three hundred meetings, gave radio speeches, "inspired" newspaper stories, and organized demonstrations and parades. He traveled sixty thousand miles by train, auto, bus, airplane, steamboat, wagon, and on foot. He covered every important city in every state in the Union. In 1924 he got thirty-six thousand votes, in 1928 fifty thousand votes, and in 1932 one hundred thousand.

. . .

For the next dozen years, however, the operations of the Communist Party in the United States were guided to a large extent by Earl Browder, general secretary of the party, partly because of the condition of Foster's health and partly because of his greater concern with Communist activities at the international level. Foster's later return to active leadership of the Communist Party in the United States came about as a result of a bitter factional struggle. The lines were drawn on theoretical grounds: orthodox Marx-Leninism versus so-called "American Exceptionalism." Browder held to the strategy of Exceptionalism. His ejection from the party, and the triumph of Foster's revolutionary policies, led to a series of actions by the United States Government beginning in 1948, directed to the liquidation of a Communist conspiracy to overthrow the Government of the United States by force and violence.

The history of the old radicals and the biographies of their leaders would be incomplete without mention of the splinter groups which split off from the Communist Party. I have selected the Socialist Workers Party, a Trotskyite splinter group, for inclusion here because of its continuing influence in radicalism. Although it is an old radical group, the Socialist Workers Party and its newspaper, *The Militant*, are still influential in radical causes, including anti-war demonstrations, women's liberation groups, and black liberation movements. It is one of the principal groups involved in the National Peace Action Coalition and the Student Mobilization Committee, two organizations which have dominated the anti-war scene in the early 1970's. In the following selections, the founding and early years of the Socialist Workers Party are described first by a biographical sketch of its founder, James P. Cannon, and then in Cannon's own account of the events which led to his split with the Communist Party.

THEODORE DRAPER

SOURCE: *From* The Roots of American Communism *by Theodore Draper. Copyright © 1957 by Theodore Draper. Reprinted by permission of The Viking Press, Inc.*

Cannon . . . was American-born. The Midwest was his native environment. His parents were born in England of Irish parentage.
They were steeped in the Irish nationalist tradition of Robert Em-
mett, the patriot who was hanged at the dawn of the nineteenth
century for an unsuccessful uprising against British rule. After
coming to the United States and settling in a suburb of Kansas
City, the father identified himself with the old Knights of Labor,
then with the Populists, then the Bryanites, and, at about the turn
of the century, the Socialists. The *Appeal to Reason* arrived weekly
at their home. At the age of twelve, the boy went to work for the
Swift packing house, a sixty-hour-a-week job. At sixteen, in 1906,
his first feeling of social consciousness was stirred by the Moyer-
Haywood-Pettibone case. He decided to go to high school at the
unusual age of seventeen—a desire for "culture" and a receptivity
to radicalism came together to rescue him from the factory and the
poolroom. After leaving school, he joined the I.W.W. as a traveling
organizer, a member of what the Wobblies called the "soap-box
union." Then came the Russian Revolution in 1917. It shook
Cannon out of the I.W.W. and steered him into the Socialist party
with the rest of the pro-Bolshevik Left Wing the following year.
While the Communist movement was struggling to be born in
1918–19, he earned a living as an office worker during the day,
went to law school three nights a week, and devoted the rest of
his time to the local Left Wing in the Socialist party.

Cannon attended the National Conference of the Left Wing in
New York in June 1919 and found himself in sympahy with the
Reed-Gitlow tendency, which opposed the domination of the for-
eign-language federations. He did not attend any of the Communist founding conventions the following September because, he
says, he was opposed to a premature split in the Socialist party.
Afterward, however, the Kansas City local went over to the Communist Labor party and Cannon was appointed secretary for the Kansas-
Missouri district. When the United Communist party was formed in
the spring of 1920 at the first Bridgman convention, he was elected
to the Central Committee and assigned as organizer of the St.
Louis–Southern Illinois district. Toward the end of 1920, he was
moved to Cleveland to edit *The Toiler*, an organ of the U.C.P. He
was shifted to New York the following year and began to take part
in the top leadership of the Communist party of America.

Cannon's own account of the founding of the Socialist Workers Party begins with his attendance at the Sixth World Congress of Comintern (Communist International) in Moscow in June of 1928. He attended as a leader of one of the factions of the American Communist Party. In the following selection he describes his first encounter with Trotsky's criticism of Stalin.

JAMES P. CANNON

SOURCE: *James P. Cannon*, The History of American Trotskyism *Reprinted by permission of Pathfinder Press. Copyright © 1944 by Pioneer Publishers, renewed 1972 by Pathfinder Press.*

1.

I was put on the program commission, partly because the other faction leaders weren't much interested in the program. "Leave that to Bukharin. We don't want to bother with that. We want to get on the political commission which is going to decide about our faction fight; on the trade union commission; or some other practical commission which is going to decide something about some little two-by-four trade union question worrying us." Such was the general sentiment of the American delegation. I was shoved onto the program commission as a sort of honor without substance. And to tell you the truth, I was not much interested in it either.

But that turned out to be a bad mistake—putting me on the program commission. It cost Stalin more than one headache, to say nothing of Foster, Lovestone and the others. Because Trotsky, exiled in Alma Ata, expelled from the Russian party and the Communist International, was appealing to the Congress. You see, Trotsky didn't just get up and walk away from the party. He came right back after his expulsion, at the first opportunity with the convening of the Sixth Congress of the Comintern, not only with a document appealing his case, but with a tremendous theoretical contribution in the form of a criticism of the draft program of Bukharin and Stalin. Trotsky's document was entitled, "The Draft Program of the Communist International: A Criticism of Fundamentals." Through some slipup in the apparatus in Moscow, which was supposed to be bureaucratically airtight, this document of Trotsky came into the translating room of the Comintern. It fell into the hopper, where they had a dozen or more translators and stenographers with nothing else to do. They picked up Trotsky's document, translated it and distributed it to the heads of the delegations and the members of the program commission. So, lo and behold, it was laid in my lap, translated into English! Maurice Spector, a delegate from the Canadian Party, and in somewhat the same frame of mind as myself, was also on the program commission and he got a copy. We let the caucus meetings and the Congress sessions go to the devil while we read and studied this document. Then I knew what I had to do, and so did he. Our doubts had been resolved. It was as clear as daylight that Marxist truth was on the side of Trotsky. We made a compact there and then—Spector and I—that we would come back home and begin a struggle under the banner of Trotskyism.

Because Trotsky was ostracized by the world communist movement, it was necessary for Cannon to keep his conversion to Trotskyism secret for the first few months and to operate surreptitiously in the U.S. to find allies and build a movement. In the next selection, one can see the tendencies toward legend-building in Cannon's chronicle of the events leading to the founding of the Socialist Workers Party.

2.

I had smuggled Trotsky's criticism of the draft program out of Russia, bringing it home with me. We came back home and I proceeded immediately with my determined task to recruit a faction for Trotsky.

You may think that was a simple thing to do. But here was the state of affairs. Trotsky had been condemned in every party of the Communist International, and once again condemned by the Sixth Congress, as counter-revolutionary. Not a single member in the party was known as an outspoken supporter of Trotskyism. The whole party was regimented against it. By that time the party was no longer one of those democratic organizations where you can raise a question and get a fair discussion. To declare for Trotsky and the Russian Opposition meant to subject yourself to the accusation of being a counter-revolutionary traitor; and being expelled forthwith without any discussion. Under such circumstances the task was to recruit a new faction in secret before the inevitable explosion came, with the certain prospect that this faction, no matter how big or small it might be, would suffer expulsion and have to fight against the Stalinists, against the whole world, to create a new movement.

Late in 1928, Cannon brought his espousal of Trotskyism out into the open and was immediately expelled from the Communist Party along with a few followers. In the following excerpt, he describes what happened next. He tells why he felt it was necessary for him to raid the Communist Party for members rather than recruit them from the general public. He also indicates how important it is for a splinter movement to publish a newspaper, an activity which may become the sole purpose of the movement.

3.

On February 15, 1929, not quite four months after our expulsion, as the Communist Party was preparing its national convention, we published the "Platform" of our faction—a complete statement of our principles and our position on the questions of the day, national and international. To compare this platform with the resolutions and theses that we, as well as other factions, used to write in the internal national faction fights, is to see what an abyss separates people who have acquired an international theoretical outlook from national-minded factionalists fighting in a restricted area. Our platform began with our declaration of principles on an international scale, our view of the Russian question, our position on the great theoretical questions at the bottom of the fight in the Russian party— the question of socialism in one country. From there our platform proceeded to national questions, to the trade union question in the United States, to the detailed problems of party organization, etc. For the first time in the long drawn-out faction fight in the American Communist movement a really rounded international Marxist document was thrown into the arena. That was the result of adherence to the Russian Left Opposition and its program.

We printed this platform in *The Militant*, first as our proposal to the convention of the Communist Party, because although expelled we maintained our position as a faction. We didn't run away from the party. We didn't start another one. We turned back to the party membership and said: "We belong to this party, and this is our program for the party convention, our platform." Naturally, we didn't expect the bureaucrats to permit us to defend it in the convention. We didn't expect them to adopt it. We were aiming at the Communist rank and file. It was this line, this technique, which gave us our approach to the rank and file members of the Communist Party. When Lovestone, Foster and Company said to them: "These fellows, these Trotskyists, are enemies of the Communist International; they want to break up the party;" we could show them it wasn't so. Our answer was: "No, we are still members of the party, and we are submitting a platform for the party that will give it a clearer principled position and a better orientation." In this way we kept our contact with the best elements in the party. We refuted the slander that we were enemies of Communism and convinced them that we, ourselves, were its loyal defenders. By this means we first gained their attention and eventually recruited many of them, one by one, into our group.

. . .

Our paper was aimed directly at the members of the Communist Party. We didn't try to convert the whole world. We took our message first to those whom we considered the vanguard, those most likely to be interested in our ideas. We knew that we had to recruit at least the first detachments of the movement from their ranks.

After our little paper was printed, then the editors, as well as the members, had to go out to sell it. We would write the paper. We would next go to the print shop, hovering over the printer's forms until the last error was corrected, waiting anxiously to see the first copy come off the press. That was always a thrill—a new issue of *The Militant*, a new weapon. Then with bundles packed under our arms we would go out to sell them on street corners in Union Square. Of course it wasn't the most efficient thing in the world for three editors to transform themselves into three newsboys. But we were short of help and had to do it; not always, but sometimes. Nor was this all. In order to sell our papers on Union Square we had to defend ourselves against physical attacks.

---

[1]Quoted in Hayim Greenberg, "Socialism Re-examined." *International Socialist Forum* (London), June 1942, p. 2120.

[2]Letter to Danielson, No. 169 in *Karl Marx and Friedrich Engels: Selected Correspondence, 1846–1895* (New York, 1834), p. 360.

[3]Letter to Schlüter, No. 222, *ibid.*, p. 497.

[4]Quoted in Goetz A. Briefs, *The Proletariat* (New York, 1937), p. 193. Communist

economists deny this material gain. A leading statistician, Jurgen Kuczynski, has stated that the living conditions of American labor in the last hundred years have actually deteriorated. Confronted with his own evidence that real wages had increased from 1790 to 1900, Kuczynski falls back on Lenin's theory that capitalism divided the workers into the labor aristocracy, bribed by higher wages, and the exploited masses. See Jurgen Kuczynski, *A Short History of Labour Conditions under Industrial Capitalism*, Vol. II, *The United States of America, 1789 to the Present Day* (London, 1943).

[5] But not because they were so adept at factional pecking. According to Gitlow, when Abraham Jakira, who stuttered badly, was heckled during a faction debate for "cackling like a goose," Amter rose to his defense by declaring that "the geese saved Rome and we shall yet save the Party." Lovestone, a bench-jockey for the opposing faction, thereupon shouted back: "All right then, from now on you're the Goose Caucus." And so it was.

NEW RADICALISM

In the 1960's, the new radicalism arose like a phoenix from the ashes of the old radical movement which burned itself out in the unsuccessful third-party movements of the first half of the century. The first new radicals were groups of intellectuals who became disaffected with the "affluent society" and militarism in foreign policy. The rapid growth of the universities in the 1950's and 1960's permitted radical intellectuals to find each other and organize movements. Many of the younger faculty members and all of the students attained maturity after the decline of McCarthyism; they were less reticent than their elders about adopting radical ideologies. Ironically, because of the university base of the new radicalism, it was much more popular among middle-class youth than among the working class it purported to serve.* Youth in the universities were on "career paths" which would bring them into middle-class professions and occupations; they were not the type of radicals who would blindly follow any leader and maintain their membership for many years. Therefore, groups such as the Students for a Democratic Society (SDS) were relatively short-lived and lacked the continuity of ideology of the older radical movement. The SDS is a particularly vivid example of organizational change under the impact of ideological change. Founded in 1962 at Port Huron, Michigan, the SDS was a successor to the Student League for Industrial Democracy, a moderate socialist group. By 1966, the League for Industrial Democracy dissolved its sponsorship of the SDS because of ideological differences that had developed in the intervening years; in short, the SDS had become too militant. The SDS lasted as an independent organization until 1969, when it split at its annual convention. Two independent factions, the "Weathermen" and the Worker-Student Alliance, survived the split; the Weathermen went underground and concentrated on "revolutionary deeds" such as "trashings" and bombings, while the Worker-Student Alliance fell under the control of the Progressive Labor Party, an old radical group. Neither of these groups represents a large segment

---

*Seymour Martin Lipset, *Rebellion in the University* (Boston: Little, Brown & Co., 1972).

of the radical student movement today.

The history of the SDS as an organization and the new radical movement as a whole illustrates the difficulties of defining social movements. Although, as noted in the first chapter, social movements tend to have rather stable organizations as a base, the new radical movement seems to be made up primarily of "followings." These are rather ephemeral and transitory groupings of people who adhere to the ideology of a few leaders.* New radicalism today seems to be composed of two distinct groups: the followers of leaders such as Tom Hayden, David Dellinger, or Jerry Rubin, and the followers of the Black Panther leaders Bobby Seale and Huey P. Newton. Even the Black Panther party has fallen prey to factionalism, as the split between Newton and Eldridge Cleaver has illustrated. Newton remains in charge of the domestic Black Panther Party, which emphasizes community organizing, but Cleaver's defection, which was joined by several large segments of the organization, has removed the internationalist and Leninist thrust of the party.

In the following selection Paul Jacobs and Saul Landau describe the conditions that led to the emergence of radicalism in the 1960's.

---

*Turner and Killian, *Collective Behavior*, p. 246.

PAUL JACOBS AND SAUL LANDAU

SOURCE: *Paul Jacobs and Saul Landau,* The New Radicals *(New York: Random House, Inc., 1966), p. 8. Reprinted by permission.*

The Movement's origins are elusive and have many strands. In the 1930's and 1940's the radical movement encompassed a broad spectrum of organizations and political beliefs: the Communists and their front groups; the socialists, Trotskyists, and other anti-Stalinist organizations; sections of the CIO and a few other unions. The Communist groups, drawing worldwide support, dominated American radicalism, since their size and prestige were greater than any of the other political tendencies. And although the American Communist Party was shaken in 1939 by the Stalin-Hitler nonaggression pact, the Nazi attack on the Soviet Union returned them to political acceptability.

But by the mid-fifties the old movement was nearly dead. The Communist Party had declined badly in the postwar period, because of government persecution and its own internal weaknesses. The trade unions were no longer crusading, many once radical anti-Communists had become supporters of the Establishment, and the socialists were barely distinguishable from the liberal Democrats.

Many of the young people in this activist generation were the children of parents who had been the radicals and left liberals of the thirties and the forties. At home they had heard the discussions about civil rights, and they knew of the political pall that hung over the country during the McCarthy era. They had learned a set of ideals from their parents and now, much to their parents' discomfiture, they were trying to put those ideals into practice.

And so by 1960 this new generation was throwing itself against American society, literally and figuratively. They found a new hero in Castro, the man of action, the man without an ideology, whose only interest seemed to be bettering the life of the Cuban people. They responded to the youthful Castro with enthusiasm and demanded "fair play" for the Cuban Revolution.

In May 1960 they were ready for an action of their own, and the opportunity was provided by the House Un-American Activities Committee. Hundreds of students from the campuses of the University of California at Berkeley and San Francisco State College, joined by some of the people who were moving away from the inactivity of the "beat" coffee houses, demonstrated physically against the Committee's San Francisco hearing. And after the demonstration, which received enormous publicity, they scorned the allegation that they had been led or inspired by the Communists. That charge, which they knew to be untrue, only reinforced their feelings of distrust for the celebrants of American society.

They identified, too, with the Freedom Riders who went South in 1960 and 1961; for this again meant taking direct action with their own bodies against segregation. They were not interested in theory, and so the long historical articles even in such left journals as *Studies* were not seen by them as being relevant.

This new activist Movement influenced even those who thought of themselves as being outside of society. As the apolitical "beats" —almost alone as symbols of protest in the fifties—turned their concern to concrete issues of racial equality and peace, their style, dress, and decor affected the activists. Arguments about politics began to include discussions of sexual freedom and marijuana. The language of the Negro poet-hipster permeated analyses of the

Cuban Revolution. Protests over the execution of Caryl Chessman ultimately brought together students and some Bohemians—the loose and overlapping segments of what was to become known as The Movement.

In the formal sense SDS is a direct descendant of the Student League for Industrial Democracy (SLID), organized in 1930 by the League for Industrial Democracy, a Fabian group closely linked to the Socialist Party. During the thirties, SLID had been a Socialist opposition to the Communist-dominated National Student Union (NSU). SLID and the NSU merged to form the American Student Union, which died a few years later, torn apart by an internal struggle between the Socialists and Communists.

After the end of World War II, SLID was revived, under the leadership of James Farmer, who later became national chairman of CORE. But the new SLID suffered from the deadening effect of McCarthyism on the campus, and by the end of the fifties its membership had dwindled. It was revived by the new activist radicals, mostly from the University of Michigan campus, who took it over in 1960 and gave it an action orientation.

SDS maintained a formal but steadily weakening link with the LID, for purposes of tax exemption and for an aura of respectability, not from any common ideology, but on January 1, 1966, there was a break. SDS is a new radical group with few ties to any of the older left groups in America. In the view of SDS, LID, once an active and vital socialist education organization, is now dominated by aging trade unionists whose anti-Communism outweighs old commitments to socialism. In turn, SDS's radical critique of American policy goes too far for most of the LID board, especially since SDS does not frame its analysis from an anti-Communist premise.

Although the Students for a Democratic Society had dissipated into factions in 1969, the remnants of SDS leadership were reassembled in 1969 in the courtroom of Judge Julius Hoffman for the "great conspiracy trial." The defendants in this trial included Tom Hayden, Abby Hoffman, Jerry Rubin and Rennie Davis, all former members of SDS and other campus radical groups. Indicted along with them, for planning and leadership of the Chicago demonstrations of 1968, were David Dellinger, John Froines, Lee Weiner and Bobby Seale. (Seale's autobiography is included in the section below on the Black

Panthers.) In 1972, the convictions of the Chicago "conspirators" (except for Seale, whose case was severed from the others) were overturned by an appeals court, which ruled the Judge Julius Hoffman's conduct was improper. Above and beyond the legal implications of the trial, there were important symbolic and historical implications, which are described dramatically by Tom Hayden.

TOM HAYDEN

SOURCE: From Trial by Tom Hayden, Copyright © 1970 by Tom Hayden. Reprinted by permission of Holt, Rinehart and Winston, Inc.

The trial became a watershed experience for an entire generation of alienated white youth. It symbolized our passage over that line separating the respectable from the criminal. From now on, even middle-class white children would no longer be safe from the paranoid wrath of the older, entrenched generation. We had seen it coming at the Pentagon, at Columbia and in the streets of Chicago, and finally at People's Park where murderous bullets were unleashed against tender white skin. The trial brought all these isolated lessons into a single focus.

Future histories will locate the late Sixties as the time when America's famous democratic pragmatism began hardening into an inflexible fascist core. To those of us living these times, however, it has come as something of a surprise. The New Leftists of the early Sixties, and many of the black radicals as well, were preoccupied not with the danger of fascist repression but that of liberal co-optation. We saw a power structure with such vast wealth and weaponry that it seemed beyond defeat. More than that, it seemed capable of preventing even the emergence of a real political challenge. Because of the generally high standard of living and the system's adaptability to social pressures, we seemed doomed to exist only as a marginal force. We accepted Mills and the early Marcuse as prophets of a new social order which had managed to stabilize all its major contradictions.

. . .

Any explanation of Chicago must begin with the fact that a violent and repressive element of the Democratic Party took power over domestic affairs, as it already had over foreign policy. The Chicago Convention marked the triumph for this element in a dispute which divided the party at the highest level in its attitude toward protest.

Some of this murky history came out at the trial in the testimony of Justice Department officials and in interviews with Ramsey Clark, who was not allowed to testify. A deep split apparently developed in 1968 between Clark and Mayor Daley over Chicago's handling of the black rebellion. Clark termed Daley's shoot-to-kill order "unlawful and unthinkable," and no real communication took place between the two men after that. In July, Clark dispatched the head of his Community Relations Service, Roger Wilkins, and a law enforcement specialist, Wesley Pomeroy, in an effort to get permit negotiations under way in Chicago. According to Clark, the Justice Department officials found Rennie Davis responsive but got nowhere with Daley.

During this same period, Clark evidently was becoming completely isolated within higher government circles. He rejected FBI evaluations of dissenters, including several members of the Conspiracy, and refused to warrant wiretapping of our phones. His handling of the Poor Peoples' campaign in the spring of 1968 drew the wrath of other federal officials. During that campaign, although Clark's mediators kept violence to a minimum around Resurrection City (an effort which certainly prepared them to handle Lincoln Park), the Attorney General was blamed for the general spectacle and for the embarrassing protests held at various government agencies.

About one week before the Convention, a critical meeting was held in the Oval Room of the White House. Present at this meeting were Lyndon Johnson, White House staff, Defense Department officials and Clark. Daley and Police Superintendent James Conlisk had called for the pre-positioning of 500 federal troops near Chicago, Conlisk having cited articles in the Berkeley Barb as part of his justification. Only the Attorney General advised against moving the troops, claiming it would have "disastrous policy implications" by creating a climate of expectation that the troops would be used.

This political conflict summarized the general crisis of the 1960's, in which those liberals who had worked with protest to improve the system (Clark, Kennedy, McCarthy) became increasingly divided from those conservatives who would prevent the spread of protest by any means necessary (Johnson, Nixon).

Our crime was our identity.

Even the sympathetic press misunderstood, billing our case as one of "dissent on trial." So did Bill Kunstler in the beginning, when he spoke of repression of "the spectrum of dissent" and implied that we differed from other Americans only in our political opinions. Although there was a certain amount of obvious truth in this claim, it always seemed superficial to us.

The vague nature of the government's case made us feel we were on trial for something deeper and unspoken. The charges against us, for example, made no sense. It was not a matter of deciding whether we were innocent or guilty; usually it was a matter of trying to comprehend what the case was all about.

Against our common sense, the government kept insisting that the trial was not "political," not about the Vietnam war, not about the Black Panther Party, but was simply the prosecution of a criminal indictment. It was, for them, a question of whether we had conspired to cross state lines with the intention or organizing, promoting or encouraging a riot. To prove their case they relied on evidence from Chicago policemen, undercover and FBI agents, Army and Navy personnel, two Chicago Tribune reporters, and only two civilians with no apparent police connections.

Despite their claims, however, the government presented little evidence of "conspiracy." In fact, government attorney Richard Shultz acknowledged that we never all met together, not even once. Bobby Seale never met any of us until coming to Chicago, and then he only met Jerry Rubin. Evidence of conspiracy in a criminal trial, however, defies the everyday imagination. The government argued that it was necessary only that we "shared a common design." But even if we did, why only the eight of us? Why not Tom Neuman, Craig Shimabokuro or several other "un-indicted co-conspirators" who seemed, from the government's evidence, to have done more in Chicago than had several of us? Why not Dick Gregory, who had announced that the convention would take place "over his dead body," and then, after withdrawing from the planning, returned to lead a march at which more arrests were made than at any other time during Convention Week? Why not Norman Mailer, whom we invited to speak and who told an angry assembly that we were "at the beginning of a war and the march immediately afterwards will be one battle in that war"?

We became the Conspiracy not because we did anything together in 1968, but simply because we were indicted together. We became closely knit because of the trial, and perhaps the government was relying on this very process for its proof. By intertwining our names through the testimony (as if the words and evidence reflected the reality of 1968) while we sat together at the defense table for five months, it might begin to appear to a jury that we always had been at interconnected unit. But evidently it never convinced the jury, and it certainly made us feel strange, like survivors of a shipwreck getting to know each other because we shared the same raft.

Tom Hayden has also provided us with a glimpse into his own background in testimony before the House Committee on Un-American Activities (HUAC). This testimony takes the form of answers to questions from the Chief Counsel of the committee, and sketches the biographical details of Hayden's life up to the founding convention of SDS in 1961.

TOM HAYDEN

SOURCE: *Reprinted by permission of The World Publishing Company from* Rebellion and Repression *by Tom Hayden, pp. 53–55. Copyright* © *1969 by the New Weekly Project, Inc.*

Conley: Mr. Hayden, would you give us a brief résumé of your educational background, please?

Hayden: Yes, I attended Royal Oak-Dondero High School in Royal Oak, Michigan, from 1954 to 1957. I attended the University of Michigan, 1957 to 1961. I returned to the University of Michigan 1962 through part of 1964, as a graduate student, and as an instructor, and I taught political science at Rutgers University in 1967.

Conley: I don't believe you mentioned it. Did you get a degree from the University of Michigan?

Hayden: I did not complete my graduate studies.

Conley: Did you get a bachelor's?

Hayden: I got a bachelor's degree in 1961.

Conley: Was this in English?

Hayden: Yes.

Conley: Now, Mr. Hayden, since your completion of your education, what particular positions have you held, since you completed your education?

Hayden: What do you mean by "positions"?

Conley: What jobs have you held, sir?

Hayden: You mean, jobs in the sense of how I get money?

Conley: Well, let us start with that, yes.

Hayden: Or political positions, or what?

Conley: Let us start with the jobs that you held where you get money.

Hayden: Well, I have done some teaching, as I said, at Rutgers University. I have been paid as an author and lecturer, published two books, one by New American Library–Signet, on North Vietnam, and another on the conditions in Newark at the time of the rebellion of July, 1967, which was published by Random House.

Conley: Was this book *Rebellion in Newark?*

Hayden: Right. And I remain under contract, writing another book on Vietnam for the same publishing house.

Conley: All right. Now have you, in connection with your book writing, also written the preface to a book called *Mission to Hanoi?*

Hayden: You mean the book by Communist Party theoretician Herbert Aptheker.

Conley: Yes, sir.

Hayden: Yes, I traveled, I was a fellow traveler to Hanoi with Herbert Aptheker in 1965, and I did write an introduction to his book, before I proceeded to write a book giving my own political views.

Conley: Now then, these are the jobs that you have held where you received pay, as I understand.

Hayden: As far as I can recall.

Conley: Now what jobs have you held in the political area, as you define it?

Hayden: Well, I consider myself an organizer of a movement to put you and your committee out of power, because I think you represent racist philosophy that has no meaning any more in the twentieth century.

Conley: What group do you refer to that you represent?

Hayden: I have worked for many groups. As you know, I worked very hard for several years for Students for a Democratic Society.

Conley: Were you president of that group from June of '62 to '63?

Hayden: I was president of SDS, yes, during the time that you designate. But before that, I was an organizer of it, and afterwards, I remained affiliated with it for some time.

Conley: Were you the author of the Port Huron Statement?

Hayden: I wish that I was, but I was merely a drafter of the original document, and the author of the document was the convention itself, that met in Port Huron.

Conley: You assisted, then, in the preparation of the document which was adopted by the convention?

Hayden: I was probably the major author of the original draft.

Conley: Was it materially changed by the convention?

Hayden: Yes. It had a better position on American Capitalism. I was not too clear about the problems of American society and the convention straightened me out by deciding that the profit system that you represent is a fundamental thing to be moved aside, so that the country can move ahead.

Jerry Rubin's book, DO IT!, is a narrative of radicalism with strongly personal bent. It opens with a biographical sketch which not only describe's Rubin's childhood but also reveals some of his philosophy.

JERRY RUBIN

SOURCE: From Jerry Rubin, DO IT! Copyright © 1970, by the Social Education Foundation. Reprinted by permission of Simon and Schuster.

I am a child of Amerika.

If I'm ever sent to Death Row for my revolutionary "crimes," I'll order as my last meal: a hamburger, french fries and a Coke.

I dig big cities.

I love to read the sports pages and gossip columns, listen to the radio and watch color TV.

I dig department stores, huge supermarkets and airports. I feel secure (though not necessarily hungry) when I see Howard Johnson's on the expressway.

I groove on Hollywood movies—even bad ones.

I speak only one language—English.

I love rock 'n' roll.

I collected baseball players' cards when I was a kid and wanted to play second base for the Cincinnati Reds, my home team.

I got a car when I was sixteen after flunking my first driver's test and crying for a week waiting to take it a second time.

I went to the kind of high school where you had to pass a test to get *in*.

I graduated in the bottom half of the class.

My classmates voted me the "busiest" senior in the school.

I had short, short, short hair.

I dug *Catcher in the Rye*.

I didn't have pimples.

I became an ace young reporter for the Cincinnati *Post and Times-Star*. "Son," the managing editor said to me, "*someday you're going to be a helluva reporter, maybe the greatest reporter this city's ever seen.*"

I loved Adlai Stevenson.

My father drove a truck delivering bread and later became an organizer in the Bakery Drivers' Union. He dug Jimmy Hoffa (so do I). He died of heart failure at fifty-two.

My mother had a college degree and played the piano. She died of cancer at the age of fifty-one.

I took care of my brother, Gil, from the time he was thirteen.

I dodged the draft.

I went to Oberlin College for a year, graduated from the University of Cincinnati, spent 1½ years in Israel and started graduate school at Berkeley.

I dropped out.

I dropped out of the White Race and the Amerikan nation.

I dig being free.

I like getting high.

I don't own a suit or tie.

I live for the revolution.

I'm a yippie!

I am an orphan of Amerika.

Radicalism in the sixties developed in two directions. There were white, middle-class, alienated intellectuals who made up the membership of the "new left." But there were also many black intellectual radicals, between two cultures, who eventually went the direction of separatism and black liberation. Beginning with the Student

Non-violent Coordinating Committee, the black radicals moved from civil rights to black power in 1966. In the late sixties, the Black Panther Party emerged as the foremost black liberation movement. The Panthers eventually absorbed some of the remnants of SNCC through a short-lived alliance. More significantly, the Panthers absorbed the radical constituency of SNCC: the black youth and black intellectuals in northern cities.

Because of its dominance of the Black liberation movement, the Black Panther Party is the principal subject of this section on new radicalism. The first selection here is a conventional historical review of the chronology of the Black Panther Party by Theodore Draper, whose credentials include expertise on the history of old radicalism (see Chapter Five). Draper combines the biographical background of Huey P. Newton and Bobby Seale, founders of the party, with a discussion of the development of the Panther ideology. He suggests that the Panthers cannot be classified as a black nationalist group but must be analyzed as new radicals.

THEODORE DRAPER

SOURCE: From The Rediscovery of Black Nationalism *by Theodore Draper. Copyright © 1969, 1970 by Theodore Draper. Reprinted by permission of The Viking Press, Inc.*

The Black Panthers, perhaps the most interesting and influential of the present-day purely political nationalist movements, have also had trouble with the concepts of a black "colony" and "nation" in the United States. They have tried to cope with the difficulties in still another way.

The Black Panther Party was formed in Oakland, California, in October 1966 by two young black nationalists, Huey P. Newton, then twenty-five, and Bobby Seale, five years older. The guiding spirit and dominant personality was—and is—Newton. His family, which he once described as "lower class, working class," moved from Louisiana, where he was born, the youngest of seven children, to California. He was graduated from two-year Merritt College, in Oakland, where he met Seale. At the school they took their first step toward nationalist political activity by joining a local Afro-American Association, which soon proved insufficiently militant for them. Newton wanted to become a lawyer, Seale an actor. About a year at San Francisco Law School convinced Newton that he was not cut out to be a lawyer. Seale spent almost four years in the Army, the last six months in the stockade because, he later claimed, "I opposed racism in the top brass, [in] a lieutenant-colonel," and he was given a "bad conduct discharge" one month before the end of his four-year term. He then drifted from odd job to odd job without getting very far in his chosen career.

One evening, during an argument at a party, Newton slashed a black auto worker with a steak knife and spent eight months in jail for the assault. After his release he and Seale got together again, and according to one version, Seale stimulated his renewed political activity by giving him *The Wretched of the Earth* by Frantz Fanon to read. When some of their younger friends at Merritt formed a Soul Students Advisory Council to demand a "black curriculum," they took an interest in it.

An incident in Berkeley apparently led them to go much further. It seems that a white policeman tried to arrest Seale for reciting poems from a chair at an outdoor café, thereby blocking the sidewalk. A fight ensued; no one was arrested. But Newton and Seale thereupon decided to give up the Soul Students Advisory Council and to form a broader organization called the Black Panther Party for Self-Defense. (The panther reference came from the symbol of Lowndes County Freedom Organization that had been launched in Alabama six months earlier.) The name was later shortened to Black Panther Party to emphasize a larger goal than "self-defense." While working in the Poverty Office in Oakland in October 1966, they wrote a 10-Point Platform and Program for the new party.

The Panthers seemed at first little more than another self-appointed local band of black nationalists in an urban ghetto. Their chief claims to publicity were their armed patrols, which drove through the streets of Oakland, and their mannerism of saying "right on" as often as possible. Their first important convert early in 1967 was Eldridge Cleaver, author of *Soul on Ice*, who, like Malcolm X, had been converted to Elijah Muhammad's Black Muslims in prison and had sided with Malcolm X after the latter's break with them. Newton impressed Cleaver, who was then working for *Ramparts*, by leading a group of armed Panthers into the office of the magazine and daring a policeman to shoot him. The police flinched that time, but in a shoot-out in Oakland in October 1967, Newton was wounded, one policeman was killed, another was wounded, and Newton was given a two-to-fifteen-year sentence for manslaughter.*

. . .

Since 1967 Black Panther ideology has become a more fully developed, if not essentially different, system. In essence, it is a hybrid made up of revolutionary black nationalism and what is by now an old friend, "Marxism-Leninism." As a result, it is not quite like any other black nationalism or any other Marxism-Leninism. For example, no other "Marxist-Leninists" have ever identified themselves with the *Lumpenproletariat*, the most rootless and degraded elements in capitalist society, whom Marx and Engels regarded as a "dangerous class" whose conditions of life destined it to play a reactionary role. The peculiar "amalgam," as Trotsky would have called it, of bits and pieces from Frantz Fanon, Malcolm X, Mao Tse-tung, Ernesto Che Guevara, Régis Debray, and others, is typical of the kind of do-it-yourself Marxism-Leninism that has come into vogue. It is especially characteristic of movements which have invited themselves into the Marxist-Leninist tradition from the outside, bringing with them their own national or particularist folkways, and shopping among all the current versions of the doctrine for those features or formulas which happen to suit or please them the most. In this respect Black Pantherism resembles Castroism but has gone much further in asserting its individuality.

Organizationally the party also shows it hybrid make-up. It is headed by a Central Committee, a term traditionally used in the Communist movement. But unlike such parties, which are headed by Secretaries or General Secretaries, the Panthers' No. 1 leader is the Minister of Defense—Huey P. Newton. The idea that the top leadership should reside in the military commander, who simultaneously fulfills the chief political role, derives directly from Régis Debray. After Newton comes Bobby Seale, the Chairman, reminiscent of Mao Tse-tung's favorite title. The next in line is the Minister of Information, Eldridge Cleaver (in absentia). No. 4 is the Chief of Staff, David Hilliard, an ex-longshoreman. The Central Committee also contains a Field Marshal, Don Cox; a Minister of Education, Ray "Masai" Hewitt; a Minister of Foreign

---

*In 1971, Newton's conviction was overturned and the government dropped the case. Newton has returned to the leadership of the Black Panther Party. (Ed.)

Affairs (unnamed); a Minister of Justice (unnamed); a Prime Minister (unnamed); a Communications Secretary, Kathleen Cleaver, wife of Eldridge Cleaver; and a Minister of Culture, Emory Douglas, who is also the party's Revolutionary Artist. With Newton in prison and Cleaver in exile, the two main leaders have been Seale and Hilliard. Local Panther groups duplicate the national set-up with a Deputy Chief of Staff and Deputy Ministers.

In October 1967 Huey Newton was arrested and charged with the murder of John Frey, a white policeman. In the following brief selection, Gene Marine describes the events that occurred during the period when Newton was removed from party leadership by his trial and imprisonment for manslaughter.

This is the period when Eldridge Cleaver dominated the Black Panther Party and created an explicit radical ideology for it. (Cleaver was later expelled from the party, apparently because he overemphasized ideology and underemphasized community service.)

GENE MARINE

SOURCE: *From Gene Marine,* The Black Panthers *(Signet Books, 1969). Reprinted by permission of The New American Library.*

. . . John Frey died on October 28, 1967; Huey Newton did not go to trial until July 15, 1968, and the verdict did not come back in until September 8. In the meantime, the rest of the story of the Black Panthers did not stop—in fact, it was only beginning. Between arrest and trial, for instance:

• Eldridge Cleaver emerged into a position of leadership as both theorist and activist.

• The Black Panthers allied themselves almost simultaneously with all-black SNCC and the nearly all-white Peace and Freedom Party, later to break with SNCC again.

• The pattern of police harrassment spread from Oakland to other Bay Area cities and then across the country as, in mid-1968, the Black Panthers set out to become a truly national organization.

• In New York alone, the Black Panther Party signed eight hundred members in a single month.

• In the meantime, the now famous but still obscure "shoot-

114

out" took place in Oakland, resulting in the wounding and rearrest of Cleaver and the murder of Panther Treasurer Bobby Hutton.

• The Panthers drew support from Tanzania and Guinea, and moved to place their case before the United Nations.

• Panthers were killed by police in Seattle and Los Angeles, and beaten in New York.

• The battle over Cleaver's teaching at the University of California began, to be followed by the whole "Cleaver affair," which at this writing has resulted in his disappearance.

All of these things, some of them little known, some of them national news, but all of them a regular part of the Bay Area press' by now hysterical campaign against Panthers, came between Huey's arrest and his trial, as did the McCarthy and Kennedy campaigns, the Johnson withdrawal, the bombing halt, the primary elections, and both national conventions. And as did the assassinations of Robert Kennedy and, much more important in this context, Martin Luther King.

Biographical portraits of black radicals would be incomplete without the inclusion of Malcolm X. Although he was assassinated before the founding of the Black Panther Party, he is regarded as a hero by the Panthers (see Chapter Fourteen). Malcolm X went through a life that included ghetto hustling, imprisonment, conversion to the Black Muslims, apostacy, the founding of his own movement, and finally assassination (some say at the instigation of the Black Muslims). In the following excerpt from the *Autobiography of Malcolm X*, he describes "hustling" and his conversion experience—an experience typical of many leaders of social movements.

MALCOLM X

SOURCE: From The Autobiography of Malcolm X. *Reprinted by permission of Grove Press, Inc. Copyright © 1964 by Alex Haley and Malcolm X, copyright © 1965 by Alex Haley and Betty Shabazz.*

There I was back in Harlem's streets among all the rest of the hustlers. I couldn't sell reefers; the dope squad detectives were too familiar with me. I was a true hustler—uneducated, unskilled at anything honorable, and I considered myself nervy and cunning enough to live by my wits, exploiting any prey that presented itself. I would risk just about anything.

Right now, in every big city ghetto, tens of thousands of yesterday's and today's school drop-outs are keeping body and soul together by some form of hustling in the same way I did. And they inevitably move into more and more, worse and worse, illegality and immorality. Full-time hustlers never can relax to appraise what they are doing and where they are bound. As is the case in any jungle, the hustler's every waking hour is lived with both the practical and the subconscious knowledge that if he ever relaxes, if he ever slows down, the other hungry, restless foxes, ferrets, wolves, and vultures out there with him won't hesitate to make him their prey.

. . .

Many a time, I have looked back, trying to assess, just for myself, my first reactions to all this. Every instinct of the ghetto jungle streets, every hustling fox and criminal wolf instinct in me, which would have scoffed at and rejected anything else, was struck numb. It was as though all of that life merely was back there, without any remaining effect, of influence. I remember how, some time later, reading the Bible in the Norfolk Prison Colony library, I came upon, then I read, over and over, how Paul on the road to Damascus, upon hearing the voice of Christ, was so smitten that he was knocked off his horse, in a daze. I do not now, and I did not then, liken myself to Paul. But I do understand his experience.

I have since learned—helping me to understand what then began to happen within me—that the truth can be quickly received, or received at all, only by the sinner who knows and admits that he is guilty of having sinned much. Stated another way: only guilt admitted accepts truth. The Bible again: the one people whom Jesus could not help were the Pharisees; they didn't feel they needed any help.

Bobby Seale was one of the co-founders of the Black Panther Party; Huey P. Newton was the other. Of the two, Seale is the only one who has written an autobiography. The following selections from Seale's book *Seize the Time* are not comprehensive, but they do reflect some of the significant conjunctions of Seale's life with growth and changes in the Black Panther Party.

BOBBY SEALE

SOURCE: From Seize the Time by Bobby Seale, pp. 4–6, 13, 61–62. Copyright © 1968, 1969, 1970 by Bobby Seale. Reprinted by permission of Random House, Inc.

I was born in Dallas, Texas, October 22, 1936. I grew up with a brother, a sister, and a cousin who lived with us named Alvin Turner. He was the son of my mother's identical twin. Off and on, I learned things like everybody else learned things. I'm no different from other people growing up and living and learning. I was raised up like the average black man, like a brother in the black community. A lot of things affected me in a way that caused me to see things. Huey was most significant, but a lot of things in the past affected me before Huey molded my attitude—unjust things that happened.

The farthest back I can remember is when I was unjustly whopped by my father—I can never forget that. My father and mother were having an argument. I was supposed to be washing some shirt in the back yard of a house we had in San Antonio. I was the oldest of three children, and was about six years old. I remember very vividly that I was playing in the back, and how my father told me to get the wash basin, put some water in it, and wash his shirt. I tried to wash his shirt, but then I guess I started playing. He was arguing with my mother, and it had something to do with that shirt. My father came outside and was mad at me because I hadn't finished the shirt; he took his belt off and really beat me. He went back inside the house and argued again with my mother. I was crying. When he came back and beat me again, my mother came out and stopped him and snatched the strap away, but he got it back from her and argued with her. Then he pushed her and beat me again. He told me to wash that shirt. I never forgot that beating. I never have, because it was an unjust beating. The argument he was having with my mother was directly related to him taking it out on me, and it wasn't right.

My father was a carpenter in Port Arthur, Texas. My mother had left him a couple of times, and one time when they got back together he built a house up from the ground. My father was a master carpenter. That's where I learned my carpentry work. I learned drafting in school, but I knew basic building structure from being around my father. He taught it to me and my brother off and on while we were growing up.

I grew up just like any other brother. We didn't always have money. During the war we had a little money, but after my father built the house he went to San Antonio, and then we were back in poverty again. It was still wartime and there was some money around, but I remember that whenever my mother and father rented a house, they would rent half out to some other people, a whole family.

I think the first time I really began to oppose things that I saw was when we were at Cordonices Village, the government housing project in Berkeley. People were living in poverty and semi-poverty. We lived in very crowded conditions with my mother's twin sister and her son. The place was always dirty. My mother always tried to save money, but the money was used up every time my father was laid off. (He wasn't able to get in the union at that time. Later, he and three other guys were the only black cats in the carpenter's union in all of California.)

We lived in poverty mostly because of my father's eighth-grade education. His father used to be rough on him. My father was a lot rougher on me in certain periods of my life, just like his father was rough on him. His father used to beat him, and one day my father left and wouldn't work for his father any more. I pulled the same thing. One day I stopped and I wouldn't work for my father any more because he wouldn't pay me. At that time I didn't know what the word exploitation meant, but that's exactly what it was, and I rejected it and opposed it.

My mother never really had any money. When I was thirteen, I used to make money on my own, hauling groceries and cutting lawns. It wasn't always profitable, but sometimes I could make a dollar or two here and there, me and a couple of brothers I used to run around with. I ran around with a couple of gangs in my younger days, when I was fourteen, fifteen, and sixteen.

. . .

Brother Huey P. Newton put the Black Panther Party into motion. Brother Huey is the Minister of Defense and leader of the Black Panther Party. He is presently a political prisoner, but he is still the philosophical theoretician, the practitioner, the head director, and top official spokesman for the Black Panther Party. It is impossible to talk about the Black Panther Party without first talking about Huey P. Newton, because brother Huey put it all into motion. We sometimes talk about "the genius of Huey P. Newton."

I met Huey P. Newton in the early Sixties, during the Cuban blockade when there were numerous street rallies going on around Merritt Junior College in West Oakland.

. . .

One day Huey said, "It's about time we get the organization off the ground, and do it now."

This was in the latter part of September 1966. From around the first of October to the fifteenth of October, in the poverty center in North Oakland, Huey and I began to write out a ten-point platform and program of the Black Panther Party. Huey himself articulated it word for word. All I made were suggestions.

Huey said, "We need a program. We have to have a program for the people. A program that relates to the people. A program that the people can understand. A program that the people can read and see, and which expresses their desires and needs at the same time. It's got to relate to the philosophical meaning of where in the world we are going, but the philosophical meaning will also have to relate to something specific."

That was very important with Huey. So, Huey divided it up into "What We Want" and "What We Believe." "What We Want" are practical, specific things that we need and that should exist. At the time, we expressed philosophically, but concretely, what we believe. So we read the program one to one. Point One of "What We Want" and Point One of "What We Believe." Point Two of "What We Want" then we got into "What We Believe." We went through everything we believed that was correlative to everything that we wanted.

Huey said, "This ten-point platform and program is what we want and what we believe. These things did not just come out of the clear blue sky. This is what black people have been voicing all along for over 100 years since the Emancipation Proclamation and even before that. These things are directly related to the things we had before we left Africa."

When we got all through writing the program, Huey said, "We've got to have some kind of structure. What do you want to be," he asked me, "Chairman or Minister of Defense?"

"Doesn't make any difference to me," I said. "What do you want to be, Chairman or Minister of Defense?"

"I'll be the Minister of Defense," Huey said, "and you'll be the Chairman."

"That's fine with me," I told him, and that's just the way that shit came about, how Huey became the Minister of Defense and I became the Chairman of the Black Panther Party. Just like that.

With the ten-point platform and program and the two of us, the Party was offically launched on October 15, 1966, in a poverty program office in the black community in Oakland, California.

OLD FUNDAMENTALISM

Fundamentalist and nativist movements in America arose in the context of social changes in which Protestant doctrines were eroded by economic and demographic shifts. The "work ethic" and associated tenets of morality were outmoded by industrialization, which displaced the small entrepreneur, and immigration, which led to the displacement of Protestant workers by Catholics.

In the following selections, Lipset and Raab lay the groundwork for our later analysis of the ideology of the Christian Crusade and the John Birch Society with a review of the major trends in American history leading to today's "radical right." Their historical review begins with a discussion of the Anti-Masonic movement, the "Know-Nothings," and the American Protective Association (APA) in the nineteenth century, and proceeds to a discussion of the Ku Klux Klan in the 1920's and the Coughlin movement in the 1930's. Each of these groups represented a "dispossessed" constituency whose values and status were displaced by change.

SEYMOUR MARTIN LIPSET AND EARL RAAB

SOURCE: From The Politics of Unreason *by S. M. Lipset and Earl Raab, pp. 61–62, 485–487. Copyright © 1970 by Anti-Defamation League of B'nai B'rith. By permission of Harper & Row Publishers, Inc.*

Right-wing extremist movements in America have all risen against the background of economic and social changes which have resulted in the displacement of some population groups from former positions of dominance. After the American Revolution, it was the growth of farmer power, as the frontier expanded, beginning to be felt by the mercantile interests of the eastern seaboard. The elite of the East and the disestablished clergy were caught up in this displacement. Behind the Know-Nothings were the technological advances which began to corrode the hegemony of the skilled craftsmen in the cities with unskilled labor, at the same time that it foreshadowed the movement back to the cities. After the Civil War, as the APA movement developed, the processes of urbanization and industrialization came into full flow. Economic power had shifted to the cities. The farmers were in increasing trouble. The workers in the city began to feel the pressure of immigrant workers. At the upper level, the old elite was feeling the pressure of the new wealthy. And in all cases, the displaced tended to be Protestants; those displacing, non-Protestant immigrants. This came to a head in the 1920's as the KKK developed: urban power had clearly become dominant; everything outside the city was becoming the backwater. The "backwater" population was streaming to the city; and on another level, labor power was beginning to challenge the economic power monopoly of the industrialists. In the 1930's of Coughlin, that challenge became thunderous for the economic elite; and the lower non-Protestant middle class became concerned for their newly won position, at the same time that they desired some change. In the 1950's of McCarthy, the displacement was on a national scale as America's corporate position in the world seemed to slip badly. And the Birch Society, perhaps the last backlash gasp of economic royalism, began to reflect a new displacement, that of white dominance. George Wallace flourished on that displacement.

In addition to identifiable group displacement, there was something more precise taking place in each of these periods: formal political alignments were shifting, and the conservative political party was usually in trouble.

The early anti-Illuminati flurry of the late 1790's coincided with the decline of Federalism. The Anti-Masons arose with the defeat of the conservative John Quincy Adams and the rise of the Jacksonian party. The emergence of the Know-Nothings as a mass movement occurred after the breakup of the conservative Whig party following its defeat in the election of 1852. Party lines had begun to crumble during this period as a result of the slavery issue. The

Republicans suffered their greatest defeat since their formation in the congressional elections of 1890, and the Democrats won the Presidency in 1892 with their first decisive plurality since before the Civil War. The 1890's saw the dramatic rise of the APA. The Republican party was not in trouble in the 1920's as it shifted back into power, along with the postwar rise of the KKK, but it had just emerged from the first shock of government interventionism. And there was a new alignment developing in the country: the first southern Democratic–northern Republican issues coalition against northern urban Democrats. In Coughlin's 1930's, of course, the Republican party collapsed. In the 1950's, McCarthy came to prominence after victory had been snatched away from a desperate Republican party at the last moment in 1948. The Birch Society came to prominence as the desperate ultraconservatives found that Republican victory no longer meant a return to Harding. George Wallace became politically potent at a time when the creaking Democratic party coalition seemed to be seriously breaking up.

The political disorganization of these periods was marked not only by dislocations of the great party coalitions but also by the process which has become known as "polarization." This term generally describes the condition whereby significant sections of the population are thrown out to both the left and the right; that is, to both ends of the preservatist-innovative axis. The early Anti-Masons were accompanied by the Jacksonian radicals and the urban-based workingmen's parties; the nativists of the 1840's and 1850's by the Abolitionists; the APA by the Populists; the Klan of the twenties by the Farmer-Labor Progressive movement; Coughlin by the active radical left movements of the 1930's; George Wallace by the "New Left" and the "Black Revolution." The history of modern European politics reveals the same recurrent phenomenon.

One meaning of the polarization process is that it poses two forces in the political arena which react not only to the issue but to each other. And as they begin to react more to each other—or to their perceptions of each other—than to the issues, the condition of ideological polarization approaches the condition of extremism or monism. The issue market place is replaced by the Armageddon of good and evil forces.

From another vantage point this means that the legitimacy of the political system is at least partially breaking down. The legitimacy of the American system exists to the extent that consensus about the rules of conflict prevail. But, as we have seen, the common commitment to the democratic rules of conflict is not internalized, but is rather more often related to a sense of loyalty to the legitimacy of the general social system. On each occasion when a major extremist movement was on the rise, the condition of political disorganization and volatility was matched and related to a condition of social disorganization and voltility. Segments of the population were feeling the press of displacement and dislocation. The traditional loyalties to social and political institutions were loosened. The low democratic restraint most prevalent among the less privileged was exposed. In the case of right-wing political movements, the natural economic interests of the concerned elite and of the disaffected lower strata were conflicting, and the political appeal had to be made on other than a class basis. It is at this point that the phenomenon of low-status backlash becomes critical to the development of extremist movements.

For a while, fundamentalism was associated with populism in America. William Jennings Bryan is the symbol of this aspect of fundamentalism: three times a candidate for president at the turn of the century, he later returned to public life as a participant in the "Scopes Trial," which challenged a Tennessee law against teaching evolution because it violated Christian doctrine. In this phase of his public career, Bryan was a symbol of the anti-intellectualism of fundamentalism. In the following selection, Richard Hofstadter describes the historical association between fundamentalism and anti-intellectualism. He also describes how fundamentalism has been emptied of religious meaning and made into ideology, a point we shall return to in Part Four.

RICHARD HOFSTADTER

SOURCE: From Anti-Intellectualism in American Life, by Richard Hofstadter. Copyright © 1962, 1963 by Richard Hofstadter. Reprinted by permission of Alfred A. Knopf, Inc.

It was appropriate that the national leadership of the anti-evolution crusade should have fallen to Bryan, a layman who combined in his person the two basic ancestral pieties of the people—evangelical faith and populistic democracy. In his mind, faith and democracy converged in a common anti-intellectualist rationale. On one side were the voices of the people and the truths of the heart; on the other were the intellectuals, a small arrogant elite given over to false science and mechanical rationalism—variously described by him as a "scientific soviet" and a "little irresponsible oligarchy of self-styled 'intellectuals.'" Religion, he pointed out, had never belonged exclusively to an elite: "Christianity is intended for *all*, not for the so-called 'thinkers' only." Mind, being mechanical, needs the heart to direct it. Mind can plan the commission of crimes as well as deeds for the benefit of society. "Mind worship is the great sin in the intellectual world today." Only the heart—which is the province of religion—can bring discipline to the things of the mind so that they work for good.

Here is the crux of the matter: the juncture between populistic democracy and old-fashioned religion. Since the affairs of the heart are the affairs of the common man, and since the common man's intuition in such matters is as good as—indeed better than—that of the intellectuals, his judgment in matters of religion should rule. Where there appeared to be a conflict between religion and science, it was the public, Bryan believed, and not "those who measure men by diplomas and college degrees," who should decide. As Walter Lippmann observed, the religious doctrine that all men will at last stand equal before the throne of God was somehow transmuted in Bryan's mind into the idea that all men were equally good biologists before the ballot box of Tennessee. In effect, Bryan proposed to put the question of evolution to the vote of Christians, and the issue was metamorphosed into a question of the rights of the majority.

One of the striking things that has occurred in the inspirational literature is that the voluntaristic and subjective impulses which I noted in commenting on the development of American Protestantism seem to have come into complete possession and to have run wild. There has been a progressive attenuation of the components of religion. Protestantism at an early point got rid of the bulk of religious ritual, and in the course of its development in the nineteenth and twentieth centuries went very far to minimize doctrine. The inspirational cult has completed this process, for it has largely eliminated doctrine—at least it has eliminated most doctrine that could be called Christian. Nothing, then, is left but the subjective experience of the individual and even this is reduced in the main to an assertion of his will. What the inspirational writers mean when they say you can accomplish whatever you wish by taking thought is that you can will your goals and mobilize God to help you release fabulous energies.

Of the two "radical right" groups included in this book, the Christian Crusade is the most direct descendant of fundamentalism. John Redekop, in his case study of the Christian Crusade, has commented on fundamentalism and set forth the reasons why it is no longer associated with populism. A portion of that commentary is included here.

JOHN REDEKOP

SOURCE: From John Harold Redekop, The American Far Right (1968) Used by permission of the Wm. B. Eerdmans Publishing Co.

An especially interesting question involves the relationship between Christian fundamentalism and Populism in the late nineteenth and early twentieth centuries. Certain areas in the United States, including much of the proverbial Bible Belt with its significant percentage of fundamentalists, gave Populism considerable support. Some scholars have argued that the post-World War II Far Right is in the tradition of American Populism. They stress the similarity of views on conspiracy, the place of prejudice, the repudiation of trained leadership, a distrust of elites, the emphasis on native practical sense (conscience), and the extent of naive emotional fervor. But what they tend to overlook is that the pivotal notion in Populism was opposition to international financiers, bankers, railroad owners, etc., because of their alleged economic exploitation of the people. Populism was essentially an economic reaction, not a crusade for a total world-view. It differed also from the Far Right in that it wanted more, not less, governmental intervention and regulation. And while Rightism shares with Populism an emphasis on mass participation, it substitutes a good bit of "Fuehrerprinzip" in place of Populist egalitarianism.

A great difference exists in the nature of methods and organization. Populist movements develop mainly from the "bottom up," while most current Far Right groups are organized from the "top down." Current Rightist leaders are convinced that the nature of the enemy necessitates a tightly knit organization, even a secret one, while Populist leaders, aware of the economic power wielded by their supposed enemy, believed that their only hope lay in co-operative mass action. Assuming that many fundamentalists actually did endorse Populism, what might have motivated them? Perhaps the lack of an immediate and specific foreign threat permitted critics to concentrate on domestic issues, such as economic exploitation, political bossism, and the rapid secularization of society. And possibly a significant part of the explanation is simply that fundamentalists think and act one way when the question of personal income is concerned, and adopt another approach when issues are remote and are viewed ideologically. One is reminded of the French peasant who, in response to the accusation that he had his political heart in the left and his economic heart in the right, responded that this constituted a reasonable and consistent inconsistency. Ideological inconsistency may well be a major flaw in the fundamentalist "Weltanschauung." In any event, it is significant that virtually all of the current studies of Populism do not stress fundamentalism as a major determinant, and some ignore it altogether.

In the following selection, Arnold Forster and Benjamin R. Epstein describe how far fundamentalism has come from populism. They describe, in somewhat polemical terms, how the Christian Crusade under Billy James Hargis has become a big business—a position far removed from the earlier anti-business attitudes of populist fundamentalism. The excerpt closes with a description of the "prayer auction" technique of money-raising employed by Hargis.

ARNOLD FORSTER AND BENJAMIN R. EPSTEIN

SOURCE: From Danger on the Right, *by Arnold Forster and Benjamin R. Epstein. Copyright © 1964 by Anti-Defamation League of B'nai B'rith. Reprinted by permission of Random House, Inc.*

"People distrust a politician trying to get elected, but listen to a preacher," Dr. Billy James Hargis once told a reporter. "They figure he has no gimmicks. I don't have a gimmick."

If people really figure that—they don't know Dr. Hargis.

As Dr. Schwarz pleads for funds to "educate" Americans about the evils of communism, the Reverend Dr. Billy James Hargis, obviously banking on the fear that communism will destroy organized religion, sends the hat around for contributions to save the church—more especially his own branch of the Disciples of Christ. The two Crusaders use different pitches, with neither showing the same major interest in building membership at the grass-roots level in the manner of the John Birch Society. Of all American evangelists propagandizing for the Radical Right, Hargis is the most zealous and energetic and perhaps leaves the greatest impact. His "religious" vehicle is the Christian Crusade—the popular name of the Christian Echoes National Ministry, Inc., a tax-exempt corporation which, for all practical purposes, is the Reverend Dr. Hargis.

This pudgy, prosperous evangelist has turned Radical Right propaganda into big business, directing it from the four-story building his Christian Crusade occupied in 1962 in Tulsa. From here his radio broadcasts reach great numbers of listeners. From here he writes weekly newspaper columns, magazine articles, religious sermons, books, tracts, and pamphlets. From here he makes tape recordings and publishes two magazines, one of which has a claimed circulation of 130,000 and may well be seen by twice as many readers.

A veritable Niagara of propaganda has flooded the Southwest and other parts of the country from this Tulsa building. All of it carries forward the wild Radical Right assertion that there is treason in high office in the United States and that Communists are everywhere. With Hargis, such exaggerations are usually followed by eloquent pleas for more money to enable the Reverend Doctor to intensify his warnings to America of the dire peril it faces. The method works, because so many middle-aged and elderly Americans, unduly frightened by what they hear from him, send Hargis lots of money in order that he and his Crusade may save our nation. The total is close to a million dollars a year, mostly in contributions in the $1 to $5 category; this is because the overwhelming majority of his followers are well along in years, and many of their dollars come out of meager savings or social security checks. From such funds Reverend Billy James Hargis takes a salary of $500 a week. The tax-exempt religious organization which he dominates bought a $44,000 home for his comfort, and they call it the "parsonage" though the Reverend has not ministered a church in fourteen years —even his own sect long ago stopped carrying Billy James's name in its yearbook list of clergymen.

In 1958, Reverend Hargis' nonprofit Christian Crusade dipped into its till of charitable contributions, originally given to "save America," for the purchase of a $6,000 Lincoln automobile, and in 1961, the organization used $7,500 of its alms for an even fancier car. Upkeep for the vehicles is borne by the Christian Crusade with money sent by Americans whom Hargis has frightened with tales of imminent catastrophe. On top of all this, Billy James, his wife and his father, as trustees of the nonprofit institution, voted $200 a week for housemaids and other domestic help for the "parsonage."

Perhaps it is because he is an ordained minister that Billy James's listeners believe he tells them only the truth. What he says makes a deadly impact. Billy James admits frankly that he seldom preaches on religion now; the concentration is on communism and how it has boldly infiltrated all aspects of American life. An enthusiastic supporter of the John Birch Society, and one of the Society's official Endorsers, the Reverend goes out of his way to praise Founder Welch and his organization.

Radical Right listeners seem rarely to ask for proof of the charges made by their leaders. For instance, in January, 1964, Dr. Hargis spoke under the sponsorship of the Central Christian Church at Ft. Lauderdale, Florida, on the theme, as usual, of communism. He gave the congregation the "lowdown" on the assassination of President Kennedy. The murder was, he said, an example of the Communist use of terror. (This was, of course, also the Birch Society explanation. But neither the FBI nor the Dallas police found any evidence whatsoever of a Red plot. To listen to Hargis and Welch, such unanimity of opinion among these agencies should not fool anyone at all.) Hargis "revealed" further that the killing of Lee Harvey Oswald, the President's alleged assassin, had been carried out in collusion with gangsters of Murder, Inc., and of the Mafia.

Hargis did not explain just how the Reds and the Black Hand had become partners. He did have, however, a fund of information, including the fact that this country was steeped in socialist groups only one step removed from communism. He named these: the American Civil Liberties Union, the National Council of Churches, the National Association for the Advancement of Colored People. He also assured his open-mouthed listeners that the American Nazi Party was tied up with the Communists.

To make these charges, he must have assumed that no one would ask him for substantiation. He was right; no one did.

Although the Christian Crusade is granted a tax-exempt status as a religious body by the Internal Revenue Service, much of the evangelist's talk on this occasion, as on most others, was politically partisan. Its main burden was the boosting of Senator Barry Goldwater for President. At the conclusion, Hargis made his inevitable appeal for donations, explaining that he had just written another book and needed $7,500 to have it published. Users went through the audience passing out charity envelopes as Hargis called for $100 checks. Each donor would get $100 worth of copies of the new tome, Billy James said.

Billy James is about forty. Jiggling a wide double chin when publicly pleading with the Almighty to bestow generosity upon his hearers, Billy James has been variously described as portly, stocky, beefy, or just fat. Les Dunnavant, a faithful follower who chauffeured Hargis' luxurious Greyhound "home and office on wheels," once told a reporter: "We can't keep any sweets around. If it's in here Billy will run to the refrigerator like a kid. We try to keep him on lean meat. He's a connoisseur of food—the consumption of it." Hargis expressed it differently: "I can't drink Metrecal and speak every night. I carry a tremendous schedule." In short, he indicated, he simply had to eat.

The Reverend Dr. Billy James Hargis delivers his nightly speeches in a moderate, conversational tone—up to a point of emphasis, and then his arms wave and a pudgy finger jabs the air as he reaches a fire-and-brimstone pitch. If only by sheer contrast to his quiet voice at the opening of his remarks, his thundering brings listeners to the edges of their seats. The speeches are peppered with a touch of cracker-barrel humor. When a phrase finds favor with an audience, he adds it to his permanent presentation. Once when he referred to the Union Theological Seminary as the "Union Theological Cemetery," the audience laughed. Now it is a standard line with Billy James.

Hargis moved toward his lucrative brand of evangelism when he was quite young. As a student he had been shy and quiet. His family was of moderate means, yet he seldom had spending money, rarely dated girls or went to parties. Scholastically, he had just made it with a C average until about midway through the eleventh grade. At that point he changed as though he had been touched by a good fairy, and his personality blossomed and his tongue unlatched. Almost overnight he became a polished speaker. Simultaneously, his scholastic ratings jumped mostly to A's. But his conversation was not of religion; it was chiefly of politics and government.

Billy James graduated from Texarkana High School and enrolled in Ozark Bible College at Bentonville, Arkansas, an institution with only twenty students. After attending this academy about a year, he was ordained at seventeen as a minister in the Disciples of Christ Church, a denomination which merged some years ago with the Christian Church. There seems to be good reason for his being dropped from his church's yearbook. "He is now engaged in a private enterprise which has no connection whatsoever with the Christian Churches (Disciples of Christ)," a church leader said.

Hargis' first pastorates were in small towns in Oklahoma and Missouri. He settled finally in Sapulpa, Oklahoma, when offered the pulpit of the First Christian Church there. The turning point in his life, Hargis says, came when he was twenty and was visiting with a minister to whom he expressed the fear that Communistic influences might be taking control of Christianity in this country. The minister's "So what?" so infuriated young Billy James that he then vowed, he says, to dedicate himself to stop the growth of communism. He persuaded his church to pay for a "religious" radio broadcast, and the response from listeners was a revelation of the numbers he could reach through this means. As an energetic young man of twenty-five, he quickly found his small-town pastorate unsatisfying. In 1950, he resigned to launch the campaign to save America from Communists and Liberals.

Within a year Billy James incorporated as a "religious, non-profit making body" called the Christian Echoes Ministry, Inc.—later, the Christian Echoes National Ministry. The bylaws of the corporation are not on file with the Oklahoma Secretary of State.

Before long, Hargis was broadcasting across a wide swath of America's heartland—from Roaring Spring, Pennsylvania, south to Eufala, Alabama; from a South Dakota station (with the call letters KORN) to the people in Thief River Falls, Minnesota, and in Muleshoe, Texas. Hargis was a man of the cloth, and his impassioned warnings of the horrendous domestic Red Plot impressed or frightened many people. They responded generously to his pleas for money to support and expand the Crusade. In 1952, his first full year of "saving America," Billy James took in over $70,000 through contributions, the sale of publications, and profits from a hotel and recreation camp for his followers. At the year's end the corporation had a nice surplus of $33,000.

As a religious preacher, Hargis intensified his theme that treason is everywhere and that communism is about to seize the country and destroy its churches. He rapidly built up a following estimated to number 75,000. In this he has been aided for almost ten years by L. E. ("Pete") White, a shrewd public relations man who earlier, in just a few years of intensive promotion, had turned the famed faith-healing preacher, Oral Roberts, into a national personality and a million-dollar enterprise.

It did not take Billy James very long to perfect his technique of raising money. Always conscious that people will tend to believe ministers, he devised a unique ritual of backwoods, fundamentalist exhortation and loud prayers to the Lord to open the eyes, hearts, and wallets of his listeners. The night he raised $38,870 to pay for twenty-six half-hour talks on a national radio hookup will illustrate the effective devices he employs:

The scene was the Third Annual Convention of the Christian Crusade. Some seven hundred Crusaders were in the audience. Hargis told them there was good news that day. He had a chance to go on the Mutual Network for six months at a special low rate— "for only $38,870," as the evangelist put it. Hargis then launched what a *New York Times* reporter described as a "prayer auction" to raise money. Using alternate appeals to God and to the seven hundred persons present, Hargis began by crying out:

"I pray to God for one man to sponsor this program for six months. I know that man exists in this audience. Will he stand up?"

No one stood.

"All right, then, we will divide this burden. I need four men who will accept God's challenge and give ten thousand dollars each to sponsor this program."

Two men stood up.

"Give us four, Oh, God, who would give five thousand dollars each. Quickly! . . . Two thousand?"

Three men stood up.

And that's how it went, down from $500 to $100. When Hargis had finished, seventy-nine men and women had pledged a total of $38,870—the exact amount needed to put the Tulsa evangelist on the air.

The entire proceeding was, in short, an auction by a skilled performer who was selling God, religion, the church, and the preservation of the United States while he held the Bible in one hand and a cash register in the other.

Billy James Hargis is more than a good businessman; he has a genius for organization. In the following selection Redekop describes how Hargis has organized his movement and attracted to it some of the celebrities of the radical right. He also describes the publication program of the Christian Crusade, a major activity for this movement, as with all social movements.

JOHN REDEKOP

SOURCE: From John Harold Redekop, The American Far Right (1968). Used by permission of the Wm. B. Eerdmans Publishing Co.

1.

The growth of Christian Crusade has been impressive. From an inconsequential local effort in 1947, it has expanded into an important national organization, largely through the personal, seemingly inexhaustible dynamism of Hargis. Its diversified enterprises include a radio network, television releases, lecture tours, pamphlet production, pamphlet sales, book publication, book sales, anti-Communist "leadership training," a youth organization (The Torchbearers), an annual convention, a summer school, a monthly magazine, a weekly magazine, sale of patriotic paraphernalia, membership promotion, and a host of minor miscellanea. The five dominant themes in this gamut of enterprises are: Hargis, Christ, the United States (flag, constitution, etc.), anti-Communism, and conservatism. Key villains in addition to Communism are: liberalism, socialism, the National Council of Churches, the Reuther brothers, the Kennedys, President Lyndon Johnson, "Hubert Horatio," U. Thant and the United Nations, most of the press, and Martin Luther King.

One reason for Christian Crusade's rapid expansion is that it is increasingly becoming a peak agency, to use group-therapy terminology. Hargis's zeal and determination have rallied a host of groups and individuals to his cause. One of the largest of these consists of military officers, mostly retired. Included are Brig. Gen. Richard Moran, Gen. Edwin Walker, Maj. George Racey Jordan, Capt. Eddie Rickenbacker, Maj. Gen. Charles Willoughby, Gen. W. P. Campbell, Col. Victor Fox, Col. Laurence Bunker, and Capt. Kenneth Ryker. Willoughby, Gen. MacArthur's former Chief of Intelligence, is an associate of Hargis and writes a Foreign Intelligence Digest in both the weekly and monthly magazines. Walker, for whom Hargis shows virtually boundless admiration, has accompanied Hargis on several extensive tours. Both Moran and Willoughby are members of Christian Crusade's Advisory Board.

Other individuals and groups which frequently speak under Christian Crusade sponsorship are: Kent Courtney (The Conservative Society of America), Tom Anderson (Farm and Ranch Magazine), Dr. Bob Jones, Sr. and Dr. Bob Jones, Jr. (Bob Jones University), Robert Welch (John Birch Society), and radio commentators Hurst Amyx and Fulton Lewis, Jr. Tape-recorded lectures by each of these are regularly offered for sale.

How big is Christian Crusade in financial terms? An audited and published financial statement for the calendar year 1963 reveals a total income of $677,152.80 and a total expense of $685,904.31. Some earlier years, prior to the mass media's widespread attacks on the organization, had brought in even larger contributions. Hargis is quoted as saying that in at least one year income surpassed the million mark. Major expense items for 1963 included: Salaries & Wages (78 employees), $128,197.82; Radio & Television, $213,793.52; and Printing & Publications, $119,883.41. Hargis himself draws a salary of $12,000 plus an expense account for official activities. Financially, Christian Crusade appears to be on the upswing once again. Hargis said in a personal conversation with this writer on October 25, 1964, that this is "the greatest year we ever had."

Sometimes accused of being a mouthpiece for a few oil barons, Hargis has vigorously denied the charge. He insists, "Christian Crusade receives few large offerings annually. The average contribution that we get in the mail is around $4.00 and we will average about $1.25 per person in the offering during our public rallies." Hargis has employed a wide array of fund-raising gimmicks, ranging from Holy Land mementos to subtle "personal" letters from his attractive wife Betty Jean, but generally there is only a straight, albeit passionate, appeal. "When people criticize my fund-raising," says Hargis, "I confess it hurts me a great deal. If I knew of ways to finance Christian Crusade other than those we have used these seventeen years, God bear me witness, I would do it. . . . I die a little each time I ask for money."

The core of Hargis's activity continues to be the radio appeal, with daily and weekly broadcasts saturating the nation. (There is a fairly rapid turnover of stations—all stations that do not carry themselves financially after three months are summarily dropped.) The stated goal at one time was "One Thousand Radio Stations by December 1, 1964." This figure was not reached. The actual count fluctuates between 400 and 450. The two giants, XEG (Monterrey, Mexico), and XERB (San Diego, California), each heard in some 40 states, continue to be the mainstays. Television has been tried, but has not become a major undertaking. Only about a dozen privately owned stations, mainly in the South and West, carry taped releases. A new technique is the 24-hour telethon in which distribution of mass-produced paperbacks is pushed to the limit. Thus the purpose of a telethon in Fresno, California, in April, 1964, was to distribute 25,000 copies of Hargis's book, *The Far Left*. The occasion revealed Hargis's almost indefatigable energy. Without a minute's sleep, "the Doctor," as his associates call him, sang, preached, prayed, lectured, and small-talked his way through a full night and day on live television, all the while urging "you folks" to "keep the phones ringing." They rang. The use of patriotic and anti-Communist films added variety to the telethon and allowed for at least momentary relaxation.

A second major enterprise is publications. The organization's monthly magazine, *Christian Crusade*, which describes itself as "The National Christian American Monthly," has a circulation of about 120,000 with a total readership of a half million. There is also the *Weekly Crusader*, at $10 a year, which puts less emphasis on fund-raising and more on what one reader called, "the inside track to truth." Pamphlets and booklets pour forth in a never-ending stream. Some of the titles written by Hargis include: "Should We Surrender to Castro or Smash Him?"; "Mental Health"; "Racial Strife"; "America—Let's Get Back to God"; "American Socialism . . . Moving America Downhill"; "How the Communists Influence American Elections"; "We Have Been Betrayed"; "The Ugly Truth About Drew Pearson"; and, "The Truth About UNESCO." Four "full-length" books by Hargis have been published by Christian Crusade. They are: *Communist America . . .*

Must It Be?; Communism, The Total Lie!; The Facts About Communism and Our Churches; and, *The Far Left*. The total circulation of these books runs into many hundreds of thousands. The first-mentioned alone reached 150,000 in the first five printings. Some of its chapter headings are: A Bird's Eye View of Treason; America Marked for Conquest; Patriotism—Once Revered, Now Smeared; Communism and Labor Unions; Communism and Racial Tension; Fantastic Foreign Aid; and United Nations—The Greatest Hoax Perpetrated on the American Public.

We have already had occasion to review some of the details of Hargis's life. In the following biographical synopsis, Redekop puts these details into order and indicates the origins of the title used by the leader of the Christian Crusade: *Dr.* Billy James Hargis.

2.

Billy James Hargis, son of a truck driver, was born on August 3, 1925, in Texarkana, Texas. There appears to be nothing particularly striking in his background. Raised in a fundamentalist, typically Southern home, he grew up during the Depression in an area which knew hard times at their worst.

On May 30, 1943, at the age of 17, Hargis was ordained a minister of the Gospel by the Rose Hill Christian Church (Disciples of Christ) of Texarkana. In 1964 his membership was still there.

After graduating from high school as a superior student, Billy James enrolled at Ozark Bible College in Bentonville, Arkansas, a small school which then had only 20 to 30 students. Reminiscing in 1962, Hargis said that the one and one-half years he spent there constitute all the formal college education he ever had. In 1954 Hargis received his first honorary doctorate (Doctor of Divinity)—one which he uses constantly—from The Defender Seminary in Puerto Rico. In 1956 Hargis completed the requirements for a Bachelor of Arts and was awarded that degree from Burton College and Seminary of Manitou Springs, Colorado, from which he also received a Bachelor of Theology two years later. It is perhaps noteworthy that Burton College was on the official list of "degree mills" issued by the United States Department of Health, Education, and Welfare in April, 1960.

A second honorary doctorate (Doctor of Laws) was conferred on Hargis in the spring of 1957 by Belin Memorial University, then located at Chillicothe, Missouri. This institution, too, was listed as a degree mill by the United States government. Recently a controversy has developed concerning the integrity of its founder-president. One account states, "Dr. Clyde Belin, president of the University, was indicted by a Federal grand jury in Kansas City on June 25, 1959, on six counts of using the mails to defraud, offered no defense, and was sentenced to a year in prison." When queried by this writer concerning the Belin doctorate, Hargis insisted that he had nothing to do with the awarding of the degree and did not attend any convocation. Nevertheless, the July, 1957 issue of *Christian Crusade* announced that "Dr. Hargis has been awarded an honorary Doctor of Laws degree from Belin Memorial University, Chillicothe, Missouri." A third honorary doctorate was received in 1961 from Bob Jones University of Greenville, South Carolina.

During the early years of his ministry Hargis was pastor of several churches: First Christian Church, Sallisaw, Oklahoma; First Christian Church, Granby, Missouri; and First Christian Church, Sapulpa, Oklahoma. He says that it was in 1947, during his pastorate in Sapulpa, that he first realized the dimensions of the leftist-Communist threat and set about organizing Christian Crusade to fight "Communism and its godless allies."

Unlike many social movements which grow out of the "experiments" of a leader with different organizational forms, the John Birch Society was pre-planned and pre-packaged as an ideological force and then delivered as a finished product to a group of businessmen in 1958. Robert Welch, a retired businessman himself, collected all of his feelings and thoughts about the political world and put them together in a two-day series of lectures which was eventually published as the *Blue Book* of the John Birch Society. In the following selection, Forster and Epstein describe the events of December 8 and 9, 1958, when Welch inspired a group of fellow businessmen to become members of the society and its Board of Directors.

ARNOLD FORSTER AND BENJAMIN R. EPSTEIN

SOURCE: From Arnold Forster and Benjamin R. Epstein, Danger on the Right, *Copyright © 1964 by Anti-Defamation League of B'nai B'rith. Reprinted by permission of Random House, Inc.*

In his years as a vice-president of the National Association of Manufacturers, and through personal business contacts, Robert Welch had made friends with men of industry who shared his political views. Late in 1958, he asked eleven such men to meet with him in an Indianapolis hotel. The men who gathered there on Monday morning, December 8, had come from nine widely scattered states.

For two days Welch delivered a breathless monologue—it was recorded and has been published as the John Birch Society's *Blue Book*. He traced the advance of communism, offered his peculiar analysis of the existing situation, and outlined the aims and the structure of an ambitious national Right Wing organization he proposed to form. Welch decided that the organization should be called the John Birch Society because a twenty-six-year-old soldier named John Birch had been "the first American casualty in World War III." The *Blue Book* quotes Welch:

"You will find that John Birch, a young fundamentalist Baptist preacher from Macon, Georgia, who did as much as any other man, high or low, to win our war and the Chinese war against the Japanese in China, was murdered by the Chinese Communists at the first opportunity after the war because of the powerful resistance he would have been able to inspire against them. You will find, and I believe, agree with me, that John Birch possesses in his own character *all* of those noble traits and ideals which we should like to see symbolized by the John Birch Society."

And he offered a ten-point program, most of which is now being carried out by Birch chapters throughout America, and which is essentially a tough campaign of membership recruitment and ultra-reactionary propaganda. Its operation ranges from issuing Far-Rightist publications to establishing reading rooms and libraries. It includes the booking of Far-Rightist speakers before civic groups across the country, firm support for the radio programs of broadcasters such as Fulton Lewis, Jr., and Clarence Manion, the use of "the powerful letter-writing weapon," the organization of front groups (a favorite tactic also of the Communists), and the exposing of alleged Communists wherever they may turn up next. The stated Birch objective is to change the pattern of American thinking, to "awaken an apathetic American people," and to build "the cumulative total of anti-Communist resistance."

This is to be achieved by organizing chapters of "from 10 to 20 dedicated patriots" to exert an impact at the local community level

—on the schools, libraries, church groups, PTAs, and thus on the whole nation—and to shock the people into enlightenment by exposing the supposed extent of the Communist conspiracy.

Two lives symbolize the ideology of the John Birch Society: those of its namesake, John Birch, and its founder, Robert Welch. In the following biographical selections we learn that John Birch was a talented young man and zealous fundamentalist whose fervent anticommunism apparently led to his death at the hands of Red Chinese troops in 1945. Robert Welch, by contrast, was a sober businessman who did not become an anticommunist "crusader" until later in life, after his attempts to influence electoral politics had failed to achieve his ideological goals.

J. ALLEN BROYLES

SOURCE: From The John Birch Society, *by J. Allen Broyles. Copyright © 1964 by J. Allen Broyles. Reprinted by permission of Beacon Press.*

John Birch earned his B.A. at Mercer in 1939 *magna cum laude*. From there he followed Frank Norris to Fort Worth where Norris was establishing Bible Baptist Seminary in connection with his church. John and another student completed the two-year course in only one year and in July, 1940, he left for China under the sponsorship of Norris and under the auspices of the World's Fundamentalist Baptist Missionary Fellowship.

John managed a workable mastery of Chinese in only seven months and began his missionary work. Following the outbreak of war between the United States and Japan in December, 1941, John fled the area of China heavily occupied by Japanese forces and continued his evangelical preaching and teaching as best he could.

Through chance circumstances, he was able to help get Colonel Doolittle and many of his flyers out of China where they had crash-landed following their bombing raid on Tokyo in 1942. This service put him in touch with the 14th Air Force under General Chennault, for whom he worked for the remainder of the war. Using his language ability, John, now Captain John Birch, was able to move about in China and do extensive and hazardous intelligence work. His main task was to observe, and report by radio, movements of Japanese troops and supplies. He carried out his work with great courage and resourcefulness through the entire war. But on August 25, 1945, ten days after V-J Day, he met a tragic death.

Captain Birch had volunteered to lead a party consisting of American, Chinese Nationalist, and Korean officers and soldiers on a special mission. The specific object of the mission has not been disclosed, but it was into a "no man's land." The withdrawal of the Japanese left a vacuum into which troops of both Red and Nationalist China poured. Captain Birch and his party, traveling by railway handcar, were stopped by a band of Red Chinese near Hsuchow. The course of events at this point blurs. But we do know that, in an ensuing argument with the leaders of this Red Chinese band, Captain Birch was shot and bayoneted to death. A Chinese Nationalist officer with him was also shot and bayoneted, but lived. The others in the party were taken prisoner, but soon released. When another party left fairly soon for a mission in the same area, a member of Captain Birch's party told its new leader of the fate of the first party. He reported that Captain Birch had unwisely tried to bluff his way out of a difficult situation, that harsh words had led to insults, and insults to arrogance, and that finally the Red Chinese leader, in a fit of anger, had shot Captain Birch. Whether acting wisely or not, John Birch did die serving his country as best he knew how. He received two decorations from his country—one of them posthumously. And there, but for Robert Welch, this story of his life would have ended.

But John Birch has been lifted up by Robert Welch as his idea of the ideal Americanist; as a perfect fusion of rural virtues, fundamentalist faith, and dedicated patriotism. But why this furor? Other fine and brave soldiers lie quiet in their graves. Why single out this one? Robert Welch and the family of John Birch reply that he was deliberately murdered by the Communists and that our government deliberately kept the truth about his death from his family. The information given them was that John was killed by stray bullets. Certainly the incidents surrounding his death are obscure, but so are many deaths in war. However, the death of Captain John Birch is heavily freighted with meaning, according to Welch. It symbolizes the determination of communism to stamp out all that is fine and good in America and "exposes" the conspiracy of our national leaders in that purpose. John Birch becomes the symbol capturing, in the words of Welch, "in the story of one American boy, the ordeal of his age."

. . .

Robert Henry Winborne Welch, Jr., was born on a large cotton farm in Chowan County, North Carolina, on December 1, 1899. Most of his paternal ancestors were either farmers or Baptist preachers, tracing their lineage to Miles Welch, who came to this country from Wales in 1720.

Robert Welch as a child was exposed to a strongly fundamentalist religious background. As he matured intellectually, he rejected many of the religious concepts and doctrines which he considered "unjustified projections of [religion's] more important certainties." He has moved religiously to a universalistic position in which he is looking for the common denominators of all our great religions. But for Welch, as for many conservatives or liberals whose economic or political views have come to assume the place of prime importance, religion is more to be used than to be followed.

Both his parents were college graduates and, because of the inaccessibility of local public schools, his mother tutored her six children at home and sent them away to school only for their last two years of high school. Under this educational program, Robert Welch progressed so rapidly that he entered the University of North Carolina at the age of twelve and earned his B.A. degree at the age of seventeen. He was described as a "boy wonder" in North Carolina newspaper reports of his graduation. His other formal education includes two years at the United States Naval Academy and two years at Harvard Law School.

While attending Law School, Robert began a candy business that so absorbed his time and energies that he left Harvard, as he had left the Naval Academy, before he graduated. In this business venture, he overextended himself and fell into financial difficulties. He invited his creditors in as an operating committee for the company, but, finding the working relationship unsatisfactory, he turned all his stock over to his creditors and pulled out. This company was eventually sold to Daggett Chocolate Company.

Welch then moved to the New York area to make another start in the candy business. Making little progress there, he was offered and accepted an executive position with E. J. Brock and Sons of Chicago. He later resigned and made one more start as a manufacturer of candy. For lack of capital, this final venture also failed. In 1934, he returned to Boston, as an employee of the James O. Welch Company, a candy manufacturing firm founded by his brother. He became one of the four vice presidents of this company and was in charge of sales and advertising, a position which took him the circuit of the sales offices of the firm in Atlanta, Pittsburgh, Chicago, Los Angeles, and Seattle.

As sales manager, Robert Welch came into close contact with business leaders in a number of cities. And he moved in business circles with the prestige of seven years of membership on the Board of Directors of the National Association of Manufacturers, three years of service as a Regional Vice President, and a two-year chairmanship of its Educational Advisory Committee. His business responsibilities have also included serving as director of a bank, and as a director of several other business corporations, the Harvard Brewing Company among them. These business contacts, coupled with a lively interest in current and past political history, gave Robert Welch a very extensive circle of acquaintances across the country. Among these were not only "business" friends but also many of the anti-Socialist and anti-Communist leaders throughout the country. Consequently he could say to the first members of the Society in Indianapolis that no matter which anti-Communist or anti-Socialist group they might name, "the chances are that the good citizens who put it together are friends of mine."

In addition to extensive travel throughout this country, Mr. Welch made it a practice to use vacations and other time for world-wide junkets. Twice in England he studied "the effects of the Socialist government," and in the course of his travels he has arranged interviews with Adenauer, Chiang Kai-shek, Syngman Rhee, and others.

Welch began to take an active part in state politics and during the 1946 campaign of Massachusetts Governor Bradford, Welch presented himself at Republican campaign headquarters, said he liked Bradford's platform and program and wanted to do his part. The man with whom he was talking leaned forward to see the size of the check Welch would write, but Welch had something else in mind. He offered to send out personal letters supporting the candidacy of Bradford to all the retail distributors and handlers of Welch candy in Massachusetts, most of whom he knew personally. Bradford's aide was pleasantly surprised. Such personal campaign material is one of the most effective ways known to gain political support for a candidate. But its cost, both in time and in the secretarial help necessary to "personalize" it, is almost prohibitive. "The costs?" Welch would take care of them himself.

The next day, Robert Welch had desks and other office equipment moved into some extra space at the campaign headquarters. He followed them in about an hour to talk with the aide about the draft of the letter he proposed to send and was, in turn, followed in about another hour by a staff of secretaries. This mailing, which approached 60,000 letters, consumed the efforts of this staff for several weeks as well as a great deal of time and effort by Welch himself. When Bradford won the campaign, Welch wanted no political favors in return.

Later, in 1950, Welch made a bid for the lieutenant governorship of Massachusetts in the Republican primary. He demonstrated a marked and rather inflexible stand for "principle," much to the dismay and chagrin of his political advisers. According to one political observer, he ran the race with tremendous drive and at a pitch very near the state of a nervous breakdown. He was then and is now a hard man to push and has an almost fanatical belief in what he's doing. In his campaign for lieutenant governor, he was always completely frank in his opinions and believed that no politician ought compromise either as he ran for office or as he served. Such a stance flies in the face of usual political strategy and it did not win him the courted candidacy. Welch came in second in a field of four candidates, but a Democratic government was elected in Massachusetts.

Welch, however, continued to take an active part in the politics of his state, often raising or personally providing financial support for candidates. In 1952, he was strongly in favor of the presidential candidacy of Robert Taft, and tried unsuccessfully to be elected as a delegate to the Republican Convention. Although Welch didn't agree with all of Taft's views, he made twenty-five radio speeches supporting him during the primary. Again, at his own expense. He shared the bitter disillusionment of many conservative Republicans when the convention by-passed Taft and nominated General Eisenhower.

Still maintaining at least a degree of faith in the conventional channels of political activity, Welch, in the same year that he founded the Birch Society, foreseeing determined liberal opposition to Goldwater's 1958 senatorial campaign in Arizona, managed to raise two thousand dollars within far-away Massachusetts to help him.

But Welch was becoming increasingly discontented with the

compromise and ineffectiveness of conventional political activity. He was also becoming more and more alarmed over what he felt to be the unchecked advance of Communist subversion in this country. He himself dates his concern with the Communist conspiracy from his first reading of Eugene Lyons' *Assignment in Utopia* in 1938. So we find his political interests and efforts shifting to other channels. He was a loyal supporter and has been a faithful memorializer of the late Senator Joseph McCarthy. He addressed state gatherings of "friends of Senator Joseph McCarthy" at least twice in 1955, and in 1956 made an address at a States Righters Conference which met in Memphis and nominated T. Coleman Andrews for President and Thomas H. Werdel for Vice President.

In addition to his other activities, Robert Welch is a prolific writer. Between 1959 and 1963, for instance, Welch himself estimates that his output totaled more than a half million words. His first book, *The Road to Salesmanship*, a fairly standard "how-to-do-it-yourself" handbook, was published in 1941. As he began to move into right-wing politics, Henry Regnery Company in 1952 published *May God Forgive Us*, Welch's analysis of the dismissal of General MacArthur by President Truman. (Interestingly enough this book was published as a "letter," a literary form later used by Welch in the "private letter," more than twice as long, entitled *The Politician*.) During 1952, reportedly 185,000 paper-bound and 9,000 hard-bound copies of the book on MacArthur were printed. In 1954, *The Life of John Birch* was published, and, according to Welch ran to 35,000 paper-bound and 3,000 hard-bound copies. Both *May God Forgive Us* and *The Life of John Birch* have since been reprinted as issues of *American Opinion*. In February, 1956, Welch embarked upon a new venture. He began to edit and publish a magazine entitled *One Man's Opinion*, which was issued somewhat irregularly and which had only a few thousand readers. The title of this publication was changed to *American Opinion* upon the founding of the John Birch Society two years later.

NEW FUNDAMENTALISM

The "Jesus Freaks," the young people who are "freaked out" on Jesus, are new fundamentalists because they participate in groups based on fundamentalist preaching.* Like all new movements, they are partly a creation of the mass media, having been featured on national television and in news magazines. Particular organizations, such as the Christian World Liberation Front of Berkeley and the "Jesus People" of Hollywood, are rather loose and open "followings" led by fundamentalist preachers such as Jack Sparks (in Berkeley) and Duane Pederson (in Hollywood). Neither of these men has theological training; they are religious leaders in the revivalist tradition, "called" to preach to a downtrodden people.

The difference between the "new fundamentalist" groups such as the Christian World Liberation Front and the "old fundamentalist" groups such as the Christian Crusade is that they have different versions of who is downtrodden and why. The new

fundamentalists, using a hip jargon and cultural style, appeal to disaffected young people (particularly students, dropouts, and former drug users) who are alienated from the "system"—that is, from the prevailing American politics and culture. The old fundamentalists employ the language and symbolism of patriotism to appeal to those who are alienated from modern society— that is, those who want to return to an earlier political and cultural era.

Because the new fundamentalist movement is so young, little scholarly research has been expended on it. The best study now available is an article which appeared in *Society* (the journal which succeeded *Trans-Action*). It is based on a survey of members of new fundamentalist groups in California. Before presenting the findings of this article, a brief introduction to two of these groups, the Jesus People of Hollywood and the Christian World Liberation Front of Berkeley, is excerpted from a journalistic study of the movement by Enroth, Ericson, and Peters. The first excerpt describes the origins of the

---

*See Lowell D. Streiker, *The Jesus Trip* (Nashville: Abingdon Press, 1971).

Hollywood group under the leadership of Duane Pederson, who began to reach out to young people through the vehicle of an "underground" newspaper, the *Hollywood Free Paper (HFP)*.

ENROTH, ERICSON, AND PETERS

SOURCE: *From Ronald M. Enroth, Edward E. Ericson, and C. Breckinridge Peters,* The Jesus People *(1972). Used by permission of the Wm. B. Eerdmans Publishing Co.*

The beginnings of the *HFP* are still somewhat hazy, though Pederson attempts to chronicle the paper's history in *Jesus People*. Armed with only the idea of a Christian underground newspaper imitating the then less established *Los Angeles Free Press*, Pederson records his initial fund-raising campaign in a few fuzzy-detailed anecdotes that he sums up typically enough: "In a very real sense, God provided the money for that first issue" (p. 17). Missing from the account is any mention of the help lent by Hollywood's First Presbyterian Church. Following his first edition, Pederson approached First Presbyterian, well known for its concern and involvement in the Hollywood youth scene, with a proposal for a partnership. The church had just opened an outreach coffee house, the Salt Company, and was toying at the time with the idea of printing an underground paper to accompany their in-person evangelistic efforts. Pederson's project dovetailed neatly with that, and it was adopted, coaxed along, and underwritten by the congregation.

In spite of the aid rendered by a bulwark of established Christianity, Pederson has little complimentary to say about the church. He often alludes to churchgoers as the "religious folk" chastised and condemned by Jesus. Nevertheless, he does continue to receive financial support from quite a few church Christians. His castigation of the church ignores the fact that his survival can be attributed to the establishment, but it blends neatly with his fabricated revolutionary self-image: "My ideas seem to be so radical and far out in left field that they're totally unacceptable to any of the religious world" (p. 70).

The union between the *HFP* and organized Christianity was brief and somewhat stormy. The bone of contention was not Pederson's idea of Christian presence on the streets through the underground media but the *HFP*'s intellectual level. The church's objection was only the paper's shallow and simplistic treatment of the gospel and its ramifications. Pederson disagreed, claiming the simple, undecorated, unexpanded message, "Jesus Loves You," was all the *HFP* needed. Pederson, with the assistance of Lawrence Young, a printer and long-time ally of evangelical causes in the Los Angeles area, garnered enough financial support to set up shop on his own.

The controversy over the intellectual and cultural level of the *HFP* has plagued Pederson since direct relations with Hollywood Presbyterian were severed. Repeatedly phrasing his articles in what he supposes to be the language of the street, Pederson sees the particular ministry of the *HFP* as aimed at the drug culture. This purpose accounts for its teeny-bopper quality: "We gear our thing to the dope scene, and this is, according to all statistics, in the junior high and high school age bracket." About the continued criticism of the paper's admitted low level, Pederson says, "I'm not concerned about that because each one of us has a different ministry, and I feel our ministry is where it's at and encourage anyone else to do what they should do."

. . .

In an effort to expand his ministry, Pederson has endeavored to establish training programs for the souls won through the evangelism of *HFP*. He founded the Jesus People Church, Inc., for the purpose, according to an article in *Truth* (March 1971), of giving "a tax exemption to his efforts in the Jesus movement." Though Pederson is harshly critical of established religion, and in fact claims the most vehement opposition to his efforts has come from the major denominations, he is quite willing to take the tax shelter offered by incorporation as a religious body. The *Truth* article goes on to note that the Jesus People Church "has ordained five ministers empowered by the state to perform marriages and function as do ministers of long established denominations."

Other Pederson efforts have not been as successful as the *HFP*. Advertised prominently in its pages is the apparently nonexistent Hollywood Free University. A staff member admitted that the entire scheme was totally unknown to him. Nor could he tell us much about the recently established Jesus People Training Centers listed in the *HFP*. Though claiming that the sessions dealt with various Bible topics, Pederson's associate was at a loss to list the topic covered in even one of the sessions and admitted that attendance was only five to seven people per session.

The most successful subsidiary of the *HFP*, and one that is crucial to its financial life, is a mail order poster and bumper-sticker shop known as the Emporium, operated by a young convert who supports himself by collecting unemployment checks. For some time the sale of "One Way" posters, "I'm High on the Love of My Jesus" bumper stickers, and a few photographic blowups of the smiling visage of Duane Pederson augmented donations and kept the *HFP*'s head above water. The mounting costs accompanying the increase in circulation, however, have been a burden that the Emporium thus far has been unable to bear. A letter recently circulated from headquarters asked those who had purchased material to consider either purchasing more or simply mailing a donation, a sign that all is not well. Finances are a sore spot with Pederson; he characterizes things only as "very tight," a trait, he claims, of all young organizations.

An important dimension of Pederson's impact on Hollywood is the series of Jesus concerts that he promotes in the Hollywood Palladium. These popular and well-attended rallies appeal to both Jesus Freaks and church youth. Pederson's role is that of emcee and evangelist. He has played a similar role at Jesus festivals elsewhere in California and other states. Next to his paper these concerts are his most successful venture.

Duane Pederson has been and will continue to be a crucial figure in the Jesus Movement. He is closer to the image of the Jesus Freak—in attitude, not appearance—than is Arthur Blessitt. Pederson admits to a charismatic experience, a subject not mentioned by Blessitt. References to the apocalypse are sprinkled through the *HFP*, a subject missing in the hip sermons of the Minister of Sunset Strip. Pederson, however, has been out-"Jesus Peopled" by the following to which he proudly points as the measure of his success. Though charismatic, he is not as charismatic as most; though convinced that these are the end times, he is less convinced than most; though anti-established church, he ordains preachers. Still, the *Hollywood Free Paper*, with few exceptions, is viewed as the newspaper of the Jesus Movement, and Duane Pederson is its leader. . . .

The CWLF has its beginnings in the work of Jack Sparks, an Indiana farm boy with impeccable establishment credentials—a bachelor's degree from Purdue and a master's and doctorate from Michigan State. He taught statistics at Penn State, where he was associated with Campus Crusade. Some time during the fall of 1968 he and his wife, along with several other Christian couples, began to feel a need to get through to the youth culture of America, especially the more radical segment of that culture epitomized by the Berkeley scene.

2.

Under the auspices of Campus Crusade, Sparks and his wife and and three other couples—Pat and Karry Matrisciana, Fred and Jan Dyson, Weldon and Barbara Hartenburg—moved to Berkeley to initiate a pilot project. They spent time on campus, talked with people, and began to pray that God would show them how to be relevant, how to share with people, how to make a Christian impact on the cutting edge of the counter-culture. Sparks explains in the March 1971 issue of *Vanguard*: "We have sought to drop into the lifestyle of the changing youth culture and—insofar as we see that culture not violating biblical standards—to adopt the culture and thereby have an increased opportunity to build a body of believers" (p. 22).

Adopt the culture he did! He let his hair and beard grow, lost about twenty pounds, and began dressing in jeans and work shirts. Those who know him well say his attitudes have changed, too. He used to be very academic and introspective. No more. His intimates say he is "for real," not just dressing up to play some phony role. He is a sincere, humble man of vision, with a sense of urgency.

When Sparks dropped into the hip Berkeley scene, he dropped out of the straight world of Campus Crusade. He and his associates felt a need to be free from the Campus Crusade bureaucracy and to develop a particular kind of literature suited to the specialized ethos of Berkeley. And an establishment-sounding organization like Campus Crusade did not go over well in Berkeley.

. . .

Probably straight Christians are most confused by the CWLF's use of revolutionary-sounding language and hip jargon. Even the organization's name, Christian World Liberation Front, is an obvious takeoff on the name of the radical Third World Liberation Front. The CWLF has no problem with this: "Jesus liberates and the world needs Jesus. The entire world needs liberating; so what's more fitting than Christian World Liberation Front?" They have no qualms about using rhetoric and jargon familiar to those in the hip and radical scenes so that the culture-free gospel of Jesus Christ can be disseminated. "What's truly needed is the sense of the power of people getting into a cultural context and being God's people there," says Sparks.

. . .

The editors of *Right On* reflect the educational level of the policy-making staff of the CWLF. David Gill was a history major at the University of California and holds a master's degree from San Francisco State; Sharon Gallagher is a graduate of Westmont College and a sociology major. All of the policy-making staff are college graduates; some hold advanced degrees. That places CWLF in a different category from all of the other Jesus groups we have discussed.

Another characteristic which distinguishes CWLF from most Jesus People is that they are not charismatic in orientation and teaching. CWLF has no official stand on the question of tongues-speaking and related phenomena. There is no official encouragement to seek speaking in tongues, though the experience is recognized as a valid spiritual gift, a tolerance lacking in many evangelical churches outside the Jesus Movement. States one staff worker: "There are brothers and sisters who speak in tongues who come to our meetings. Fine. If they start laying their trip on us, that everybody needs to, we'll show them from Scripture that it's not so."

One indication that the Jesus Freak movement represents a new version of fundamentalism is the fact that it appeals to young people. In the following selection, Robert Lynn Adams and Robert John Fox report the reasons they discovered for the appeal of the movement to adolescents—young people who have tried the counter-culture and want to return to conventional religion; they would like to retain what they consider the creative aspects of the counter-culture, however, and they reject only those aspects of it which they consider "sinful."

ROBERT ADAMS AND ROBERT FOX

SOURCE: From Robert Lynn Adams and Robert John Fox, "Mainlining Jesus." Copyright © February 1972, Society Magazine by Transaction, Inc., New Brunswick, New Jersey.

The Jesus trip seems tailor-made for adolescents. Not only does commitment to Jesus preserve childhood morality with its absolutistic definitions of right and wrong, but it also provides an ideology based on personal, internal and, for the most part, unexplainable experience rather than on critical, rational or realistic analysis. Indeed, the ideology is unchallengeable and thereby not available for analysis by the uninitiated.

The Jesus trip also provides adolescents with the necessary peers, rituals, creeds and programs—brothers, baptisms, speaking in tongues and a source for the ideology, the Bible. Approval and affirmation by peers are guaranteed within the movement. To the droves of young teens who fill Gethsemane Chapel on the nights that the professional music groups perform, Rennie issues the invitation in these words, "Accept Jesus Christ. Don't get left out. Come right now."

The Jesus trip can be seen as an attempt to resolve the crisis of the onset of sexuality by denying sexual feelings. Previous to puberty, the individual has developed to some degree an identity based upon his or her experiences and needs. With the onset of the physiological revolution within and with the growing awareness of adult roles, this identity is threatened; suddenly he must accept a new aspect of identity—sexuality. Successful growth depends on the individual's ability to meet his new needs and expand his identity without threatening the self. Rather than risk the trauma of this adjustment, the individual may resolve the crisis in neurotic fashion: by establishing an ideal by which to deny his feelings. Adolescent idealism represents one such attempt to keep oneself separate from one's real feelings. An example of such denial is this statement by a 16-year-old who had been on drugs and sexually active prior to his conversion:

I am free, free from the garbage of the world—the kind of stuff that you're a slave to. Jesus said, "Whoever commits sin is a servant of sin." I've quit taking drugs, I've quit getting it on the girls—I've changed, man! Don't you understand? I'm free, free, free—all the time and not just for six to eight hours—all the time.

I still have problems, but I don't hassle with them, because I'm free!

We believe that religion as represented in this movement is a step backwards. The Jesus trip, like drugs, appears to be used in such a way as to avoid coming to terms with the anxieties related to the identity crisis. In normal development the new dimensions of identity are added to the previously established identity, modifying it to some degree; some parts of one's previous identity will be discarded, submerged or eradicated by new behavior. Instead of progressing toward adult ethics, the Jesus person clutches tenaciously to childhood morality, with its simplistic black-and-white, right-and-wrong judgments. Rather than developing behavior oriented towards reality, he flies into ideational, ideological abstractions to numb his awareness of his newly arisen needs. Spurning a reality that begins with individual feelings, he subordinates himself to peer approval. For these reasons we term the Jesus trip a pseudo-solution to the identity vs. role confusion crisis.

COMPARING DRUG AND JESUS CULTURES

Members of the Jesus movement have a high incidence of past drug use, with 62 percent of those over 18 and 44 percent of those under 18 having used dope. Only a few individuals were extremely light users, usually of marijuana.

Continuities between the drug and Jesus experiences are as follows: 1) both are outside the modal American life style, in fact, both are anti-establishment in their attempts to create alternatives to the American middle-class life style. Middle-class denominational religion, in the words of one pastor, "is as phony as it can be." 2) Both are subjective and experientially oriented, as opposed to the dominant cultural style, which is objective, scientific and rationally oriented. 3) The nature of the religious experience at Gethsemane Chapel and other holiness-type congregations is wholly consonant with previously experienced drug highs. A common description of the conversion experienced is: "It's a rush like speed."

We found a number of discontinuities between the dope and Jesus trips. As compared with the drug culture, the Jesus trip offers an extremely limited repertoire for action. For the Jesus person, life revolves entirely around Jesus, his acceptance and missions. All events are either of the Lord or of the devil. Brothers and sisters of the faith meet each other with religiously-infused greetings, and "God bless" substitutes for "goodbye." The drug culture as a whole exhibits a much greater variety. Certainly there are drug users whose lives center solely around dope, its procurement and use, but drug use has become quite generalized among a wide variety of people many of whom have a broader range of action alternatives in dealing with reality than the Jesus people.

The Jesus trip represents an almost violent ideological swing from far left to far right, a type of "reaction formation." A shift toward a conservative position in solving world problems is reported by 76 percent of those interviewed. Only two persons have changed toward the left. Of those who reported no change in position, none were "drop-outs" in the usual sense of the word. They represent a more consistent ideological history—no rebellion against parents, a continuity between their childhood religious faith and the adult Jesus movement. Their feelings toward American society, for example, are that it is "pagan like the Roman Empire at the time of Christ" or it is "too complex" for an opinion to have been formed. A slightly more liberal outlook was articulated by one respondent who observed that "the system is great, but people pervert justice." The focus here is still typically on the individual rather than on system change.

Four out of five of those reporting a shift in outlook state that the change coincided with their religious conversion. World problems, they now believe, "can only be solved through finding Christ;" "We can't have peace on the outside if we don't on the inside;" "If everyone was a Christian there wouldn't be any world problems."

For Jesus people, sexual behavior also undergoes profound alteration when they leave the drug culture. Although 62 percent of the Jesus people in the sample report premarital sex prior to conversion, in most cases asceticism has become the dominant rule since being saved. A few slips are reported "once after conversion," but these can hardly be classified as libertine. Less than 5 percent openly differ with the sexual ethics of the movement and continue to practice premarital sex after their conversion. Another divergency is that the Jesus culture entails re-entering the system, returning to a middle-class work ethic and closing the generation gap. After coming from middle-class backgrounds (72 percent of those reporting father's occupation are from white-collar homes and over two-thirds of these are clearly upper-middle-class occupations), dropping out represents downward mobility; these youth are now reentering the system, preparing to participate in the work force.

The movement's strong anti-intellectualism, however, is prompting some young people to drop out of college at a time when their re-entry into the system requires additional training. Many Jesus people, however, are still involved in routine educational views. Of the 89 young people who answered the questionnaire, 17 had completed high school, 19 were still in college, three had some college, two were college graduates, and many were young high school students.

Several in the sample, who had dropped out of college, cite their religious experience as the motivating force in this decision. A songwriter-itinerant singer for gospel causes asserts that "The more education one has, the less likely one is to join (the) Jesus movement . . . (the) less one becomes childlike . . . becomes hardened." He elaborates that school teaches that science is God, that truth is relative, and that there can be good and evil at the same time, but this is not true.

College graduates are included among the ranks of commune dwellers who tend gardens as a livelihood. Generally, though, the older persons in the movement had dropped out during or after high school and now represent a most interesting sociological phenomenon: downward mobility and movement from church to sect (many come from church-affiliated families). Thus in closing the gap between themselves and their parents by rejoining the system, they have created fresh conflict over their education and religion. However, many parents are so pleased with their return to the system that they are financing their offspring's stay in the commune. One youth mentioned the possibility of going to Europe to an evangelical convention, explaining that his father would pay his expenses.

Preachers at Gethsemane Chapel admonish the audience to "honor they father and thy mother." Many youth noted their conscious attempts to help them rebuild relationships with their families. Prayers in communes often concern members of the family who have problems and "need to be saved."

Whereas the drug trip represents a quest, the Jesus trip is a panacea. Despite its attendant problems, the drug culture is admirable in its affirmation of the individual's quest for experience and discovery of truth; in this it is not unlike the basis of modern liberal education. The Jesus trip, however, is a cure-all. No problem is too great to be answered easily; the believer desists from solving problems, "leaves it up to the Lord."

Another difference between the two cultures relates to authoritarianism. The free-lance drug culture is by definition nonauthoritarian. The Jesus culture, on the other hand, sees the world in either-or terms. No experience is free from being of God or of the devil. This unequivocal embracing of authoritarianism may be a by-product of the scanty education of many young believers combined with a background of family conflict.

The Jesus culture escapes the leadership problem posed by the individualism of the drug culture. Lewis Yablonski observes how the individualism of the drug scene often leads to a lack of leadership—a vacuum which sometimes allows "deviants" from the scene to wreak havoc on the peace and tranquility desired by the majority. Although leadership in the Jesus movement is attributed to God, there is no want of self-anointed human leaders around to make suggestions: the hierarchy ranges from the deacons in the commune (often young Christians with less than one year's experience of being saved) to the ministers of Gethsemane Church. The ministers are consulted on Biblical and other problems which the deacons in the commune cannot solve.

Duane Pederson was a night-club entertainer who "retreated" from a harsh reality through drugs. His experience, described in the following excerpt from his book, was a model for his followers, who have had to go through the same conversion experience to free themselves from the death-grip of drugs. Pederson is now a successful "missionary" to the drug culture in Hollywood, and much of his success can be attributed to his identification with alienated youth.

DUANE PEDERSON

SOURCE: *From Duane Pederson with Bob Owen,* The Jesus People *(Pasadena: Compass Press, 1971), pp. 12–15. Reprinted by permission.*

My world was exciting and I loved it. I didn't know at that time that this glitter was soon to tarnish. But it did.

Several years later, totally disillusioned, and no longer starry-eyed with wonder at the glare of footlights and smell of grease paint, I was working the night club circuit. My little dreams were beginning to disappear. I had long since learned that applause did not provide total satisfaction.

So I tried to retreat from the world of harsh reality through drugs, booze . . . and about everything else. But none of those things did the job I hoped they would. Each escape effort failed. Each "return" to reality found me lonely. I still lived pretty much in a world of fantasy. I was nowhere . . .

I honestly believe that the deep love I have for street people— and all the others that might be called "society rejects"—is because I have experienced everything they have. During my 14 years as an entertainer I was always on the road. And I had no real home either . . .

But all that changed in a night club in Minneapolis. A friend of mine who had been a singer and dancer for the Lawrence Welk Show came into the club. I said, "Let's have lunch together."

"All right," he said. And we set the time and place.

When we got together the next day he began to share Jesus Christ with me. He started back in the Old Testament and talked about David and Jonathan.

"Duane, the love that they shared was the kind of love that far surpassed anything either of them had ever known."

I nodded, taking it all in, my heart growing hungry for something I couldn't quite define. Then he jolted me. "In fact, Duane, Jesus Christ shows the very same love to each of us . . ."

"He does?" I stammered. "Jesus does?"

"That's right." Then he paused for what seemed like a long time.

To break the silence, I said, "Is it for real?"

"Yes, every word of it. You know, my life used to be—all messed up."

"Yes. But, where does this Jesus fit into the picture? He's for the good guys, isn't He?"

My friend chuckled. "Not really. Jesus said, 'I didn't come to call the righteous and all the religious people to repentance. But I came to call sinners.' And, Duane, I was a sinner. No question about that . . ."

Not knowing what else to say, I said, "You're sure right."

He leaned toward me and his eyes bored right into mine.

"Duane, that's all over with now. Jesus Christ has given me something I never had. It's groovy. Neat. I've never felt this way before."

Another pause. My friend drummed his fingers on the table and waited. Almost hesitantly I finally said, "How about me? I need to get hold of the same thing you've got." And to myself I was thinking: Please let it be for me, too. This is what I want. What I've been wanting for all my life.

"Sure. All you've got to do is just ask Him to take over your life. And He'll do it."

"When?"

"Right now."

"Right here?"

"Yes, right here."

So I bowed my head. There were people all around, but that didn't matter. In a plain, simple way I said, "Jesus, I'm a sinner. My life's all messed up. I've got no goal. No future. My highs don't satisfy anymore. Please forgive my sins . . . And, how about taking over Duane Pederson's life . . . from right now."

And something happened at that moment.

I felt different, and yet I wasn't different. I didn't know what had happened to me until some time later as I was reading in the Bible, where the Apostle Paul was trying to describe the experience I had just had. He said, "Therefore, if any man be in Christ, he is a new creature. Old things are passed away. Behold, all things are become new" (2 Corinthians 5:17)

I left the club that day.

As I left I said to the manager, "Something great has happened to me. My life is different . . ."

He laughed. "Sure, Duane. You've had a couple. Sure, it's different."

"I mean it. Things are not the same. I'm leaving."

He grinned knowingly. "You'll be back."

I said, "No, I won't." That was several years ago, and I never did go back. I never will. I've got something too great to give up.

PART III

IDEOLOGY
AND
PROPAGANDA

OLD AND NEW RHETORICS

WILLIAM McPHERSON
SOURCE: Written for this volume.

Aristotle wrote: "The whole affair of Rhetoric is the impression [to be made upon an audience]; and hence delivery must be cared for, not on grounds of justice, but as something we are bound to do. Strict justice, of course, would lead us, in speaking, to seek no more [of an emotional effect] than that we should avoid paining the hearer without alluring him; the case should, in justice be fought on the strength of the facts alone, so that all else besides demonstration of fact is superfluous. Nevertheless, as we have said, external matters do count for much, because of the sorry nature of an audience."[1]

Aristotle's discussion of rhetoric makes it clear that he feels it is a political necessity, even though it is "superfluous" to the facts. He argues that one of the purposes of rhetoric is to "prevent the triumph of fraud and injustice,"[2] a purpose which many leaders of social movements use to justify their rhetoric.

REBELLION AND RHETORIC

Rhetoric is defined here as communication which uses political and religious symbols to express the ideology of a social movement. This definition incorporates the concept of "propaganda" but extends beyond the usual perjorative meaning attributed to that concept. "Rhetoric" is being used increasingly in social science literature because rhetoric is viewed as an end in itself and not simply as a means to an end.[3]

Rhetoric is a verbal form of collective behavior,[4] embodied in speeches and periodicals which are produced by leaders of movements and given wide circulation. Most social movements devote a large share of their resources to the production of rhetoric by publishing a newspaper or magazine. Karl Mannheim has observed that "oppressed groups" are "so strongly interested in the destruction and transformation of a given condition of society that they unwittingly see only the elements in the situation which tend to negate it."[5] This way of "seeing" society is expressed through speeches and articles by leaders of movements.

Social movements which find themselves in opposition to the prevailing culture fit Robert Merton's definition of "rebellion": a mode of adaptation which "leads men outside the environing social structure to envisage and seek to bring into being a new . . . social structure."[6] As both Mannheim and Merton suggest, rhetoric is cultural deviance. Rhetoric is a form of rebellion because it expresses rejection (the "destruction" of values) and urges the substitution of alternative values ("transformation").

All social movements tend to have internal needs which are different from their external needs, because they are conflict groups.[7] Rhetoric promotes the internal strength and stability of movements through images of the "ideal member"[8] and through symbols of strength and virtue.[9] Rhetoric propagates an external "image" of growth and influence through symbolic leadership and reference-group orientation.[10] Thus, rhetoric enables a social movement to survive as a conflict group because it externalizes tension and conveys an aggressive, activist image of the movement. Combining the behavioral concepts of "rebellion" with the functional concepts of internal and external needs, we derive the following typology:

REBELLION

Functional Level	Rejection	Substitution
Internal:	Counter-Mythology	Counter-Elitism
External:	Alienation	Absolutism

COUNTER-MYTHOLOGY

Counter-mythology is a form of rhetoric which employs myths and legends to reject the dominant mythology of the society. In counter-mythology, social movements interpret historical and social events differently from the prevailing definition of reality in order to establish their own definitions. "Truth" is not at issue here; it is assumed that questions of validity apply equally to the dominant mythology of a society and to the counter-mythology of social movements.

In American society, mythology takes the form of a "civil religion" which supersedes denominational doctrines.[11] The American mythology incorporates myths of national origin and national mission: (1) "new world myths," originating in the settlement of America by Europeans, and (2) "frontier myths," originating in the westward movement of immigrants and their descendants. These historical processes, which occurred throughout the eighteenth and nineteenth centuries, created myths and legends about the "land of opportunity" and the "conquest of nature."

The dominant mythology of a society tends to be general and abstract. A counter-mythology, in the rhetoric of social movements, tends to be specific and detailed; it is based on a reinterpretation of the same historical events in the light of the particular movement's own experiences and beliefs. The myths and legends of a social movement may involve the leaders and programs of the movement itself, or they may involve other selected heroes and historical events. But these myths and legends are usually contrary to the dominant mythology because they are based on the lives of men viewed as "deviant" or events viewed as "peculiar."

Counter-mythology varies by types of movements. The older movements view the past nostalgically, dwelling on a "golden age" when heroes came forth to lead the revolution or to restore lost virtues. Old radical movements explicitly reject American beliefs and values by substituting the virtues of socialist revolution. The rhetoric of the communist movements dwells on the glory of the Russian Revolution and its heroes, Lenin, Trotsky and Stalin. Contemporary Russian leaders do not play an important role in the old radical counter-mythology.

The older fundamentalism in America is patriotic with reference to the past and sorrowful with reference to the present. The rejection of the dominant mythology does not involve complete disavowal of American history, but rather a denial of the secular elements in it. There is an emphasis on the Christian basis of American culture and institutions. Trends away from Christian virtues are regarded as evidence of apostasy. The virtues of the past are reasserted through myths and legends about the religious basis of American society.

Newer movements invest their hope in the future society which they are trying to create. The new radical rhetoric portrays members of the younger generation as heroes and exemplars. They are leading the way to a new society through a struggle with the older generation. There is no virtue in tradition; legends are created by those who have a vision of the new society and seek to implement it through their own lives.

In the new fundamentalist rhetoric, counter-mythology uses the symbolism of salvation to articulate hope for a better future. All sinners are eligible for salvation, including hippies, drug users, and other drop-outs from society. Patriotism and the work ethic are absent from the new fundamentalist rhetoric; they are not the basis of virtue, as they are in the old fundamentalist rhetoric.

As social movements age, their rhetoric changes. The counter-mythology becomes less hopeful and more traditionalistic. The expectation of immediate and sweeping changes in society declines; the concentration of specific events and models from the past increases. There is still the same intensity of rejection of the dominant mythologies in the older rhetorics; but they do not offer the same sense of immediacy as the newer rhetorics.

COUNTER-ELITISM

Counter-elitism is the rhetorical substitution of the internal authority of the movement for allegiance to external authority. Social movements, to varying degrees, compete with other sources of authority—churches, educational institutions, political organizations—for allegiance. The dominant authority patterns in modern society, at least ideally, are based on rational-legal authority; that is, bureaucratic authority is based on the rule of law rather than the rule of men. Social movements tend to challenge this type of authority with charismatic authority (in the newer movements) or traditional authority (in the older movements).[12] As movements become older, they revert to traditional authority. The problem of succession of leadership is solved through hereditary authority patterns in which inheritance is based on ideological discipleship rather than kinship. Considerations of loyalty override questions of competence for leadership. Leadership skills are emphasized less than commitment to the ideology of the movement, at least in the rhetoric.

Prevailing authority norms of modern societies rest on economic, educational, and political institutions which make expertise and merit the basis of status. Elites in American society are not purely meritocratic, as Mills and others have shown.[13] However, their status is justified with values stressing open recruitment and promotion based on ability.

Social movements tend to counter these values when constructing their models of leadership. The rhetoric of counter-elitism holds out to the members the promise of status through recruitment into leadership ranks based on commitment alone. Commitment may involve allegiance to specific doctrines or to more general values, but it always involves a non-rational component. For voluntary groups such as social movements, ideological commitment is essential. However, non-rational commitment is not necessarily a basis for stability or effectiveness in social movements, which is one reason why they are ephemeral groups.

In the rhetoric of counter-elitism a variety of leadership values are promoted, but there is a common theme: the special status of the leaders.[14] Radical movements tend to define leadership status in "revolutionary" terms: "revolution as a profession" and the "vanguard party" are Leninist concepts incorporated into the rhetoric of communist movements and the new radical movements. The older radical groups stress revolutionary orthodoxy as a qualification for leadership, while newer radical movements stress revolutionary creativity.

Fundamentalist movements define leadership status in devotional terms, as in devotion to a cause or to a personal savior. In the older fundamentalist movements devotion is measured by ability to cite scripture or the classics for "proof" of the authority of their statements. Fundamentalist preachers such as Billy James Hargis or Duane Pederson constantly quote scripture to bolster their arguments. Robert Welch of the John Birch Society uses an analogous method of rhetorical proof: he assiduously footnotes his writings to "document" his charges of communist control and moral decay. Newer fundamentalists also use the "testimonial" technique of rhetorical proof, citing personal experiences as support of their claims to exemplary status.

Counter-elitism in the rhetoric of older movements of both the radical and fundamentalist persuasion tends to stress experience and long-term loyalty. This is understandable in light of the "careers" of the leaders of the older movements. They build their authority on successful accomplishments and on their investment of time and energy over the years. The counter-elitism of the newer movements cannot assume long service or steadfast loyalty among the leadership because the groups are so recently formed. Rather, the rhetoric tends to stress extraordinary deeds and exceptional qualities of leaders who emerge at critical turning points to build the movement. Media exposure is an important vehicle of leadership in new movements because of the sometimes sensational activities of the leaders. Often a new movement is little more than a "following" for a well-known young radical or charismatic preacher.

ALIENATION

Alienation as a sociological concept is the disaffection with life or with social institutions that results from the loss of social bonds—kinship networks, community ties, and so forth—in a mass society. In the rhetoric of social movements, alienation is expressed through symbols of discontent and advocacy of the change or destruction of institutions in society. The "push" of alienation leads people to join social movements;[15] they are then available for the "pull" of the movement's own solutions. The concept of alienation was introduced by Marx; the most useful discussion of the concept for our purposes lies in an article by Melvin Seeman. Of Seeman's five definitions of alienation, the term "powerlessness" is useful for analyzing the rhetoric of radical movements and the term "meaninglessness" is useful for analyzing the rhetoric of fundamentalist movements. With some modifications, Seeman's term "normlessness" is useful for analyzing the rhetoric of older movements and his term "self-estrangement" is useful for analyzing the rhetoric of newer movements.[16] Each of these terms requires further elaboration.

Powerlessness is the feeling that political efforts to change society are futile; it is the basis for the concept of revolution. Radical movements tend to regard reforms as worse than useless; they prevent the "masses" from realizing the extent of their oppression and therefore forestall the drastic changes that are needed. Thus the "liberal," reformist institutions of society—political parties and governmental agencies, educational institutions and economic institutions—are seen as the most dangerous enemies of change.

Meaninglessness is the feeling that the goals and ideals to which one is committed are devoid of meaning. Fundamentalist movements tend to blame social institutions such as the family and the educational system for the decline of values. "Permissive" child-rearing practices and education which does not stress morality are considered responsible for moral decay.

Normlessness is the feeling that older values and norms are being forgotten and losing their influence in society. Older movements tend to view contemporary society as hypocritical or cavalier about traditional virtues. Even the older radical movements view social change with some trepidation because they feel that their established models are being overlooked by agents of change. They feel left out of the new trends and fads in radicalism and they fear the effects of the new radicals on society. Older fundamentalists are even more fearful of change. They feel that the best examples and models of society are found in history and tradition, and that the further the society moves away from these models the worse it becomes.

Self-estrangement is the feeling that one's own life is not under control. The newer movements tend to describe a collective estrangement in their rhetoric, contending that society is not under the control of rational or enlightened elites. The new radicals feel that American foreign and domestic policy is leading toward disaster for the masses at home and abroad. The new fundamentalists feel that American life is spiritually bankrupt and that there will be an apocalyptic end to the current malaise.

As social movements move from newer to older phases, their rhetoric tends to move from "estrangement" to "normlessness." The newer movements tend to have a very broad perspective and therefore are alienated from a wide range of institutions and elites. The older movements narrow their perspective somewhat and tie their critique to particular institutions and elites which conflict with their established models. The rhetoric of the older movements tends to focus on the same institutions year after year.

ABSOLUTISM

Absolutism is the analysis of social and personal problems in simplistic alternatives. In the rhetoric of social movements, absolutism is the obverse of alienation. It portrays ideological solutions as alternatives to the real problems of the members. Even though the movement may offer a simplistic program of solutions, the rhetoric exaggerates the significance of the program to provide the movement with "symbolic uniqueness."[17]

Absolutism is a resolution of the dilemma of social life. In any society, people are subjected to uncertainties arising from the complexity of social systems. Everyone is compelled to make decisions on the basis of incomplete information or precarious predictions, and there are people who cannot handle the resultant ambiguities. People with low tolerance for ambiguity are attracted to movements with absolutist rhetoric because absolutism is the removal of ambiguity in social analysis.[18] Many movements base their ideology on absolutist premises such as "inevitablity of history" or "righteousness of the saved." Flowing from these premises, the rhetoric becomes an expression of intolerance. Intolerance may be threatening to other groups because it challenges rules of social interaction. Movements which use absolutism in their rhetoric thus become conflict groups; they may deliberately or unwittingly create opposition. Many social movements have become increasingly isolated as they build up opposition to their doctrines in society; their response to isolation has often been increased intolerance. Thus the effects of absolutism in rhetoric lead to increasing isolation and polarization of social interaction.

The process of polarization is most evident among older movements because their longer history has permitted the spiraling process of isolation and intolerance to occur. The rhetorical polarization of the social world into friends and foes is often a reflection of the experience of the groups. The suppression of radical groups, which has occurred in the United States under the Wilson administration, the Smith Act, and McCarthyism, has led to more intolerance in their own rhetoric. [19] Conflict between the party and society is viewed as an expression of ideological conflict between a progressive system and a decadent one. The old fundamentalists have also developed a polarized view of the social world; it is a mirror-image of the rhetoric of the old radicals. Just as communists view capitalism as an unmitigated evil, radical rightists view communism as an absolute evil. Although they have not been suppressed, many of the old fundamentalist movements have experienced isolation, and their rhetoric has often become strident when they have felt most isolated.

Newer social movements are less likely to express absolutism in the form of polarization and more likely to seek purification of society. Their hopes for changing society are fresh and untarnished by bitter experience, and their rhetoric reflects this optimism. However, the rhetoric is no less absolutist; it still uses simplistic views of the social world to promote ideological purification. Thus, the new radical rhetoric invokes cultural change as a means of purifying the decadent old system. New radicals tend to express political issues as struggles between older and younger generations, struggles in which the younger generation has a vision of a new and better society. The new fundamentalists tend to express religious doctrines in counter-cultural terms. They see conversion as a purification process in which cultural symbols express the inner purification of the soul as well as the external purification of social institutions.

The contrast between old and new rhetorics in the area of absolutism is thus a contrast between rhetorical devices of polarization and of purification. Older ideologies, as established doctrines, rely more on the commitment of members to eternal principles against which the world is judged and found wanting. Newer ideologies, as emerging doctrines, elicit conversion experiences from members who find that they can purify their own lives by participating in a movement which promises purification of society.

CONCLUSION

An analysis which uses the terms defined in this chapter will permit the student of social movements to classify similarities and differences in rhetoric. The concepts used here are based on a dynamic model of ideology and propaganda which assumes that rhetoric changes as social movements grow older and change over time. Classification of the rhetoric is only the beginning of analysis, however. The functions of the different types of rhetoric must be discovered; these functions have been suggested in this chapter and will be explored further in subsequent chapters.

Theoretically, the rhetoric of all social movements should incorporate all aspects of the typology introduced in this chapter. In other words, any social movement might be expected to have equal amounts of counter-mythology, counter-elitism, alienation, and absolutism in its rhetoric, according to whatever measures we devise. In practice, however, different movements will have different emphases in their rhetoric. Older social movements will tend to place more emphasis on counter-mythology because they have a longer history; older movements will also have a more stable authority structure and thus their counter-elitism will be more elaborate. Hence the older movements tend to emphasize the internal functional level of their rhetoric. Conversely, we might expect newer movements to stress the external functional level— alienation and absolutism—because they have a fresh view of society and its problems.

When movements are analyzed along another dimension, that of radicalism versus fundamentalism, their rhetorical emphases also vary. The radical movements tend to be more removed from core American values, and their rhetoric tends to emphasize rejection of American culture. Therefore we would expect to find radical movements emphasizing counter-mythology and alienation, in contrast to the emphasis on counter-elitism and absolutism in fundamentalist movements. The fundamentalists tend to accept dominant American myths up to a certain point, and to be less concerned with problems in American society. However, the tendency of fundamentalists to rely on revealed truth means that their leaders will tend to emphasize their spiritual authority (which is counter-elitism) and the righteousness of their program of salvation (which is absolutism).

While different movements can be expected to emphasize different aspects of their rhetoric, all movements will have elements of the four components of rhetoric outlined in this chapter. In the examples of rhetoric reprinted in Part Four, all four concepts will be employed to classify the rhetoric of the movements represented there.

[1]Lane Cooper, ed., *The Rhetoric of Aristotle* (New York: Appleton-Century-Crofts, Inc., 1932), pp. 184–185. Brackets in original.

[2]*Ibid.*, p. 5.

[3]For example, Kenneth Burke, *The Rhetoric of Religion* (Boston: Beacon Press, 1961), p. 42; Joseph Gusfield, *Symbolic Crusade* (Urbana: University of Illinois Press, 1966), p. 170.

[4]Collective behavior, contrary to popular opinion, represents not a complete lack of patterned social behavior but the failure of established organizations to "afford direction and supply channels of action." In the arena of collective behavior, social movements supply alternative directions and channels of action through their rhetoric. Turner and Killian, *Collective Behavior*, p. 30.

[5]Karl Mannheim, *Ideology and Utopia* (New York: Harcourt, Brace & Co., 1936), p. 40.

[6]Robert Merton, *Social Theory and Social Structure* (Glencoe, Ill.: The Free Press, 1968), p. 209.

[7]Lewis Coser, *The Functions of Social Conflict* (Glencoe: The Free Press, 1956).

[8]Hans Toch, *The Social Psychology of Social Movements* (Indianapolis: Bobbs-Merrill, 1965), p. 198.

[9]Orrin Klapp, *Collective Search for Identity* (New York: Holt, Rinehart and Winston, 1969), p. 277.

[10]Murray Edelman, *The Symbolic Uses of Politics.* (Urbana: University of Illinois Press, 1964), p. 166.

[11]Robert Bellah, *Beyond Belief* (New York: Harper and Row, 1970).

[12]Max Weber, *The Theory of Social and Economic Organization* (Glencoe: The Free Press, 1947).

[13]C. Wright Mills, *The Power Elite* (New York: Oxford University Press, 1956); and E. Digby Baltzell, *The Protestant Establishment* (New York: Vintage Books, 1964).

[14]Robert Michels, *Political Parties* (Glencoe, Ill.: The Free Press, 1949).

[15]Hans Toch, *The Social Psychology of Social Movements* (Indianapolis: Bobbs-Merrill, 1965).

[16]Melvin Seeman, "On the Meaning of Alienation," *American Sociological Review*, December 1959. Seeman's fifth synonym for alienation, "isolation," does not apply to the rhetoric of social movements because they tend to relieve members' of feelings of isolation through the mechanisms of collective behavior described by Turner and Killian and others.

[17]Orrin Klapp, *Collective Search for Identity*, p. 264.

[18]Milton Rokeach, *The Open and Closed Mind* (New York: Basic Books, 1960).

[19]David Shannon, *The Decline of American Communism* (excerpted in Part Two).

"CRUSADES" AND "SYMBOLIC POVERTY"

In his own way, Orrin Klapp reinforces many of the concepts used in the previous chapter of this book. He explains the processes by which rhetoric transforms social movements into crusades. He discusses "mystiques" in a manner analogous to the concept "counter-mythology" used in the previous chapter. He discusses the role of heroes in a manner analogous to "counter-elitism." He also discusses the functions of symbolism for the members of social movements and explains the operation of the "crusading role" in transforming the members from alienated people into true believers. In the section on "symbolic poverty" Klapp develops the argument which was used in Chapter Nine: the frustrations and disorientations of society lead men to search for absolutes. Klapp explains that search in terms of the "symbolic barrenness" of a mass society. Members of social movements attempt to break out of the dullness that blankets their lives by violating norms of propriety and becoming nonconformists. Thus they become "rebellious" and resort to beliefs in rhetorical absolutes.

ORRIN KLAPP

SOURCE: From Orrin Klapp, Collective Search for Identity. *Copyright* © *1969 by Holt, Rinehart and Winston. Reprinted by permission of Holt, Rinehart and Winston, Inc.*

Heroes take people on vicarious journeys, but crusades take them on real ones. If one starts acting like a hero, he may become a crusader. A crusade may require him to act like a hero. A crusade is a type of movement that rises above ordinary life because it requires one to leave business-as-usual and commit himself earnestly to something he believes in deeply. It is, therefore, capable of producing powerful effects, both on society and on one's conception of oneself. It is, to use various metaphors, a game in which the stakes are high, a plunge, a path from which there is no return. It requires faith in something good enough to justify the trouble and risk. A statement of one of the original crusaders is not foreign to the spirit of all crusaders: "I am marching with a goodly band, and we have placed ourselves entirely in the hands of God, for we go forth as His servants to accomplish His will."[1] Because of such spirit, one may say a crusade is a movement which carries both a cross and a sword. The sword signifies attack on wrong, defense of right, and cutting the bonds of ordinary concern. The cross signifies commitment to higher ideals, mystiques—indeed, every crusade has a cultic aspect, whatever its practical goals, because it needs and uses ritual and achieves redemption of identity along with its practical work. So I would treat crusading as a prime route of identity transformation, one of the few kinds of movement besides cult that does for its members internally as much as it does to society at large.

This is far from implying that a crusade must be a religious movement; rather, I propose to treat it as a generic kind of movement that might arise in any era—though more likely in some than in others. History *does* repeat itself, if one can ignore enough particulars. Many historians will support such a contention: Crane Brinton, searching for recurring patterns of revolution; or Richard Hofstadter, noting that the propaganda appeals of fascist demagogues of the 1940s resembled those of Populism in America in the 1880s: "There seemed to be certain persistent themes in popular agitation of this sort that transcend particular historical eras."[2]

. . .

THE CRUSADER AS A SOCIAL TYPE

What kind of person is a crusader and what is his role? If we are to go beyond a mere dictionary definition (one who undertakes a "remedial enterprise with zeal and enthusiasm"), it might be by considering people such as Harriet Beecher Stowe, William Lloyd Garrison, Margaret Sanger, and William Booth, often called crusaders by historians and biographers; or persons most often thought of as crusaders—Billy Graham, Martin Luther King, Carry Nation, George Lincoln Rockwell, Adolf Hitler, Susan B. Anthony, Gandhi, Jesus Christ, Richard the Lion-Hearted, Martin Luther, Dorothea Dix, and Mario Savio.[3] It is plain that Americans do not automatically consider crusading good or bad, but feel that various people of whom one approves or disapproves can play the role. The commonest things said in describing crusaders were: works or fights for a cause in which he believes, effectiveness in rallying people, and rebel or pioneer who broke new ground. The range of personal traits—from Carry Nation to Mario Savio, from Martin Luther King to George Lincoln Rockwell—is great; we seek, therefore, something that might be shared by diverse persons, such as a stereotypical image, a role, and perhaps a mentality or outlook which different kinds of people could share. This is what I mean by saying that a crusader is a social type rather than a personality type.[4]

. . .

CRUSADE AS A MOVEMENT

You cannot have a crusade by yourself. Like any collective process—a social party, a game, a conversation, a fight, a crowd, a culture—the whole is prior to the part. A crusade comes into being, then forms its members—their disposition, mentalities, and roles—according to its requirements. We have described the crusader as a type; individuals such as William Booth or Harriet Beecher Stowe are perfect—even stereotypic—examples. Still, it is fairly obvious that many more people enter a crusade and *acquire* its mentality and role than have it to begin with. Even those who lead become transformed from mere idealists, intellectuals, and reformers into eloquent speakers and battle-hardened veterans. Those who enter later become transformed not only by the struggle itself but by the models of the leaders and martyrs who went before. All acquire a certain aura of heroism. So, from the point of view of the recruit, the crusade is a role opportunity: to form oneself according to a pattern not ordinarily available, to rise to a higher level of input (commitment) and output (heroism), to test oneself by mortal encounter and engagement; above all, then, to find a new conception of oneself.

For this reason, then, we wish to examine a crusade as a collective process: the kind of self-finding opportunity it affords. We are especially interested in features which seem to mark the cru-

sade off from ordinary movements—such as militance, righteousness, sense of uphill struggle, and image of evil. While all activities
called crusades do not equally have such features, one might say
that those which do approach the ideal type of the perfect crusade
and thereby gain power to transform their members and generate
esprit de corps. Take, for example, three crusades announced in the
newspapers in the same town at the same time: (1) a "United Crusade" to raise funds for community welfare, which started its drive
with these words: "Let's roll up our sleeves and get to work"; (2) a
"Stamp Out Crime" crusade inaugurated by the Independent Insurance Agents Association to honor individuals who come to the aid
of the police; (3) a "Christian Anti-Communism Crusade" led by
Dr. Fred Schwarz, which began its meetings with the national
anthem, a flag salute; and a prayer that we may be "stirred" to-
night for the "cause of freedom," concluding its program of anti-
communist songs and a speech by Schwarz with the statement
"We have tried to survey the evil forces loose in the world."

There is little doubt which of these is really most crusade-like in
spirit. So one might arrange activities called crusades on a scale of
moral elevation and intensity, with the "United Crusade" at one
end and Garrison fighting slavery at the other. The point is that
people do not really care about many worthy social programs, but
they *do* care about a real crusade. Moral intensity and elevation
seem to describe two of these dimensions of caring: the feeling of
rightness and the sense of being called upon to work for a higher
purpose, performance beyond the requirements of ordinary duty. In
general, bureaucracy has no crusading spirit. Military operations
may or may not have it. Zeal, or caring beyond matter-of-fact job
requirements, is the beginning of a crusading spirit. Fanaticism is
its end point.

. . .

The crusade is precisely that kind of movement which blends
the ritual and mystique of cult with practical goals of work and
struggle for something. Unlike cult, however, it focuses primarily
not on emotional centering but on the job it has to do. But, because
it takes one away from a hundred trivial tasks to one supreme task,
it is a wonderful opportunity to redefine oneself by action and
center oneself on the supreme good; and, for this purpose, the
more evangelistic it becomes the better.

For example, some anticommunist groups in the United States—

as Billy James Hargis' Christian Anti-Communist Crusade [sic],
Fred Schwarz's group, and the John Birch Society—are doing
something other than helping the FBI detect threats to the Constitution. They add nothing to the amount of available information,
but do much to stir up emotion about things we already know, and,
regarding domestic communism at least, arouse a vigilance far out
of proportion to the actual size of a party estimated to have about
20,000 members, which the FBI feels fully able to handle. This
evangelism not only does not inform but interferes in many ways
with liberal education, furthering a climate of fear among edu-
cators—not of the communists but of the anti-communists! What,
then, is it achieving? If we assume that a crusade, like a cult, is
doing something at a dramatic-ritual level for its members—
possibly for society-at-large—that a matter-of-fact movement or
police action could not, then it may be earning its keep for many
Americans in giving them roles as modern Paul Reveres.

Such dramatic-ritual functions have two main aspects: cultic
(internal) emotional payoff to members, and dramatic (external)
to society-at-large.

Cultic (Internal Ritual) functions. A visit to a John Birch Society
meeting shows clearly enough what crusading does for its members. We see Robert Welch giving a speech to about 500 members
in a packed convention room in a California hotel. An over-life-
size photograph of John Birch is displayed on the platform beside
the American flag. The meeting begins with a flag salute and prayer
invocation. Then, after some business, Welch begins. He is obviously the "big moment" the crowd has been waiting for. He apolo-
gizes at the beginning because he "doesn't want to talk too long."
A member in the audience calls out, "Go ahead and talk for five
hours! We'll listen." Indeed, he does give a long speech. The
crowd hangs on his words, drinking them up as though it cannot
get enough. His speech is a ranting, rather bad-tempered, but not
humorless, tirade against the whole of American society as an
"insane asylum" going to pot morally. He gives vivid examples of
corruption and bad behavior. Americans are insane because they
cannot see the communist menace in all this. Drastic measures are
needed, but no one does anything. The implication is that *we* are
the ones who are sane and right. In his talk, Welch makes no
specific action proposals, reminding his audience that the John
Birch Society is not a political party—indeed is nonpolitical as an

organization though members as individuals may be political. The crowd enjoys the tone and the feeling of his speech, as one would a sermon that makes one feel good; they are not disappointed that specific action proposals are not made. On this occasion, at least, evangelism is enough. Welch has been spelling out in his words and living presence a role model for them. The meeting ends with discussion and testimonials from the floor; a man rises to tell how his life has become more meaningful since he joined the Society: "I'm a new man since joining, life has started over for me." Unlike an evangelical meeting, however, nobody comes forward to be saved; most were apparently already converts. But the emotional ritual of such proceedings shows that its function is like that of a church service for the faithful. They come away confirmed and uplifted, feeling that life has more significance.

. . .

But beyond the general values of emotional revivalism, we wish to consider more specifically how the crusading *role* contributes to identity. What is it that it gives that workaday life usually does not? I wish to point out there the contribution to identity of: (1) the feeling of return home; (2) the test by which to prove oneself; (3) the break with normal life; (4) reorientation of life; (5) the opportunity for a heroic role; (6) the purgative function of the image of evil; and (7) the vision of the good.

1. The first thing to note is that the crusader role has an unusual capacity for giving the feeling of "rightness"—more so, even, than rational certification procedures, such as court decisions, licensing, conferring of diplomas, or professional promotions. The crusade's power of conferring rightness resembles that of a cult in giving a deep moral, rather than a merely technical, sense of rightness, and in making life more exciting. . . . The sense of rightness that a crusade gives might, I think be summarized by the following statement: "After all the things that I have done in my life, many of which I was not particularly proud of, *this is right!*" This is what I mean by the feeling of a return home morally. A person may live much of his life with programs, institutions, ideas, and people he has no heart for; he is not even sure they are moral. The crusade allows him to return home. Bandages, scars, and jail time can further signify the sense of right, what Cameron calls "status-through-militancy."

2. The crusade offers not merely a freshened perception of right,

but the kind of thing one can *do* to actualize that feeling and prove oneself. Actions vary greatly in their power to confer rightness. A public demonstration or testimony is likely to do more than a private resolution or deed. A Christian crusader who had for the first time professed his faith publicly said, "Through this experience (of witnessing) I now find joy. I went with real fear in my heart. Now, my life has taken on new meaning." Donating blood is symbolically more significant than money to buy the same amount of blood; somehow it gives an "in" feeling, bridging the alienation of man from man in a mysterious way. Work "beyond the call of duty" gives one a sense of right by its sacrificial element (whereas much modern work not only gives no sense of rightness but actually makes a man feel wrong, as in "deals" or sales in which he has to compromise morality). A fight involving risk and sacrifice has the mystique of the donation of blood, multiplied by the gravity of the danger. A crusade offers some kind of test by which a person can prove himself morally, a moment to "stand up and be counted"—an occasion that may never have come before, especially unlikely in a bureaucracy. The commonest forms of this test are, perhaps, the "baptism of fire," an ordeal with risk in which one conquers fear.

. . .

3. Another contribution of the crusade to new identity is that it helps, indeed requires, a person to break with the routines and obligations of normal life and start a new life. With the crucial step he puts his old life behind him, perhaps renounces friends, job, church—much as does many a sect convert. Family and friends often object to the crusader devoting so much time, effort, and money, which is at the same time inconvenient to them and a sacrifice for him. So, during the time of the famous Sacco-Vanzetti case, men quit jobs and mortgaged their homes to "save Sacco and Vanzetti." . . . The justification for such renunciation is the nobility of the role undertaken, compared with the relative worthlessness of the relationships neglected. The crusader does not feel any more at fault for leaving old friends than would a monk for devoting himself to begging. Crusades vary, of course, in the degree to which they demand a break with normal obligations. Some, such as Billy Graham's or Moral Rearmament, make less demands than movements like Jehovah's Witnesses or the Communist Party; perhaps this is a fault in the former, namely, that the more truly crusade-

like a movement is the more demands it makes. . . . So the crusader, once he has joined, even if still accepted by his former friends, feels dislocated and set apart. Jail experience, or suffering the status of outcast, of course, greatly helps the break with normal life. . . . Though set apart, he does not feel outcast or to blame, but may rebuke those who do not join him—as Martin Luther King said of churches which "remain silent behind the safe security of stained glass windows." He feels that others belong on *his* side, not that he has stepped out of bounds. If he feels set apart, it is by dignity and dedication to higher calling, rather like Sir Galahad among the sinful knights. So the set-apartness is not a loss of status but a gain. Though judged heretic, apostate, oddball, troublemaker, traitor by some, he breaks with normal life to embark on a new life—rather like a cultic rebirth.

4. As compensation for dislocation from the social structure, the crusade offers a reorientation of life with a sense of courage and purpose. . . . The crusade converts the "cat on the street" in Watts, Los Angeles, into the young lion (Simba) of Black Nationalism. Its action on the mass[5] is that of a magnet on iron particles: it draws rioting mobs into disciplined regiments, "lost souls" into corps with trumpets and tambourines. This orientation is like a cultic one, except that it is directed toward action upon society—whether by agitation, evangelism, nonviolent pressure, or outright war. When a movement is at the same time religion and crusade, it is hard to tell how much of the identity reclamation is due to the cultic and how much to the crusading aspect. A perfect crusade offers the paradoxical combination of the joy of righteous combat with the promise of perfect peace. Whatever may be its effect upon society, it offers a cure for the individual's anomie.

5. Like the cultic path, the way of a crusader is not ordinary, but heroic. The difference between ordinary life and a heroic role is the difference between climbing stairs and climbing Mr. Everest. It is achievement which sets a person above others—the straight-and-narrow path, the bridge of swords over which the quest hero must crawl with bleeding hands. Defeat allows a crusader to think of himself not as loser but as martyr. Hence, the power of uplift comes from the inherent exultation of the heroic role: the sense of having fought the "good fight," identification with leaders even more heroic, and cancellation of any guilt by merit and suffering.

Therefore, one of the prime duties of a crusade leader is to provide a firm, inspiring model for his fellows. He should be the first to swing the axe, begin the march, apply the boycott, go on the hunger strike, and the last to recant or retreat. His personal style should be austere, expressing devotion to the cause. Aggressive, forthright, opinionated, morally courageous individuals who despise compromise make the best crusaders—such figures as Carry Nation, Billy Graham, Malcolm X, Martin Luther King, Robert Welch, Barry Goldwater—to all of whom the remark of a Goldwater follower in 1964 would be equally applicable: "What I admire most about him is his absolute honesty and idealism."[6] By his assurance he helps all of those around him to feel like new men: he is clear and they find out where they stand; he is firm and they become resolute; he is opinionated and they become sure of themselves; he "knows" and they understand. Thus a crusade leader refreshes identity; through him a mass can experience an uplift without personal contact, as is true of most symbolic leaders.[7]

This does not imply that crusade followers—though they get psychological rewards—have the same personal characteristics as the leader, however much they may identify with him. It would be a mistake to put all "fanatics" in the same mold. He is strong, they are dependent; he has initiative, they imitate; he is authoritarian, they are suggestible. Their strength is a facsimile of his, produced partly by imitation, supported by whatever inner strength they may have. Likewise, what a leader gets out of a crusade psychologically must be distinguished from what his followers get: a mix in which for the former there is a greater amount of realization of abilities, and for the latter more moral confirmation.[8]

6. The heroic role by which the crusade takes a person away from his old life pits him against evils which he now sees clearly, though he may have been complacent about them before. We must, therefore, consider the contribution of the image of evil to identity. A heightened melodramatic image of an enemy at whom to lance, or of apocalyptic evil looming, gives a person not only a sense of battle but an elevated image of himself; he may feel the stature of the heroic role and gird himself to meet the evil. Indeed, the image of the villain changes the aspect of the whole world for the crusader. Thus, as Malcolm X's sister explained, once the "demonology" of the Black Muslims is accepted by any black man, he will never again see the white man with the same eyes. Likewise,

the Ku Klux Klan leader complains of the moral menace of "strangers" who have taken over the land, invaded the cities, broken down moral strandards, desecrated the Sabbath, and threatened Nordic Americans.[9] If the villain has changed the world for the worse, then getting rid of him will change it for the better. From attack on him, the crusade gains a purgative function, providing a relief rather like that of lancing a boil, both for the individual and for society. So the idea of cleansing or sweeping away evil in order to restore goodness and save society is part of the mystique of the crusade and puts it in the category of the ritual of purity and danger.[10] This is the (I think mistakenly called) "paranoid" mentality of people like Birchers and fluoridation fighters, which may reflect no more than a need for the ritual of a fight for the right and a little romance brought into otherwise meaningless lives.

7. Likewise, the vision of the good that will be achieved after the fight is over needs to be sharpened for the crusader. It need not be a Utopia, but it should be purged of villains and radically improved. So the rebellious university student described the world he wanted after reform:

"Most middle-class students see their role as going back to supplant daddy when he retires. . . . What I want is a world where people are free to make the decisions that affect their own lives, a world in which they are not trapped on a vast merry-go-round of concealed power, not forced into situations where the choice is already made for them. I want a "participatory democracy" . . . a nonexploited system in which no one is making money off another man's work. I want people to be happy, too. More than anything else, I want a world where we're free to be human to each other."[11]

Without some such image, however short of pie-in-the-sky, no crusade would have the power to stir people, for getting rid of the villain is not enough unless there is a better world ahead.

As a result of such features—emotional revivalism, the feeling of return home, a test by which to prove oneself, the break with normal life, reorientation, the heroic role, the purgative function of the image of evil, and the vision of good—the crusade is able to offer a deeper change of self-conception and identity than would be possible in ordinary life. So people who have participated in crusades tell of the changes that have occurred in their outlook. . . .

SYMBOLIC POVERTY

Man has entered an era in which he is making his own environment. He prefabricates entire dwelling units, together with their contents, and stacks them where he pleases. He creates artificial climates under geodesic domes. He fills the world with synthetic goods, including replicas of nature. More than politics, technology, architecture, and city planning seem to hold the promise of Utopia.

But he has not been so successful with making symbols; he has had less success in fabricating symbols than things. Functional design fights continually against the tendency of technology and mass production to sameness—that stainless-steel sameness which one so often feels in modern design, however conscientious the efforts to vary it and give it identity. The loss of individuality in mass production is only part of the problem, however. Another— and to my mind more important—part is the assumption either that the environment of man is made up merely of things rather than of symbols, or that needed symbols can be arbitrarily designed and created as the occasion calls for it.

The first of these assumptions which helps to make a meaningless society is illustrated by commerical land use. When one looks at an activity like real estate development, one sees a class of professionals just moving things around without conern for symbols other than those found on the face of the dollar in their own pockets. And so much activity in America (even in public communication!) has only this object so that it is no surprise to find a lack of meaning Nor do suburban developments with names like Golden Oaks or Sun City solve the problem of creating an environment of places with meaning for people to live in. Indeed, such developments, if more than mere labels, are skillfully designed pseudoplaces, like Disneyland, except that you stay there longer.

The other assumption, that one can invent symbols, is shown by the design of sanctuaries. Sanctuaries highlight the problem, because here the requirement that a building be a symbol as well as a thing is most plain. Yet how grotesquely inappropriate are many designs for new church buildings—both inside and outside— ranging from bareboards dullness and plainness to startling buildings that look like automobile engines or launching pads for rockets. Occasionally a designer intervenes to create a stunningly appropriate and expressive contemporary symbol—as in Coventry Cathedral using charred beams to memorialize the German bombing and also Christian forgiveness. But, more often, the shock and bewilderment of the public-at-large is testimony enough that the problem of creating meaningful common symbols of man's highest hope has not been solved. To repeat, the fault, as in the case of church building, is not ignoring symbolism, but the architect's or artist's presumption, once he strays from tradition, that he knows what a significant design is—that meaning is produced by a designer's will rather than by a crescive growth in the interactions and responses of people, as when sanctuaries become hallowed by use.

The price of innovation, when ones does not know how to create symbols, is symbolic barrenness. In the midst of this barrenness, artists, architects, public relations experts, musicians, and ministers are often called upon to provide some kind of meaning for an occasion—to give a public building dignity, to affirm a sense of purpose, to give some individual a feeling of importance. But few know whether such efforts are successful. And artists often have not lived up to their responsiblity—whether from their own choice and fault, or from conditions beyond, and possibly stifling to, their creative powers—of finding out the symbols the public needs. A great many artists disdain the effort to create symbols; they are the first to admit their work has no meaning, beating critics to the punch. And how many of those who produce the new things that make up our life—manufacturers, fashion designers, builders, architects, city planners, legislators—worry about symbols, either the ones they are displacing or those they ought to be creating? Aside from the special field of semantics dealing with the communication of precise information, the public meaning of symbols has been badly neglected.

Although we enjoy many new and beautiful things, our country suffers from symbolic poverty, resulting from the assumption that things are enough and the ignorance of how to make symbols—on some occasions, the sheer murder of symbols. People look around at their world—at things manufactured, at things produced by artists, at organizations and relationships with people, at things they themselves are doing—not knowing what they mean. Few recognize the obligation to make and preserve public symbols, and fewer still know how to do it.

What is symbolic poverty? Not lack of factual information, but of kinds of symbols which make a person's life meaningful and interesting. At the discursive level, this is not so much in term of factual information as such things as stories, legends, romances, gossip, and conversation which is engaging and expressive of vital concerns rather than banal. But at the nondiscursive level modern society suffers a more serious poverty of symbols, including a lack of: reassurance from the gestures of others (that one is loved, understood, needed, somebody special)—what Eric Berne calls "strokes"; ritual which gives a person a sense of himself and fills his life with valid sentiments; place symbols, the familiar world where one belongs, home; the voice of the past, a sense of contact with prior generations; psychological payoffs in recognition for work; and, above all, centering.

Such things result from, or themselves constitute, interactional deficiencies. In a society like ours, which stresses abundance, it is especially painful to suffer identity deprivations from interactional deficiencies. The keenness of identity deprivation is due to the fact that we expect so much and get so little: we live in a society which extols, proclaims, teases, and gratifies the ego—but fails to sustain it with adequate interaction. Not only does our modern society fail to provide adequate interaction for the sick and deviant, but even the "successful" feel a kind of hollowness. As I pointed out in Chapter 1, identity is a delicate psychosocial equilibrium requiring various kinds of support for its maintenance. But in the very society that proclaims abundance for everybody, we see interactional and symbolic deficiencies: the boredom of mechanized sameness, both in job and at home; the wiping away of traditions and places; shallow, inconsistent relationships which, though labeled "friendships," are really impersonally categorical and changeable; an inability of people to get through façades and roles to each other; a piling up of impersonal information which fails to identify because it is not "mine" or "ours"; a weakness of basic social sentiments, such as love, loyalty, and faith; and a lack of ritual by which to intensify either social sentiments or a sense of one's own importance; and, finally, the perishability of fads and styles as status symbols, which because they do not last, cannot be reliable pegs for identity.

In such a milieu, a man has little with which to identify himself.

His family is a small, unstable group which, as sociologists say, is more voluntary association than an institution. His family name means little in a society in which people coming and going makes it impossible to build family reputation, and the whole question of kinship and progenitors is unimportant. Possessions can do little to identify a man when major items—even one's home—are replaced every few years and turnover is increased by abundance and faddism. Anyway, how can one get a sense of ownership of technology, which is made by others, is just like the property of millions of others, and becomes obsolescent before one can be attached to it? Place cannot provide identity when it becomes merely space, as I have explained in Chapter 1. One's job or business is the main peg of identification in modern society; but even this offers little to identity because for the majority it is only a category—such as a civil service rating—in an impersonal bureaucracy. Few, even among leaders of business, have personal reputations that amount to much; and, for almost all, loss of job by retirement or unemployment turns a person easily into "nobody." Above it all is the lack of mystique, of faith in something "more," so characteristic of secular society.

Such features are symbolic deficiencies when considered in contrast with the meaning that a human needs in his life; they are interactional deficiencies when seen in terms of the support and psychological payoff that a person needs from others. Such deficiencies, though glaringly accentuated in the United States, are characteristic of mass societies and may reasonably be predicted of all modern and modernizing societies sooner or later.

From the standpoint of social policy, the nub of the matter is that we do not know how to design a context of human relations in the abundance of mobile, modernistic, traditionless society which will provide the individual with nondiscursive symbols to give him an interesting life and a satisfying identity.

This is the problem of banality. A person whose interactions lack psychological payoffs will find life unutterably boring. The success symbols, though he has them, will seem empty. Practical measures, such as economic progress, political reform, even welfare legislation, will seem irrelevant to him, because they do not deal with the real problem—of banality. He will, therefore, have a tendency to be a dropout or a deviant, turning to escapes or kicks for compensation. Deviants come from those who, in increasing numbers, feel themselves cut loose from attachments to the social system and so are likely to take directions of identity search of which squares (satisfied with the identity they get from the status quo) disapprove. They do not mind becoming visible—as oddballs, rebels, ego-screamers, faddists, and poseurs, whose experiments in self-revision represent the new romanticism.

My basic theory, which I have tried to justify in this book, is that a deviant has a special motive, an identity deprivation from which the square does not suffer. An ego-deprived person turns to a kick outside the accepted order when he cannot find a *summum bonum* within. The kick is for the deviant what conversion is for the cultist—his centering and salvation. An identity-deprived person takes kicks much more seriously than does someone who is satisfied with identity—what to the latter is merely fun is to the former his big moment. Because of this identity need, the deviant feels he has a right to deviate. His argument might be as follows: If the social order denies me a feeling of integrity as a person, something is wrong with *it*; therefore, I have a right to go outside its codes to the extent necessary to find myself. Such a point of view divides people—not between haves and have-nots, or political parties—but between those who feel dissatisfied with their identity and cheated by the social order—therefore searching, escaping, unconventional, rebel, extremist—and those who are satisfied with their identities because the psychological payoffs are satisfactory to them.

The former will be likely to turn to the responses and movements dealt with in this book—major kinds of mass response to symbolic poverty and banality. They may turn to cults. They may try voyages of identity through the roles of celebrities and heroes. They may try ego-screaming—in various kinds of style experimentation, faddism, posing, and rebellion. They may try to define themselves by action and ordeal; to return home morally by commitment to crusades. From the standpoint of the individual seeking to gain himself a more meaningful life, these are all searches. But from the societal standpoint, they are efforts to restore symbolic balance. Let us consider this.

[1]Volkmar of Gretz, an original crusader, quoted in James A. Michener, *The Source* (New York: Random House, 1965), p. 554.

[2]He refers to a study by Leo Lowenthal and Norbert Guterman, *Prophets of Deceit* (New York: Harper & Row, 1949). As examples of persistent themes transcending particular historical eras (common to Populism and fascism) Hofstadter mentions: the conception of history as a conspiracy; the notion that the world is moving toward apocalypse; the attention to "greed and other personal vices" of wicked people rather than to structural analysis of the social system; and the concept of the "native simplicity and virtue of the folk." *The Age of Reform* (New York: Random House, 1955), pp. 72, 73.

[3]Most often mentioned in 365 nominations of crusaders by 74 junior and senior students (36 males, 36 females), San Diego State College, 1966. See also crusaders mentioned in Klapp, *Heroes, Villains and Fools*, p. 46.

[4]Klapp, *Heroes, Villains and Fools*, pp. 9–16.

[5]For theory of the mass and availability of people for social movement, see Arthur Kornhauser, *The Politics of Mass Society* (New York: Free Press, 1959), which distinguishes between communal, pluralistic, and mass societies in terms of availability of people for movements. For basic theory of the mass and its "convergence" of interests, see Herbert Blumer, "Collective Behavior," in A. M. Lee (ed.) *Outline of Principles of Sociology* (New York: Barnes & Noble, 1946), pp. 185–189.

[6]BBC 1 television, London, July 31, 1964.

[7]See Klapp, *Symbolic Leaders*.

[8]Eric Hoffer, *The True Believer* (Harper & Row, 1961), analyzes the reward of the "fanatic" as the assurance of sheep-like belief for which he surrenders his old spoiled identity. This, I think, is a little too strong to apply to all—perhaps even most—crusaders, many of whom, leaders especially, are markedly inner-directed.

[9]Hiram Wesley Adams, Klan Imperial Wizard, quoted in Hofstadter, *The Age of Reform*, pp. 295–296.

[10]Mary Douglas, *Purity and Danger, an Analysis of Concepts of Pollution and Taboo* (New York: Praeger, 1966). In more mythic terms, the crusade is a repetition of the hero-monster-deliverance theme (St. George, Beowulf, Perseus, Sigird, Rama). See O. E. Klapp, "The Folk Hero," *Journal of American Folklore*, Jan.—March 1949, pp. 17–25.

[11]David Smith, student, Tufts University, *Life*, April 30, 1965, p. 30.

CONTROL OF THE COLLECTIVE UNCONSCIOUS AS A PROBLEM OF OUR AGE

Here and in Chapter Twelve, two noted sociologists comment on the social consequences of ideology. The title of this chapter is indicative of the concern and anxiety of European intellectuals during the rise of fascism. Karl Mannheim was deeply disturbed by events in Europe in the 1920's and 1930's, when mass movements in Germany and Italy upset the dominant belief systems. Like many intellectuals of the time, he was strongly influenced by Freud, hence the term "collective unconscious." By regarding the "collective unconscious" as a problem, Mannheim reveals his proclivities for social equilibrium and his fears of the effects of aggressive social movements.

Unlike many other social commentaries, however, Mannheim's writings rise above the immediate concerns and problems and provide a basis for analysis of any ideology. His distinction between "ideology" and "utopia" is especially useful here. It enables us to see that there are elements in the dominant belief system of any society which give rise to opposing beliefs; hence, the discussion of social movements must recognize the value conflict which underlies the rhetoric of the movements. Concepts such as "counter-mythology" and "counter-elitism," introduced in Chapter Nine and used in Chapters Thirteen through Sixteen, are based on a conflict model of belief systems. The concept of "absolutism" also follows from such a conflict model, involving the polarization of beliefs between opposing groups.

KARL MANNHEIM

SOURCE: Ideology and Utopia *by Karl Mannheim. Reprinted by permission of Harcourt Brace Jovanovich, Inc. Copyright 1936.*

The emergence of the problem of the multiplicity of thought-styles which have appeared in the course of scientific development and the perceptibility of collective-unconscious motives hitherto hidden, is only one aspect of the prevalence of the intellectual restiveness which characterizes our age. In spite of the democratic diffusion of knowledge, the philosophical, psychological, and sociological problems which we presented above have been confined to a relatively small intellectual minority. This intellectual unrest came gradually to be regarded by them as their own professional privilege, and might have been considered as the private preoccupation of these groups had not all strata, with the growth of democracy, been drawn into the political and philosophical discussion.

The preceding exposition has already shown, however, that the roots of the discussion carried on by the intellectuals reached deeply into the situation of society as a whole. In many respects their problems were nothing else than the sublimated intensification and rational refinement of a social and intellectual crisis which at bottom embraced the entire society. The breakdown of the objective view of the world, of which the guarantee in the Middle Ages was the Church, was reflected even in the simplest minds. What the philosophers fought out among themselves in a rational terminology was experienced by the masses in the form of religious conflict.

When many churches took the place of one doctrinal system guaranteed by revelation with the aid of which everything essential in an agrarian-static world could be explained—when many small sects arose where there had formerly been a world religion, the minds of simple men were seized by tensions similar to those which the intellectuals experienced on the philosophical level in terms of the co-existence of numerous theories of reality and of knowledge.

At the beginning of modern times, the Protestant movement set up in the place of revealed salvation, guaranteed by the objective institution of the Church, the notion of the subjective certainty of salvation. It was assumed in the light of this doctrine that each person should decide according to his own subjective conscience whether his conduct was pleasing to God and conducive to salvation. Thus Protestantism rendered subjective a criterion which had hitherto been objective, thereby paralleling what modern epistemology was doing when it retreated from an objectively guaranteed order of existence to the individual subject. It was not a long step from the doctrine of the subjective certainty of salvation to a psychological standpoint in which gradually the observation of the psychic process, which developed into a veritable curiosity, became more important than the harkening to the criteria of salvation which men had formerly tried to detect in their own souls.

Nor was it conducive to the public belief in an objective world-order when most political states in the period of enlightened absolutism attempted to weaken the Church by means which they had taken over from the Church itself, namely, through attempting to replace an objective interpretation of the world guaranteed by the Church, by one guaranteed by the State. In doing this, it advanced the cause of the Enlightenment which at the same time was one of the weapons of the rising bourgeoisie. Both the modern state and the bourgeoisie achieved success in the measure that the rationalistic naturalistic view of the world increasingly displaced the religious one. This took place, however, without the permeation into the broadest strata of that fullness of knowledge required for rational thinking. Furthermore, this diffusion of the rationalistic world-view was realized without the strata involved in it being brought into a social position which would have allowed an individualization of the forms of living and thinking.

Without, however, a social life-situation compelling and tending toward individualization, a mode of life which is devoid of collective myths is scarcely bearable. The merchant, the entrepreneur, the intellectual, each in his own way occupies a position which requires rational decisions concerning the tasks set by everyday life. In arriving at these decisions, it is always necessary for the individual to free his judgments from those of others and to think through certain issues in a rational way from the point of view of his own interests. This is not true for peasants of the older type nor for the recently emerged mass of subordinate white-collar workers who hold positions requiring little initiative, and no foresight of a speculative kind. Their modes of behavior are regulated to a certain extent on the basis of myths, traditions or mass-faith in a leader. Men who in their everyday life are not trained by occupations which impel toward individualization always to make their own decisions, to know from their own personal point of view what is wrong and what is right, who from this point on never have occasion to analyse situations into their elements and who, further, fail to develop a self-consciousness in themselves which will stand firm even when the individual is cut off from the mode of judgment peculiar to his group and must think for himself—such individuals will not be in a position, even in the religious sphere, to bear up under such severe inner crises as scepticism. Life in terms of an inner balance which must be ever won anew is the essentially novel element which modern man, at the level of individualization, must elaborate for himself if he is to live on the basis of the rationality of the Enlightenment. A society which in its division of labour and functional differentiation cannot offer to each individual a set of problems and fields of operation in which full initiative and individual judgment can be exercised, also cannot realize a thoroughgoing individualistic and rationalistic *Weltanschauung* which can aspire to become an effective social reality.

Although it would be false to believe—as intellectuals easily tend to do—that the centuries of the Enlightenment actually changed the populace in a fundamental way, since religion even though weakened lived on as ritual, cult, devotion, and ecstatic modes of experience, nonetheless their impact was sufficiently strong to shatter to a large extent the religious world-view. The forms of thought characteristic of industrial society gradually penetrated into those areas which had any contact whatever with industry and sooner or later undermined one element after another of the religious explanation of the world.

The absolute state, by claiming as one of its prerogatives the setting forth of its own interpretation of the world, took a step which later on with the democratization of society tended more and more to set a precedent. It showed that politics was able to use its conception of the world as a weapon and that politics was not merely a struggle for power but really first became fundamentally significant only when it infused its aims with a kind of political philosophy, with a political conception of the world. We can well dispense with sketching in detail the picture of how, with increasing democratization, not only the state but also political parties strove to provide their conflicts with philosophical foundation and systematization. First liberalism, then haltingly following its example conservatism, and finally socialism made of its political aims a philosophical credo, a world-view with well established methods of thought and prescribed conclusions. Thus to the split in the religious world-view was added the fractionalization of political outlooks. But whereas the churches and sects conducted their battles with diverse irrational articles of faith and developed the rational element in the last analysis only for the members of the clergy and the narrow stratum of lay intellectuals, the emergent political parties incorporated rational and if possible scientific arguments into their systems of thought to a much greater degree and attributed much more importance to them. This was due in part to their later appearance in history in a period in which science as such was accorded a greater social esteem and in part to the method by which they recruited their functionaries, since in the beginning, at least, these were chosen largely from the ranks of the above-mentioned emancipated intellectuals. It was in accord with the needs of an industrial society and of these intellectual strata for them to base their collective actions not on a frank enunciation of their creed but rather on a rationally justifiable system of ideas.

The result of this amalgamation of politics and scientific thought was that gradually every type of politics, at least in the forms in which it offered itself for acceptance, was given a scientific tinge and every type of scientific attitude in its turn came to bear a political colouration.

This amalgamation had its negative as well as its positive effects. It so facilitated the diffusion of scientific ideas that ever broader strata in the whole of their political existence had to seek theoretical justifications for their positions. They learned thereby—even though frequently in a very propagandistic manner—to think about society and politics with the categories of scientific analysis. It was also helpful to political and social science in that it gained a concrete grip on reality and in so doing gave itself a theme for stating its problems, which furnished a continuous link between it and that field of reality within which it had to operate, namely, society. The crises and the exigencies of social life offered the empirical subject-matter, the political and social interpretations, and the hypotheses through which events became analysable. The theories of Adam Smith as well as those of Marx—to mention only these two—were elaborated and extended with their attempts to interpret and analyse collectively experienced events.

The principal liability, however, in this direct connection between theory and politics lies in the fact that while knowledge always has to retain its experimental character if it wishes to do justice to new sets of facts, thinking which is dominated by a political attitude can now allow itself to be continuously readapted to new experiences. Political parties, because of the very fact of their being organized, can neither maintain an elasticity in their methods of thought nor be ready to accept any answer that might come out of their inquiries. Structurally they are public corporations and fighting organizations. This in itself already forces them into a dogmatic direction. The more intellectuals became party functionaries, the more they lost the virtue of receptivity and elasticity which they had brought with them from their previous labile situation.

The other danger which arises from this alliance between science and politics is that the crises affecting political thinking also become the crises of scientific thought. Out of this complex we will concentrate on only one fact which, however, became significant for the contemporary situation. Politics is conflict and tends increasingly to become a life-death struggle. The more violent this struggle became, the more tightly did it grip the emotional undercurrents which formerly operated unconsciously but all the more intensively, and forced them into the open domain of the conscious.

Political discussion possesses a character fundamentally different from academic discussion. It seeks not only to be in the right but also to demolish the basis of its opponent's social and intellectual existence. Political discussion, therefore, penetrates more profoundly into the existential foundation of thinking than the kind of discussion which thinks only in terms of a few selected "points of view" and considers only the "theoretical relevance" of an argument. Political conflict, since it is from the very beginning a rationalized form of the struggle for social predominance, attacks the social status of the opponent, his public prestige, and his self-confidence. It is difficult to decide in this case whether the sublimation or substitution of discussion for the older weapons of conflict, the direct use of force and oppression, really constituted a fundamental improvement in human life. Physical repression is, it is true, harder to bear externally, but the will to psychic annihilation, which took its place in many instances, is perhaps even more unbearable. It is therefore no wonder that particularly in this sphere every theoretical refutation was gradually transformed into a much more fundamental attack on the whole life-situation of the opponent, and with the destruction of his theories one hoped also to undermine his social position. Further, it is not surprising that in this conflict, in which from the very start one paid attention not only to what a person said but also the group for which he was the spokesman and with what action in view he set forth his arguments, one viewed thought in connection with the mode of existence to which it was bound. It is true that thought has always been the expression of group life and group action (except for highly academic thinking which for a time was able to insulate itself from active life). But the difference was either that in religious conflicts, theoretical issues were not of primary significance or that in analysing their adversaries, men did not get to an analysis of their adversaries' groups because, as we have seen, the social elements in intellectual phenomena had not become visible to the thinkers of an individualistic epoch.

In political discussion in modern democracies where ideas were more clearly representative of certain groups, the social and existential determination of thought became more easily visible. In principle it was politics which first discovered the sociological method in the study of intellectual phenomena. Basically it was in political struggles that for the first time men became aware of the unconscious collective motivations which had always guided the direction of thought. Political discussion is, from the very first, more than theoretical argumentation; it is the tearing off of disguises—the unmasking of those unconscious motives which bind the group existence to its cultural aspirations and its theoretical arguments. To the extent, however, that modern politics fought its battles with theoretical weapons, the process of unmasking penetrated to the social roots of theory.

The discovery of the social-situational roots of thought at first, therefore, took the form of unmasking. In addition to the gradual dissolution of the unitary objective world-view, which to the simple man in the street took the form of a plurality of divergent conceptions of the world, and to the intellectuals presented itself as the irreconcilable plurality of thought-styles, there entered into the public mind the tendency to unmask the unconscious situational motivations in group thinking. This final intensification of the intellectual crisis can be characterized by two slogan-like concepts "ideology and utopia" which because of their symbolic significance have been chosen as the title for this book.

The concept "ideology" reflects the one discovery which

emerged from political conflict, namely, that ruling groups can in their thinking become so intensively interest-bound to a situation that they are simply no longer able to see certain facts which would undermine their sense of domination. There is implicit in the word "ideology" the insight that in certain situations the collective unconscious of certain groups obscures the real condition of society both to itself and to others and thereby stabilizes it.

The concept of *utopian* thinking reflects the opposite discovery of the political struggle, namely that certain oppressed groups are intellectually so strongly interested in the destruction and transformation of a given condition of society that they unwittingly see only those elements in the situation which tend to negate it. Their thinking is incapable of correctly diagnosing an existing condition of society. They are not at all concerned with what really exists; rather in their thinking they already seek to change the situation that exists. Their thought is never a diagnosis of the situation; it can be used only as a direction for action. In the utopian mentality, the collective unconscious, guided by wishful representation and the will to action, hides certain aspects of reality. It turns its back on everything which would shake its belief or paralyse its desire to change things.

The collective unconscious and the activity impelled by it serve to disguise certain aspects of social reality from two directions. It is possible, furthermore, as we have seen above, to designate specifically, the source and direction of the distortion. It is the task of this volume to trace out, in the two directions indicated, the most significant phases in the emergence of this discovery of the role of the unconscious as it appears in the history of ideology and utopia. At this point we are concerned only with delineating that state of mind which followed upon these insights since it is characteristic of the situation from which this book came forth.

At first those parties which possessed the new "intellectual weapons," the unmasking of the unconscious, had a terrific advantage over their adversaries. It was stupefying for the latter when it was demonstrated that their ideas were merely distorted reflections of their situation in life, anticipations of their unconscious interests. The mere fact that it could be convincingly demonstrated to the adversary that motives which had hitherto been hidden from him were at work must have filled him with terror and awakened in the person using the weapon a feeling of marvellous superiority.

It was at the same time the dawning of a level of consciousness which mankind had hitherto always hidden from itself with the greatest tenacity. Nor was it by chance that this invasion of the unconscious was dared only by the attacker while the attacked was doubly overwhelmed—first, through the laying bare of the unconscious itself and then, in addition to this, through the fact that the unconscious was laid bare and pushed into prominence in a spirit of enmity. For it is clear that it makes a considerable difference whether the unconscious is dealt with for purposes of aiding and curing or for the purpose of unmasking.

To-day, however, we have reached a stage in which this weapon of the reciprocal unmasking and laying bare of the unconscious sources of intellectual existence has become the property not of one group among many but of all of them. But in the measure that the various groups sought to destroy their adversaries' confidence in their thinking by this most modern intellectual weapon of radical unmasking, they also destroyed, as all positions gradually came to be subjected to analysis, man's confidence in human thought in general. The process of exposing the problematic elements in thought which had been latent since the collapse of the Middle Ages culminated at last in the collapse of confidence in thought in general. There is nothing accidental but rather more of the inevitable in the fact that more and more people took flight into scepticism or irrationalism.

THE END OF IDEOLOGY
IN THE WEST

Daniel Bell is the leading advocate of the "end of Ideology" school of social commentary. This group of sociologists and social critics claims that ideology is exhausted in the political life of Western, industrialized countries. (They do allow for the continued importance of nationalist ideologies in non-industrialized nations.) However, Bell and others do admit that pockets of society will continue to expound their ideologies and that leaders will come forth to create movements around the ideologies. Since 1960, when this essay was first published, it is evident that ideology still has an impact on Western societies, especially among youth and minority groups. It is no accident that the new radicals have criticized Bell for proclaiming the end of ideology. In an article written for *Our Generation*, Robert Haber contends that the "end of ideology" argument is itself ideology, namely an apology for corporate liberalism and an intellectual suppression of radicalism.* However, the new radicals do not seem to have created a successful and coherent ideology for themselves (see Chapters Six and Fourteen); so Bell may have been right after all.

*Robert A. Haber, "The End of Ideology as Ideology," *Our Generation*, November 1966, pp. 51–68.

DANIEL BELL

SOURCE: From Daniel Bell, The End of Ideology. *Reprinted with permission of The Macmillan Company from* The End of Ideology *by Daniel Bell. Copyright © 1960 by The Free Press, A Corporation.*

There have been few periods in history when man felt his world to be durable, suspended surely, as in Christian allegory, between chaos and heaven. In an Egyptian papyrus of more than four thousand years ago, one finds: "... impudence is rife ... the country is spinning round and round like a potter's wheel . . . the masses are like timid sheep without a shepherd . . . one who yesterday was indigent is now wealthy and the sometime rich overwhelm him with adulation." The Hellenistic period as described by Gilbert Murray was one of a "failure of nerve"; there was "the rise of pessimism, a loss of self-confidence, of hope in this life and of faith in normal human effort." And the old scoundrel Talleyrand claimed that only those who lived before 1789 could have tasted life in all its sweetness.[1]

This age, too, can add appropriate citations—made all the more wry and bitter by the long period of bright hope that preceded it— for the two decades between 1930 and 1950 have an intensity peculiar in written history: world-wide economic depression and sharp class struggles; the rise of fascism and racial imperialism in a country that had stood at an advanced stage of human culture; the tragic self-immolation of a revolutionary generation that had proclaimed the finer ideals of man; destructive war of a breadth and scale hitherto unknown; the bureaucratized murder of millions in concentration camps and death chambers.

For the radical intellectual who had articulated the revolutionary impulses of the past century and a half, all this has meant an end to chiliastic hopes, to millenarianism, to apocalyptic thinking—and to ideology. For ideology, which once was a road to action, has come to be a dead end.

Whatever its origins among the French *philosophes*, ideology as a way of translating ideas into action was given its sharpest phrasing by the left Hegelians, by Feuerbach and by Marx. For them, the function of philosophy was to be critical, to rid the present of the past. ("The tradition of all the dead generations weighs like a nightmare on the brain of the living," wrote Marx.) Feuerbach, the most radical of all the left Hegelians, called himself Luther II. Man would be free, he said, if we could demythologize religion. The history of all thought was a history of progressive disenchantment, and if finally, in Christianity, God had been transformed from a parochial deity to a universal abstraction, the function of criticism—using the radical tool of alienation, or self-estrangement— was to replace theology by anthropology, to substitute Man for God. Philosophy was to be directed at life, man was to be liberated from the "specter of abstractions" and extricated from the bind of the supernatural. Religion was capable only of creating "false consciousness." Philosophy would reveal "true consciousness." And by placing Man, rather than God, at the center of consciousness, Feuerbach sought to bring the "infinite into the finite."[2]

If Feuerbach "descended into the world," Marx sought to transform it. And where Feuerbach proclaimed anthropology, Marx, reclaiming a root insight of Hegel, emphasized History and historical contexts. The world was not generic Man, but men; and of men, classes of men. Men differed because of their class position. And truths were class truths. All truths, thus, were masks, or partial truths, but the real truth was the revolutionary truth. And this real truth was rational.

Thus a dynamic was introduced into the analysis of ideology, and into the creation of a new ideology. By demythologizing religion, one recovered (from God and sin) the potential in man. By unfolding of history, rationality was revealed. In the struggle of classes, true consciousness, rather than false consciousness, could be achieved. But if truth lay in action, one must act. The left Hegelians, said Marx, were only *littérateurs*. (For them a magazine was "practice.") For Marx, the only real action was in politics. But action, revolutionary action as Marx conceived it, was not mere social change. It was, in its way, the resumption of all the old millenarian, chiliastic ideas of the Anabaptists. It was, in its new vision, a new ideology.

Ideology is the conversion of ideas into social levers. Without irony, Max Lerner once entitled a book "Ideas Are Weapons." This is the language of ideology. It is more. It is the commitment to the consequences of ideas. When Vissarion Belinsky, the father of Russian criticism, first read Hegel and became convinced of the philosophical correctness of the formula "what is, is what ought to be," he became a supporter of the Russian autocracy. But when it was shown to him that Hegel's thought contained the contrary tendency, that dialectically the "is" evolves into a different form, he became a revolutionary overnight. "Belinsky's conversion," comments Rufus W. Mathewson, Jr., "illustrates an attitude toward ideas which is both passionate and myopic, which responds to them on the basis of their immediate relevances alone, and inevitably reduces them to tools."[3]

What gives ideology its force is its passion. Abstract philosophical inquiry has always sought to eliminate passion, and the person, to rationalize all ideas. For the ideologue, truth arises in action, and meaning is given to experience by the "transforming moment." He comes alive not in contemplation, but in "the deed." One might say, in fact, that the most important, latent, function of ideology is to tap emotion. Other than religion (and war and nationalism), there have been few forms of channelizing emotional energy. Religion symbolized, drained away, dispersed emotional energy from the world onto the litany, the liturgy, the sacraments, the edifices, the arts. Ideology fuses these energies and channels them into politics.

But religion, at its most effective, was more. It was a way for people to cope with the problem of death. The fear of death— forceful and inevitable—and more, the fear of violent death, shatters the glittering, imposing, momentary dream of man's power. The fear of death, as Hobbes pointed out, is the source of conscience; the effort to avoid violent death is the source of law. When it was possible for people to believe, really believe, in heaven and hell, then some of the fear of death could be tempered or controlled; without such belief, there is only the total annihilation of the self.[4]

It may well be that with the decline in religious *faith* in the last century and more, this fear of death as total annihilation, unconsciously expressed, has probably increased. One may hypothesize, in fact, that here is a cause of the breakthrough of the irrational, which is such a marked feature of the changed moral temper of our time. Fanaticism, violence, and cruelty are not, of course, unique in human history. But there was a time when such frenzies and mass emotions could be displaced, symbolized, drained away, and dispersed through religious devotion and practice. Now there is only this life, and the assertion of self becomes possible--for some even necessary—in the domination over others.* One can challenge death by emphasizing the omnipotence of a movement (as in the "inevitable" victory of communism), or overcome death (as did the "immortality" of Captain Ahab) by bending others to

---

*The Marquis de Sade, who, more than any man, explored the limits of self-assertion, once wrote: "There is not a single man who doesn't want to be a despot when he is excited . . . he would like to be alone in the world . . . any sort of equality would destroy the despotism he enjoys then." De Sade proposed, therefore, to canalize these impulses into sexual activity by opening universal brothels which could serve to drain away these emotions. De Sade, it should be pointed out, was a bitter enemy of religion, but he understood well the latent function of religion in mobilizing emotions.

one's will. Both paths are taken, but politics, because it can insti-
tutionalize power, in the way that religion once did, becomes the
ready avenue for domination. The modern effort to transform the
world chiefly or solely through politics (as contrasted with the religious transformation of the self) has meant that all other institutional ways of mobilizing emotional energy would necessarily
atrophy. In effect, sect and church became party and social movement.

A social movement can rouse people when it can do three things:
simplify ideas, establish a claim to truth, and, in the union of the
two, demand a commitment to action. Thus, not only does ideology
transform ideas, it transforms people as well. The nineteenth-century ideologies, by emphasizing inevitability and by infusing
passion into their followers, could compete with religion. By identifying inevitability with progress, they linked up with the positive
values of science. But more important, these ideologies were linked,
too, with the rising class of intellectuals, which was seeking to
assert a place in society.

The differences between the intellectual and the scholar, without being invidious, are important to understand. The scholar has
a bounded field of knowledge, a tradition, and seeks to find his
place in it, adding to the accumulated, tested knowledge of the past
as to a mosaic. The scholar, qua scholar, is less involved with his
"self." The intellectual begins with *his* experience, *his* individual
perceptions of the world, *his* privileges and deprivations, and
judges the world by these sensibilities. Since his own status is of
high value, his judgments of the society reflect the treatment accorded him. In a business civilization, the intellectual felt that the
wrong values were being honored, and rejected the society. Thus
there was a "built-in" compulsion for the free-floating intellectual
to become political. The ideologies, therefore, which emerged
from the nineteenth century had the force of the intellectuals
behind them. They embarked upon what William James called
"the faith ladder," which in its vision of the future cannot distinguish possibilities from probabilities, and converts the latter into
certainties.

Today, these ideologies are exhausted. The events behind this
important sociological change are complex and varied. Such calam-
ities as the Moscow Trials, the Nazi-Soviet pact, the concentration
camps, the suppression of the Hungarian workers, form one chain;

such social changes as the modification of capitalism, the rise of the Welfare State, another. In philosophy, one can trace the decline of simplistic, rationalistic beliefs and the emergence of new stoic-theological images of man, e.g. Freud, Tillich, Jaspers, etc. This is not to say that such ideologies as communism in France and Italy do not have a political weight, or a driving momentum from other sources. But out of all this history, one simple fact emerges: for the radical intelligentzia, the old ideologies have lost their "truth" and their power to persuade.

Few serious minds believe any longer that one can set down "blueprints" and through "social engineering" bring about a new utopia of social harmony. At the same time, the older "counter-beliefs" have lost their intellectual force as well. Few "classic" liberals insist that the State should play no role in the economy, and few serious conservatives, at least in England and on the Continent, believe that the Welfare State is "the road to serfdom." In the Western world, therefore, there is today a rough consensus among intellectuals on political issues: the acceptance of a Welfare State; the desirability of decentralized power; a system of mixed economy and of political pluralism. In that sense, too, the ideological age has ended.

And yet, the extraordinary fact is that while the old nineteenth-century ideologies and intellectual debates have become exhausted, the rising states of Asia and Africa are fashioning new ideologies with a different appeal for their own people. These are the ideologies of industrialization, modernization, Pan-Arabism, color, and nationalism. In the distinctive difference between the two kinds of ideologies lies the great political and social problems of the second half of the twentieth century. The ideologies of the nineteenth century were universalistic, humanistic, and fashioned by intellectuals. The mass ideologies of Asia and Africa are parochial, instrumental, and created by political leaders. The driving forces of the old ideologies were social equality and, in the largest sense, freedom. The impulsions of the new ideologies are economic development and national power.

And in this appeal, Russia and China have become models. The fascination these countries exert is no longer the old idea of the free society, but the new one of economic growth. And if this involves the wholesale coercion of the population and the rise of new elites to drive the people, the new repressions are justified on the ground that without such coercions economic advance cannot take place rapidly enough. And even for some of the liberals of the West, "economic development" has become a new ideology that washes away the memory of old disillusionments.

It is hard to quarrel with an appeal for rapid economic growth and modernization, and few can dispute the goal, as few could ever dispute an appeal for equality and freedom. But in this powerful surge—and its swiftness is amazing—any movement that instates such goals risks the sacrifice of the present generation for a future that may see only a new exploitation by a new elite. For the newly-risen countries, the debate is not over the merits of Communism—the content of that doctrine has long been forgotten by friends and foes alike. The question is an older one: whether new societies can grow by building democratic institutions and allowing people to make choices—and sacrifices—voluntarily, or whether the new elites, heady with power, will impose totalitarian means to transform their countries. Certainly in these traditional and old colonial societies where the masses are apathetic and easily manipulated, the answer lies with the intellectual classes and their conceptions of the future.

Thus one finds, at the end of the fifties, a disconcerting caesura. In the West, among the intellectuals, the old passions are spent. The new generation, with no meaningful memory of these old debates, and no secure tradition to build upon, finds itself seeking new purposes within a framework of political society that has rejected, intellectually speaking, the old apocalyptic and chiliastic visions. In the search for a "cause," there is a deep, desperate, almost pathetic anger. The theme runs through a remarkable book, *Convictions*, by a dozen of the sharpest young Left Wing intellectuals in Britain. They cannot define the content of the "cause" they seek, but the yearning is clear. In the U.S. too there is a restless search for a new intellectual radicalism. Richard Chase, in his thoughtful assessment of American society, *The Democratic Vista*, insists that the greatness of nineteenth-century America for the rest of the world consisted in its radical vision of man (such a vision as Whitman's), and calls for a new radical criticism today. But the problem is that the old politico-economic radicalism (pre-occupied with such matters as the socialization of industry) has lost its meaning, while the stultifying aspects of contemporary culture (e.g., television) cannot be redressed in political terms. At the same time,

American culture has almost completely accepted the avant-garde, particularly in art, and the older academic styles have been driven out completely. The irony, further, for those who seek "causes" is that the workers, whose grievances were once the driving energy for social change, are more satisfied with the society than the intellectuals. The workers have not achieved utopia, but their expectations were less than those of the intellectuals, and the gains correspondingly larger.

The young intellectual is unhappy because the "middle way" is for the middle-aged, not for him; it is without passion and is deadening. Ideology, which by its nature is an all-or-none affair, and temperamentally the thing he wants, is intellectually devitalized, and few issues can be formulated any more, intellectually, in ideological terms. The emotional energies—and needs—exist, and the question of how one mobilizes these energies is a difficult one. Politics offers little excitement. Some of the younger intellectuals have found an outlet in science or university pursuits, but often at the expense of narrowing their talent into mere technique; others have sought self-expression in the arts, but in the wasteland the lack of content has meant, too, the lack of the necessary tension that creates new forms and styles.

Whether the intellectuals in the West can find passions outside of politics is moot. Unfortunately, social reform does not have any unifying appeal, nor does it give a younger generation the outlet for "self-expression" and "self-definition" that it wants. The trajectory of enthusiasm has curved East, where, in the new ecstasies for economic utopia, the "future" is all that counts.

And yet, if the intellectual history of the past hundred years has any meaning—and lesson—it is to reassert Jefferson's wisdom (aimed at removing the dead hand of the past, but which can serve as a warning against the heavy hand of the future as well), that "The present belongs to the living." This is the wisdom that revolutionists, old and new, who are sensitive to the fate of their fellow men, rediscover in every generation. "I will never believe," says a protagonist in a poignant dialogue written by the gallant Polish philosopher Leszek Kolakowski, "that the moral and intellectual life of mankind follows the law of economics, that is by saving today we can have more tomorrow; that we should use lives now so that truth will triumph or that we should profit by crime to pave the way for nobility."

And these words, written during the Polish "thaw," when the intellectuals had asserted, from their experience with the "future," the claims of humanism, echo the protest of the Russian writer Alexander Herzen, who, in a dialogue a hundred years ago, reproached an earlier revolutionist who would sacrifice the present mankind for a promised tomorrow: "Do you truly wish to condemn all human beings alive today to the sad role of caryatids . . . supporting a floor for others some day to dance on? . . . This alone should serve as a warning to people: an end that is infinitely remote is not an end, but, if you like, a trap; an end must be nearer—it ought to be, at the very least, the labourer's wage or pleasure in the work done. Each age, each generation, each life has its own fullness. . . ."[5]

---

[1]Karl Jaspers has assembled a fascinating collection of laments by philosophers of each age who see their own time as crisis and the past as a golden age. These— and the quotations from the Egyptian papyri as well as the remark of Talleyrand— can be found in his *Man in the Modern Age* (rev. ed., London, 1951), Chapter II. The quotation from Gilbert Murray is from *Five Stages of Greek Religion* (2d ed.; New York, 1930), Chapter IV.

[2]The citation from Marx is from the celebrated opening passages of *The Eighteenth Brumaire of Louis Napoleon* [which] has a general discussion of alienation, but I have followed here with profit the discussion by Hans Speier in his *Social Order and the Risks of War* (New York, 1952), Chapter XI.

[3]Rufus W. Mathewson, Jr., *The Positive Hero in Russian Literature* (New York, 1958), p. 6.

[4]See Leo Strauss, *The Political Philosophy of Hobbes* (Chicago, 1952), pp. 14–29.

[5]To see history as changes in sensibilities and style or, more, how different classes or people mobilized their emotional energies and adopted different moral postures is relatively novel; yet the history of moral temper is, I feel, one of the most important ways of understanding social change, and particularly the irrational forces at work in men. The great model for a cultural period is J. H. Huizinga's *The Waning of the Middle Ages*, with its discussion of changing attitudes toward death, cruelty, and love. Lucien Febvre, the great French historian, long ago urged the writing of history in terms of different sensibilities, and his study of Rabelais and the problem of covert belief (*Le problème de l'incroyance du XVIème siècle*) is one of the great landmarks of this approach. Most historians of social movements have been excessively "intellectualistic" in that the emphasis has been on doctrine or on organizational technique, and less on emotional styles. Nathan Leites' *A Study of Bolshevism* may be more important, ultimately, for its treatment of the changing moral temper of the Russian intelligentsia than for the formal study of Bolshevik behavior. Arthur Koestler's novels and autobiography are a brilliant mirror of the changes in belief of the European intellectual. Herbert Leuthy's study of the playwright Bert Brecht (*Encounter*, July, 1956) is a jewel in its subtle analysis of the changes in moral judgment created by the acceptance of the image of "the

Bolshevik." The career of Georg Lukacs, the Hungarian Marxist, is instructive regarding an intellectual who has accepted the soldierly discipline of the Communist ethic; other than some penetrating but brief remarks by Franz Borkenau (see his *World Communism* [New York, 1939], pp. 172–75), and the articles by Morris Watnick (*Soviet Survey* [London, 1958], Nos. 23–25), very little has been written about this extraordinary man. Ignazio Silone's "The Choice of Comrades" (reprinted in *Voices of Dissent* [New York, 1959]) is a sensitive reflection of the positive experiences of radicalism. An interesting history of the millenarian and chiliastic movements is Norman Cohn's *The Pursuit of the Millenium*. From a Catholic viewpoint, Father Ronald Knox's study *Enthusiasm*, deals with the "ecstatic" movements in christian history.

PART IV

OLD
AND
NEW RHETORICS

13

OLD RADICALISM

Sources of Rhetoric   William Z. Foster and James P. Cannon, two communist leaders (see the biographies in Chapter Five), have written books with a rhetorical cast. While ostensibly written as histories of their respective movements, these books incorporate all of the rhetorical devices described in Chapter Nine, especially counter-mythology and counter-elitism. Excerpts from the books illustrating these themes are included in this chapter. The two movements which Foster and Cannon led, the Communist Party and the Socialist Workers Party, publish newspapers which are a contemporary source of rhetoric. The Communist Party publishes *The Daily World* (formerly *The Daily Worker*) and the Socialist Workers Party publishes *The Militant*. Excerpts from both news articles and editorials are included in this chapter.

Counter-Mythology   The origins of old radicalism in the labor movements of the late nineteenth century have provided sources for the counter-mythology of socialism and communism in America. Eugene V. Debs was the foremost leader of American socialism (see Chapter Five), and his experiences in the American Railway Union are described in glowing terms in the first excerpt. Some observers regard the railroad strike which Debs led a failure, but in the counter-mythology of socialism it becomes a success.* In any case, it illustrates how dramatic confrontations with capitalism led many labor leaders to become socialists and communists.

William Z. Foster, in *The Twilight of World Capitalism*, discusses the growth of the communist movement worldwide in the context of its confrontation with capitalism. His historical review, excerpted here, contains dramatic descriptions of the growth of communism and

---

*Sidney Lens, *Radicalism in America*. (New York: Thomas Y. Crowell, 1969), p. 205.

208

predictions of its eventual triumph. Contemporary communist leaders use the same rhetoric in their glowing accounts of the current activities of the communist party. In an article from *The Daily World*, Conrad Komorowski claims that the 20th Convention of the Communist Party, U.S.A., will be the historic beginning of the triumph of communism in the United States.

James P. Cannon, in his *History of American Trotskyism*, conveys some of the excitement he felt during the early days of the Socialist Workers Party. His counter-mythology betrays the sectarian nature of the Trotskyist movement; he was more excited about recruiting members away from the Communist Party, and confronting the party over the issue of Trotsky's break with Stalin, than he was in finding new converts to communism.

EUGENE V. DEBS

SOURCE: Eugene V. Debs, "How I Became a Socialist," from H. Wayne Morgan, Ed., American Socialism, 1900–1960, © 1964. Reprinted by permission of Prentice-Hall, Inc., Englewood Cliffs, N. J.

On the evening of February 27, 1875, the local lodge of the Brotherhood of Locomotive firemen was organized at Terre Haute, Ind., by Joshua A. Leach, then grand master, and I was admitted as a charter member and at once chosen secretary. "Old Josh Leach," as he was affectionately called, a typical locomotive fireman of his day, was the founder of the brotherhood, and I was instantly attracted by his rugged honesty, simple manner and homely speech. How well I remember feeling his large, rough hand on my shoulder, the kindly eye of an elder brother searching my own as he gently said, "My boy, you're a little young, but I believe you're in earnest and will make your mark in the brotherhood." Of course, I assured him that I would do my best. . . .

My first step was thus taken in organized labor and a new influence fired my ambition and changed the whole current of my career. I was filled with enthusiasm and my blood fairly leaped in my veins. Day and night I worked for the brotherhood. To see its watchfires glow and observe the increase of its sturdy members were the sunshine and shower of my life. To attend the "meeting" was my supreme joy, and for ten years I was not once absent when the faithful assembled.

At the convention held in Buffalo in 1878 I was chosen associate editor of the magazine, and in 1880 I became grand secretary and treasurer. With all the fire of youth I entered upon the crusade which seemed to fairly glitter with possibilities. For eighteen hours at a stretch I was glued to my desk reeling off answers to my many correspondents. Day and night were one. Sleep was time wasted and often, when all oblivious of her presence, in the still small hours my mother's hand turned off the light, [and] I went to bed under protest. . . .

My grip was always packed; and I was darting in all directions. To tramp through a railroad yard in the rain, snow or sleet half the night, or till daybreak, to be ordered out of the roundhouse for being an "agitator," or put off a train, sometimes passenger, more often freight, while attempting to deadhead over the division, were all in the program, and served to whet the appetite of the conqueror. . . .

Through all these years I was nourished at Fountain Proletaire. I drank deeply of its waters and every particle of my tissues became saturated with the spirit of the working class. I had fired an engine and been stung by the exposure and hardship of the rail. I was with the boys in their weary watches, at the broken engine's side and often helped to bear their bruised and bleeding bodies back to wife and child again. How could I but feel the burden of their wrongs? How could the seed of agitation fail to take deep root in my heart? . . .

In 1894 the American Railway Union was organized and a braver body of men never fought the battle of the working class.

Up to this time I had heard but little of Socialism, knew practically nothing about the movement, and what little I did know was not calculated to impress me in its favor. I was bent on thorough and complete organization of the railroad men and ultimately the whole working class, and all my time and energy were given to that end. My supreme conviction was that if they were only organized in every branch of service and all acted together in concert they could redress their wrongs and regulate the conditions of their employment. The stockholders of the corporation acted as one, why not the men? It was such a plain proposition—simply to follow the example set before their eyes by their masters—surely they could not fail to see it, act as one, and solve the problem.

It is useless to say that I had yet to learn the workings of the capitalist system, the resources of its masters, and the weakness of its slaves. Indeed, no shadow of a "system" fell athwart my pathway; no thought of ending wage-misery marred my plans. I was too deeply absorbed in perfecting wage-servitude and making it a "thing of beauty and a joy forever."

It all seems strange to me now, taking a backward look, that my vision so focalized on a single objective point that I utterly failed to see what now appears as clear as the noonday sun—so clear that I marvel that any workingman, however dull, uncomprehending, can resist it. . . .

Next followed the final shock—the Pullman strike—and the American Railway Union again won, clear and complete. The combined corporations were paralyzed and helpless. At this juncture there was delivered, from wholly unexpected quarters, a swift succession of blows that blinded me for an instant and then opened wide my eyes—and in the gleam of every bayonet and the flash of every rifle the class struggle was revealed. This was my first lesson in Socialism, though wholly unaware that it was called by that name.

An army of detectives, thugs, and murderers was equipped with badge and beer and bludgeon and turned loose; old hulks of cars were fired; the alarm bells tolled; the people were terrified; the most startling rumors were set afloat . . . injunctions flew thick and fast, arrests followed, and our office and headquarters, heart of the strike, was sacked, torn out, and nailed up by the "lawful" authorities of the federal government; and when in company with my loyal comrades I found myself in Cook County Jail at Chicago with the whole press screaming conspiracy, treason, and murder, . . . I had another exceedingly practical and impressive lesson in Socialism. . . .

The Chicago jail sentences were followed by six months at Woodstock and it was here that Socialism gradually laid hold of me in its own irresistible fashion. Books and pamphlets and letters from Socialists came by every mail and I began to read and think and dissect the anatomy of the system in which workingmen, however organized, could be shattered and battered and splintered at a single stroke. The writings of Bellamy and Blatchford early appealed to me. The "Cooperative Commonwealth" of Gronlund also impressed me, but the writings of Kautsky were so clear and conclusive that I readily grasped, not merely his argument, but also caught the spirit of his Socialist utterance—and I thank him and all who helped me out of darkness into light.

It was at this time, when the first glimmerings of Socialism were beginning to penetrate, that Victor L. Berger—and I have loved him ever since—came to Woodstock, as if a providential instrument, and delivered the first impassioned message of Socialism I had ever heard—the very first to set the "wires humming in my system." As a souvenir of that visit there is in my library a volume of "Capital," by Karl Marx, inscribed with the compliments of Victor L. Berger, which I cherish as a token of priceless value.

The American Railway Union was defeated but not conquered—overwhelmed but not destroyed. It lives and pulsates in the Socialist movement, and its defeat but blazed the way to economic freedom and hastened the dawn of human brotherhood.

WILLIAM Z. FOSTER

SOURCE: From William Z. Foster, The Twilight of World Capitalism. Copyright © 1949. Reprinted by Permission of International Publishers Co., Inc.

In this general period of the decline of world capitalism, encompassed within the span of my life, a fundamentally dynamic development has been the birth and growth of the world communist movement. The Communist Party is the party of socialism, and as the worldwide surge of the masses towards socialism expands, the Communist Party, its leader, develops with it. In every significant country, from the most advanced capitalist nations to backward colonial lands, a Communist Party is to be found. It is the party with the historic role of leading harassed humanity out of the present jungle society onto the higher social level of socialism. I have devoted most of the best years of my life in helping to build this great movement in the United States, the heartland of world capitalism.

The Communist parties of the world now have about 20,000,000 actual members. This total figure does not include, of course, the many millions of Communist sympathizers in trade unions, youth organizations, peasant bodies, women's clubs, etc. This number gives no indication of the immense mass following of communism. Today almost one-third of the human race (counting China), is under the direct political leadership of Communists, and large numbers of the rest of the peoples are more or less influenced by communism. Among the largest Communist parties are those of Soviet Russia 7,000,000 (or over), China 3,000,000 (a year ago), Italy 2,250,000, Czechoslovakia 2,000,000, France, Poland, Hungary, and Rumania, about 1,000,000 each, and Bulgaria, 600,000. There are Communist parties in almost every country in the world.

The capitalists everywhere realize the significance of the Communist Party and are striken with alarm at its progress. Frightened also at the precarious condition of their beloved profit-system, they watch with dread the growth of the Communist Party and they concentrate all their venom and hatred against it. They have no such revulsion towards the opportunist Social-Democratic Party, because they have seen it in political power in many countries and they have found out in practice that, despite its use of socialist phrases, it never establishes socialism. But they have also learned from experience that the Communist Party, once in power, does surely bring about socialism. They see in our party their Nemesis, the leader of the revolutionary workers, whom Marx called "the gravediggers of capitalism."

The Communist Party has been developing since the turn of the century. The chief architect of this "party of a new type" was Lenin, master organizer, leader of the Russian Revolution, and the profoundest political thinker since Marx and Engels. Their successor, another great party builder, is Stalin, the outstanding living Marxist. Lenin outlined all the basic propositions around which Communist parties everywhere are being built. The party of Lenin has nothing in common with the fantastic caricatures of it that are now current in capitalist circles. The total falsification of the Communist Party, its theory, structure, practice, and objectives, by the capitalist enemy is a key phase of the latter's utter misrepresentation of everything connected with socialism.

. . .

The crowning political development of our period is the appearance upon the world scene of the socialist man and woman. These new-type people are both the main goal and highest achievement of socialism. They will reach their highest development under communism, which is the next social stage beyond socialism. One of the charges most commonly directed against Communists, and also one of the most false, is the allegation that the Communist movement has in mind only the state and never the individual; that communism seeks to create individuals who are so warpedly collectivist in spirit as to have no other goal in life but selflessly to serve an all-powerful state. President Truman repeated this slander in his Inaugural Address. But such charges bear no relation to Communist reality. The supreme purpose of communism, on the contrary, is precisely to develop to the maximum the individual human being; to bring about a freer, happier, higher type of man and woman. If Communists now place so much emphasis upon discipline this is because of the exigencies of the class struggle, the supreme need of the workers and the whole socialist people to stand solidly together in the face of the still powerful capitalist enemy.

No other political movement aims so consciously for the cultivation of the highest possible type of individual as does communism. The distinction of the Communists is that, as no others, they seek to develop an integrated, well-balanced individual, one who, while enjoying personal freedom to the maximum degree, also knows how to utilize fully the basic principles of collectivism. Collectivism and the development of the individual, under socialism and communism, are not antagonistic but complementary principles. In the communist conception the fundamental aim is of creating such free collectivist individuals that the state must serve the people, and not the other way around. Although that country is still young and is combating world difficulties from hostile capitalism, in the U.S.S.R. the new socialist type of social being is rapidly developing. Soviet citizens live together in fruitful co-operation, and do not war upon each other, as under capitalism, in frantic efforts for self-preservation or self-aggrandizement.

CONRAD KOMOROWSKI

SOURCE: From "Rising struggles reflected in Communists' convention," by Conrad Komorowski, The Daily World, February 24, 1972, p. 3.

NEW YORK, Feb. 23—Historic steps were taken by the 20th Convention of the Communist Party of the USA, General Secretary Gus Hall said in his summary remarks.

The burst of applause from the 254 delegates from 36 states showed they felt the same way.

Reports from the field to the convention testified to a ferment of struggle rapidly developing through the United States. It was reflected in the convention proceedings and decisions. . . .

The struggle against monopoly and the building of an anti-monopoly coalition, revitalization of the labor movement by building rank-and-file committees and movements, the fight for black-white unity, support to the struggles of oppressed peoples, advancing the struggles of youth and women were the central issues which engaged the delegates' energies.

The building of the Party assumes greater urgency and has open to it greater opportunities than before, Daniel Rubin, Organizational Secretary, declared in his report. The Party, Rubin said, has been only partly geared to the new situation described by Hall in the main report and testified to by the delegates.

The key to building the Party, Rubin said, is involvement of Communists in mass struggles. Where that has occurred, as in the Free Angela Davis campaign, the Hall-Tyler election campaign, Black liberation, Chicano and other struggles, the Party has been built.

Building the party, he added, also means establishing and strengthening mass ties, and developing the role of progressive and Left organizations. . . .

JAMES P. CANNON

SOURCE: From James P. Cannon, The History of American Trotyskism. Copyright © 1944 by Pioneer Publishers, renewed 1972 by Pathfinder Press. Reprinted by permission of Pathfinder Press.

I will never forget the day we got our first recruit in Philadelphia. Soon after we were expelled, while the hue and cry was raging against us in the party, there came a knock on my door one day and there was Morgenstern of Philadelphia, a young man but an old "Cannonite" in the factional fights. He said, "We heard about your expulsion for Trotskyism, but we didn't believe it. What is the real low-down?" In those days you didn't take anything for good coin unless it came from your own faction. I can remember to this day going into the back room, getting out the precious Trotsky document from its hiding place and handing it to Morgie. He sat down on the bed and read the long "criticism"—it is a whole book—from beginning to end without stopping once, without looking up. When he finished, he had made up his mind and we began to work out plans to build a nucleus in Philadelphia.

We recruited other individuals the same way. Trotsky's ideas were our weapons. We ran the "criticism" serially in *The Militant*. We had only the one copy, and it was a long time before we were able to publish it in pamphlet form. Because of its size we could not get it mimeographed. We had no mimeograph of our own, no typist, no money. Money was a serious problem. We had all been deprived of our positions in the party and had no incomes of any kind. We were too busy with our political fight to seek other jobs in order to make a living. On top of that we had the problem of financing a political movement. We could not afford an office. Only when we were a year old did we finally manage to rent a ramshackle office on Third Avenue, with the old "El" roaring in the window. When we were two years old we obtained our first mimeograph machine, and then we began to sail forward.

. . .

Within a few weeks, on January 8, 1929 we organized the first Trotskyist public meeting in America. I looked over the first bound volume of *The Militant* today and saw the advertisement of that meeting on the front page of the issue of January 1, 1929. I admit I felt a little emotion as I recalled the time we threw that bombshell into the radical circles of New York. In front of this Labor Temple a big sign announced that I was going to speak on "The Truth About Trotsky and the Russian Opposition." We came to this meeting prepared to protect it. We had the assistance of the Italian group of Bordigists, our Hungarian comrades, a few individual sympathizers of Communism who didn't believe in stopping free speech, and our own valiant newly-recruited forces. They were deployed around the platform in the Labor Temple and near the door to see to it that the meeting wasn't interrupted. And that meeting did go through without interruption.

The hall was filled, not only with sympathizers and converts, but also with all kinds of people who came there from all kinds of motives, interest, curiosity, etc. The lecture was very successful, consolidated our supporters and gained some recruits. It also threw greater alarm into the camp of the Stalinists, and pushed them further along the road of violence against us.

Counter-elitism In their view of the political world, the communists see themselves as an embattled minority which confronts the capitalist power structure on behalf of the masses. Even though they are a militant movement, the communists claim that they can maintain internal democracy in the face of persecution. They employ a doctrine of "democratic centralism" in their rhetoric. The first excerpt from Foster's book illustrates the use of this doctrine. Communists do participate in democratic elections, as the excerpt from *The Daily World* illustrates, but they do so primarily to further their ideological goals.

James P. Cannon again illustrates the sectarian nature of the Socialist Workers Party in his discussion of how recruits from the Communist Party were in need of discipline when they came to the Trotskyists. Cannon also describes how a small, disciplined cadre can control a massive strike in his chronicle of the Minneapolis Teamster's Strike of 1934. Finally, an editorial from the Socialist Workers Party newspaper, *The Militant*, illustrates how radicals try to discredit the capitalist press and counter it with their own leadership of the masses.

WILLIAM Z. FOSTER

SOURCE: From William Z. Foster, The Twilight of World Capitalism *Copyright © 1949. Reprinted by permission of International Publishers Co., Inc.*

No organization in the whole history of mankind has had such a magnificent record of sacrifice and achievement as the Communist Party of the Soviet Union, and none is more beloved by its people. What doubly appalls the capitalists is their realization that the Communist parties of other countries, even if they are as yet less developed, are nevertheless all made of the same invincible stuff as the great party of Lenin and Stalin. Just now the world is being given a dramatic demonstration of this decisive fact by the Communist Party of China, led by the brilliant Mao Tse-tung. With its 3,000,000 members, the gallant people's army, and the backing of the masses, it is resolutely cleaning away the trash of feudalism, and smashing the reactionary Chiang Kai-shek government, which American imperialism has long been bottle-feeding. It is in the process of leading its vast people along the road to people's democracy, industrialization, and eventual socialism. To carry out this monumental task will require literally miracles of work, but we can be assured that the great Chinese Communist Party, in the spirit of Lenin, will be able to accomplish them. Those who are now hoping that the Communist Party will never be able to lead backward China to freedom and prosperity are in for a sad awakening.

The Communist Party in every country is a voluntary organi-

zation. Its organizational effectiveness is greatly strengthened by
the high sense of discipline with which its members are infused.
Capitalist enemies fiercely attack this Communist discipline, which
they deeply fear. They try to discredit the party among the masses
by picturing its discipline as a mechanical, military-like domination
of the leaders over the rank and file members. But such a charac-
terization has no connection with reality. Communist parties are
far and away the most democratic of all political parties, whether
in socialist or capitalist countries. Selecting their leaders upon a
democratic-efficiency basis, which constantly brings the best and
most capable elements to the fore, they have a minimum of the evil
of bureaucratic clique control that hamstrings so many other political parties and trade unions. The Communist Party discusses
its problems in a democratic way (and no other party has such penetrating discussions), works out its general political line, concen-
trates its attention on "the key link that can move the whole chain,"
and then mobilizes its forces energetically for the task in hand. The
Communist Party is a fighting organization, not a talking machine.
Once the decision has been taken, the minority is expected to abide
by the will of the majority, or, if its differences are fundamental,
to sever its connection with the party. This resolute method of the
party greatly enhances its power and efficiency.

Still another vital Leninist principle that basically strengthens
Communist parties is their practice of self-criticism. In this most
important respect, no other party can even remotely compare with
the Communist Party. Non-Communist parties habitually try to
cover up their political errors and to defend their policies, right or
wrong. We constantly see this illustrated by American capitalist
parties during elections, and the practice seriously weakens their
effectiveness. Communist parties, on the other hand, make no pre-
tense of infallibility. They frankly admit such mistakes as they may
make and they freely alter their political line to meet changed political conditions. They are not interested in saving their "face,"
and they are not held back by attempts of their enemies to capitalize
on Communist admissions of errors. A Communist leader who is not
self-critical is not worth his salt and will sooner or later come to
grief in the party. As a result of this self-criticism, the Communist
Party is enabled to learn the vital lessons from the path that has
been traversed, and it can then see more clearly the road that lies
ahead. Self-criticism, in the practice of which the great Lenin was

without a peer, is one of the most dynamic features of Communist political organization and activity. It gives Communist parties a huge advantage over the conceited, self-satisfied parties of the usual bourgeois and Social-Democratic stripe. As Lenin says, "The attitude of a political party towards its own mistakes is one of the most important and surest ways of judging how earnest the party is, and how it in practice fulfills its obligations towards its class and the toiling masses."

THE DAILY WORLD

SOURCE: From "The CP Campaign," in the Daily World's *"World Magazine," February 26, 1972, p. M–3.*

The following excerpts are from a report by Henry Winston, National Chairman of the Communist Party, to the Party's National Committee last November. The report is available in a pamphlet, "The Politics of People's Action—The Communist Part in the '72 Elections," from New Outlook Publishers, 32 Union Square East, New York 10003. It costs 50 cents.

The main content of the work of the Party as a whole for the year 1972 is the election campaign. By this is meant that the election campaign, in content, involves the totality of the Party's mass work.

We are saying then, that the election campaign is not merely for this or that speaker, for this or that meeting. The election campaign is the alpha and omega of the work of the Party in 1972.

The potential is great for organizing the mass fighting power of the people, in which the working class is the core, fighting monopoly, fighting trade union bureaucracy, class collaboration and social democratism. Our Party must emerge in a new way among masses who are not only listening today, but insist on hearing more about communism. They will come closer and closer to us, and among them there will be many thousands who will join this Party.

The denial of ballot rights to Communists by law, and/or impossible qualification requirements, is at one and the same time a denial of ballot rights to all minority parties and a conscious class act of monopoly to prevent the emergence of a popular people's party. Here is a clear example which shows how in practice the fight against democracy in general always begins with an attack against the Communist Party. The fight for the ballot rights of the Communist Party is a battle for democracy as a whole.

The year 1972 is decisive. What we do is important, not only for our own country, but for the entire world. The opportunities are great. What is needed is for our Party to be there.

JAMES P. CANNON

SOURCE: From James P. Cannon, The History of American Trotskyism. Copyright © 1944 by Pioneer Publishers, renewed 1972 by Pathfinder Press. Reprinted by permission of Pathfinder Press.

Many people came to us who had revolted against the Communist Party not for its bad sides but for its good sides; that is, the discipline of the party, the subordination of the individual to the decisions of the party in current work. A lot of dilettantish petty-bourgeois minded people who couldn't stand any kind of discipline, who had either left the CP or been expelled from it, wanted, or rather thought they wanted to become Trotskyists. Some of them joined the New York branch and brought with them that same prejudice against discipline in our organization. Many of the newcomers made a fetish of democracy. They were repelled so much by the bureaucratism of the Communist Party that they desired an organization without any authority or discipline or centralization whatever.

All the people of this type have one common characteristic: they like to discuss things without limit or end. The New York branch of the Trotskyist movement in those days was just one continuous stew of discussion. I have never seen one of these elements who isn't articulate. I have looked for one but I have never found him. They can all talk; and not only can, but *will*; and everlastingly, on every question. They were iconoclasts who would accept nothing as authoritative, nothing as decided in the history of the movement. Everything and everybody had to be proved over again from scratch.

Walled off from the vanguard represented by the Communist movement and without contact with the living mass movement of the workers, we were thrown in upon ourselves and subjected to this invasion. There was no way out of it. We had to go through the long drawn-out period of stewing and discussing. I had to listen, and that is one reason my gray hairs are so numerous. I was never a sectarian or screwball. I never had patience with people who mistake mere garrulousness for the qualities of political leadership. But one could not walk away from this sorely beset group. This little fragile nucleus of the future revolutionary party had to be held together.

. . .

All modern strikes require political direction. The strikes of that period brought the government, its agencies and its institutions into the very center of every situation. A strike leader without some conception of a political line was very much out of date already by 1934. The old fashioned trade union movement, which used to deal with the bosses without governmental interference, belongs in the museum. The modern labor movement must be politically directed because it is confronted by the government at every turn. Our people were prepared for that since they were political people, inspired by political conceptions. The policy of the class struggle guided our comrades; they couldn't be deceived and outmaneuvered, as so many strike leaders of that period were, by this mechanism of sabotage and destruction known as the National Labor Board and all its auxiliary setups. They put no reliance whatever in Roosevelt's Labor Board; they weren't fooled by any idea that Roosevelt, the liberal "friend of labor" president, was going to help the truck drivers in Minneapolis win a few cents more an hour. They weren't deluded even by the fact that there was at that time in Minnesota a Farmer-Labor Governor, presumed to be on the side of the workers.

THE MILITANT

SOURCE: From "Truth and the Press," The Militant, Editorial, October 15, 1971. Reprinted by permission of The Militant Publishing Association. Copyright © 1971.

The reason the capitalist papers lie as they did during the Attica events is because they are controlled by and run in the interests of the ruling class—bankers, businessmen, financiers and landlords. To tell the truth to the American people is not in their interests. It is not in their interests to help make the masses of people aware of the dehumanization, racism, sexism and exploitation of this entire capitalist system including the prisons.

Every newspaper must have a "bias"—that is, it must take a stand, either on the side of the oppressors or on the side of the oppressed. And every newspaper does take a stand, whether it admits it or not.

The Militant, unlike the whole spectrum of the capitalist press, did not take the word of the prison officials in Attica as fact. In fact, we doubted the official accounts from the beginning and sent staff writer Derrick Morrison up to Attica to attempt to get the truth.

The Militant readily and proudly admits that it is a newspaper which serves the interests of the oppressed. It takes the side of working people, Blacks, Puerto Ricans, Chicanos, Native Americans, gay people, women, youth, prisoners and all who are struggling for a new, humane world. These are the forces which are exposing hypocrisy and seeking the truth about how this system is run.

Readers of *The Militant* can help get out the truth by joining in the campaign to introduce this paper to 30,000 new readers by Dec. 1.

Alienation   Two brief excerpts from the newspapers of the old radical movements indicate the depth of alienation in the old radical rhetoric. The first, from *The Daily World*, blames capitalism for the effects of racism—urban decay, suppression of black liberation groups, and so forth. This use of the orthodox Marxist doctrines for analysis of contemporary issues exemplifies the old radical form of alienation in the rhetoric of the movement. The second illustration comes from *The Militant*, which blames the Nixon Administration for economic troubles such as unemployment, inflation, and exploitation at home and abroad. As an alternative to administration policies, *The Militant* suggests voting for the Socialist Workers Party candidates for President and Vice-President.

THE DAILY WORLD

SOURCE: *From "Heal the Rift, Unite the Fight," by William L. Patterson, The Daily World, February 26, 1972, p. M-4.*

On every front of human relations—on an international as well as national level—U.S. reaction faces problems it cannot resolve in its favor. The moral crisis that has emerged out of imperialism's racism makes an impact upon all ruling class problems. It exposes the viciousness and infamy of bourgeois society in the USA. Every branch of government in the United States—city, state and federal—

is polluted and diseased by the virus of racism. White nationals are being dehumanized by racist mythology.

The Black liberation struggle is an Achilles' heel of U.S. imperialism. To unify, strengthen, intensify and deepen the struggle against America's racist ruling class is a historic task facing all progressive peoples and none more so than Black America. This is part of its responsibility to itself, our country and mankind. The split in the SCLC can only do the opposite unless out of that breach, through discussion and struggle, there comes a class understanding of the need for Black unity in organization and an understanding of its great value to all segments and phases of the struggle in this, the main arsenal of world reaction.

To prevent that understanding and the sharpening of the liberation struggle, which would inevitably follow, the racist leaders of the U.S. will stop at nothing. We have witnessed their murderously destructive attacks upon the Black Panthers. We have seen the corruptive role the monopolists' Foundations (such as Ford, Rockefeller, etc.) have played in patronizing SNCC and CORE. In recent years we have been confronted with the murder of the beloved Dr. Martin Luther King, Malcolm X and other liberation fighters. The role Big Business philanthropy has played in seeking to corrode the integrity of Black scholars is notorious. We have seen the bloody hand of America's banking consortium passing out gold to fascism in Portugal, Rhodesia and South Africa.

Today Big Business is in a frenzy of fear of the Black Liberation Movement, its potentialities for unity, the growing militancy of Black Americans and the developing appreciation of both white and Black of the values of mass movements. It will stop at nothing in its frantic efforts to make segments of the Black fighting forces a reserve of reaction. Without Black America's contributions to the democratic struggles of this country the few remaining inalienable rights and constitutional guarantees Americans have won would not now exist or be enjoyed.

THE MILITANT

SOURCE: From "Callous Disregard," The Militant, *Editorial, December 17, 1971. Reprinted by permission of The Militant Publishing Association. Copyright © 1971.*

The U.S. Labor Department reported Dec. 3 that unemployment rose to 6 percent during November. According to Herbert Stein, chief of Nixon's Council of Economic Advisers, the rise in unemployment since June of this year has been the largest five-month increase since 1955. The number of people who have been out of work for 15 weeks or more did not decrease in November, but remained at about 1.3 million, or nearly one-fourth of the total unemployed.

When Nixon announced his New Economic Policy on Aug. 15, he claimed that he was going to lower unemployment. But what he called a program for reducing the number of workers on the unemployment rolls was really a program to give more money to big business.

Nixon presently has a proposal pending before Congress that would give investment tax credits to capitalists so they will expand their production and supposedly create more jobs. This so-called "trickle-down" theory is nothing but a giveaway to the rich. It shows that Nixon has no real concern about the hardships endured by the growing numbers of unemployed workers and their families. Nixon's callous disregard was further revealed by his announcement of a 5 percent cut in federal jobs.

The whole thrust of Nixon's economic program has been to improve U.S. businesses' position in the international competition for profits—not to eliminate inflation and unemployment. Nixon's policies have meant holding down wages while giving full rein to speedup and automation in order to sweat more out of the hides of American workers. This will help American capitalists compete with foreign capitalists, who have cheaper labor costs. A certain amount of unemployment is useful in the context of Nixon's aims, because it creates greater competition among workers for jobs, thus making it easier to hold down wages.

What is needed to halt the rise of unemployment and alleviate the situation of the jobless is a crash program of public works projects to build low-cost housing, hospitals, parks and schools. The workweek should be cut with no reduction in pay in order to spread the work to everyone who wants a job. And full union wages should be paid to the unemployed, whether or not they have been previously employed.

This is the program of the Socialist Workers Party presidential and vice-presidential candidates, Linda Jenness and Andrew Pulley, the only candidates who have a serious and effective plan for ending unemployment.

Absolutism   Polarization, as a rhetorical device, is evident in William Z. Foster's description of the socialist society of the future. He contrasts the economic virtues of socialism with the economic vices of capitalism. The same rhetorical device is used in the *Daily World* editorial on the Angela Davis case. The efforts of communists and other radicals to free Angela are contrasted with the efforts of Governor Reagan and President Nixon to use the "powers of capital and evil" to keep her in jail.

WILLIAM Z. FOSTER

SOURCE: From William Z. Foster, The Twilight of World Capitalism. *Copyright © 1949. Reprinted by Permission of International Publishers Co., Inc.*

In the past two generations world capitalism has passed its zenith and begun to sink into decline but, on the other side of the international picture, world socialism has grown into lusty youth. Indeed, so clearly has this double process of declining capitalism and rising socialism shown itself that there are now strong reasons to believe that socialism has already become the more powerful of the two systems on a world scale. Historians will probably record that the years immediately following World War II constituted the time when the world balance of forces were definitely tipped on the side of socialism.

Under socialism the decisive industries, the land, the banks, the transportation systems, and all other major means of production and distribution are in the hands of the people, and not of private capitalists. Production is carried on for social use instead of for private profit. The whole national economy is operated according to plan, not by chance, as under the competitive system of capitalism. The workers and their democratic allies, the farmers and professionals, control the government completely. This system of society, based upon science, abolishes the great contradictions with which capitalism is afflicted. There is no further exploitation of man by man. Without capitalists, democracy is assured and there can be no fascism. In this planned society, free of exploitation and capitalist chaos, there can be no cyclical crises and no unemployment. War, too, is unthinkable in a socialist world. Socialism is the preliminary stage to communism, the highest form of society. Under communism, the wages system and the state, both of which exist in special forms under socialism, will eventually disappear. In the Soviet Union the question of the evolution from the present-day socialism to communism has now become a matter of practical politics. Socialism and communism cast off the economic, political, and ideological fetters from man and open up before him a boundless prospect for human happiness, well-being, and development.

Socialism is the first phase of communism, and the period of the dictatorship of the proletariat is the transition between capitalism and socialism. This scientific Marxist term has been grossly misused and distorted by enemies of socialism. Reduced to its simplest terms, it simply means the rule of the workers supported by their democratic allies. Under capitalism, in the United States as elsewhere, there exists the rule of the capitalists, or the dictatorship of the bourgeoisie. The basic difference between these two systems is that the dictatorship of the bourgeoisie is exercised by the relatively small employing class to repress and exploit the working class, against the interests of society as a whole. The dictatorship of the proletariat is exercised in behalf of the overwhelming mass of the people, to prevent exploitation of man by man, and in the general interests of society.

The Communist Party is the leading force of the dictatorship of the proletariat; it is not the dictatorship itself, which is the rule of the working class. The proletarian dictatorship is the means by which the workers and their allies clear away the economic and political remnants of capitalism and lay the foundations of the new, free society.

The dictatorship of the bourgeoisie, especially in this period of the decline of capitalism, is highly reactionary and its ultimate expression is brutal, tyrannical, imperialist, war-making fascism. The dictatorship of the proletariat, or the rule of the workers and their democratic allies, on the other hand, is the world standard bearer of democracy. As Lenin said, the dictatorship of the proletariat is a thousand times more democratic than any capitalist democracy. Its ultimate goal is communism, under which system classes will disappear and so, also, the state. The Soviet Union, with its one-party system, is a dictatorship of the proletariat. In the new democracys of Eastern and Central Europe—Poland, Czechoslovakia, etc.—the coalition governments are based upon the working class. The United States, too, will undoubtedly produce its own specific type of the rule of the working class when it eventually adopts socialism.

I was 36 years old and had already been a socialist 17 years when, like a lightning bolt, socialism scored its first decisive victory over capitalism in 1917. This was the great Russian Socialist Revolution.

THE DAILY WORLD

SOURCE: From "Victorious Step," Editorial, The Daily World, *February 25, 1972, p. 7.*

Angela is free on bail today because of
—her militant and unwavering spirit,
—the irrepressible rise of protest throughout the U.S., among the nation's young people, in the Black communities, and in the ranks of union men and women,
—the tidal wave of anger on all continents, demanding that she be freed,
—the unsparing efforts by the Communist Party, Angela's party, and its members, in her defense.

Days earlier, the long struggle to save the prisoners sitting in California's death cells had been won when the state Supreme Court outlawed capital punishment.

Angela and the more than 100 condemned California prisoners, one-third of them Black and Chicano, faced the same enemy—Governor Ronald Reagan, who was determined that they die.

Reagan initiated the persecution of Angela Davis when she was an instructor at the University of California, Los Angeles.

Behind Reagan looms the threatening shadow of Richard Nixon, though he is in Peking. Nixon was in on the ground floor in Angela's persecution, represented by J. Edgar Hoover, his ace "contract" man.

There have been those who doubted that Angela could be saved from the powers of capital and evil led by Nixon and Reagan.

The victory shows that it is possible to smash the whole frameup; it is possible to win freedom for Angela Davis.

Throughout the nation, those who fought valiantly for bail for

Angela, will draw the renewed confidence from the victory that will amass an unconquerable popular force for her complete freedom.

Throughout the world, those who worked diligently for the Black, American woman Communist, thousands of miles away, will recruit new millions to insure Angela's final victory.

As Henry Winston, Communist Party national chairman, told its 20th national convention last Sunday, the "fight for Angela Davis is not only the fight for bail, but for her freedom, her complete freedom."

The road of struggle was indicated to the convention by Gus Hall, general secretary, who said that though the "struggle to free Comrade Angela Davis . . . has a broad base in the United States," though it is already a "worldwide movement," the key "to win Angela's freedom," is to broaden the movement still further.

14

NEW RADICALISM

Sources of Rhetoric Many of the new radical groups of the 1960's have dissipated into factions, but their leaders are still producing rhetoric. This rhetoric is not published in periodicals, except in the case of the Black Panther Party, because the periodicals are no longer representative of the entire movement.* However, the new radical leaders have published a number of books, and the writings of Tom Hayden, Abbie Hoffman, Jerry Rubin, David Dellinger, Bobby Seale, and Eldridge Cleaver have provided us with a rich source of rhetoric. Writing books is not the principal concern of most new radicals, but it has become a major preoccupation of some. Abbie Hoffman was quoted in the *Los Angeles Times* of June 2, 1970: "I have a disdain for my own

writing. I don't view myself as an author. I just exert a lot of energy. Sometimes I write it down on paper . . . It's embarrassing. You try to overthrow the government and end up on the best-seller list."

Of course, Hoffman's "disdain" does not prevent him or other new radical leaders from producing a lot of rhetoric. In fact, the production of rhetoric may become one of the mainstays of the new radical movements now that the organized groups are gone.

Counter-Mythology In the rhetoric of the "new left" radicals, specific events are emphasized more than in the rhetoric of the new black radicals (see below). On the other hand, heroes are almost absent from the "new left" counter-mythology. "The movement" as a whole is regarded as the vessel of liberation.

Specific events which play a major role in the liberation rhetoric of the new radicals include: (1) the Free Speech incident at the University of California at Berkeley, 1964; (2) the antics of the Yippies, here illustrated

---

New Left Notes, the periodical of the Students for a Democratic Society, is now published by the "Worker-Student Alliance" faction of SDS, which is under the control of the Progressive Labor Party, an old left group. Two other periodicals which represent some intellectual segments of the new left are *The Guardian* and *Liberation*.

by the Stock Market incident in 1967; (3) the Pentagon March in 1967; and (4) the Chicago demonstrations of 1968. Each of these is the subject of a counter-mythological statement by Jerry Rubin, Abbie Hoffman, or David Dellinger.

JERRY RUBIN

SOURCE: *From Jerry Rubin,* Do It! *Copyright © 1970 by the Social Education Foundation. Reprinted by permission of Simon and Schuster.*

It began with a 14-word edict issued by a Berkeley campus dean outlawing political tables and leafleting for the purpose of organizing demonstrations off the campus.

We were amazed. Surely it must be a problem of "communication." But every dean we talked to said: "I can't do anything about it. I'm not responsible. But you'll have to obey the rules."

And the president of the university, Clark Kerr? No one even knew what *he* looked like.

Then we learned the *inside story:* The previous year we used the campus to organize massive civil rights demonstrations against the hotel and auto industries in San Francisco. The very same racists who controlled the business world controlled the university too! And they were trying to protect their businesses by attacking us at our base, the university. They were the Regents.

The Regents were at their Country Clubs, and they would rather shit on a student than talk to him.

We put up civil rights tables in the middle of the campus.

We decided to deliberately break the new rules.

A police car pulled onto Sproul Plaza. Cops were leading one arrested activist into the car when somebody shouted, "Sit down!"

Within seconds the car was surrounded by a few hundred people. Within minutes our numbers grew to 2,000.

Inside the police car was Jack Weinberg, a prisoner of the pigs. But we surrounded the pigs, and they were our prisoners.

We demanded *his* release in exchange for *their* release. The cops would have to drive the car over our bodies to take our brother to jail.

We climbed on top of the police car to rap about what was going down. For the next 10 hours into the night, 5,000 people packed into the Berkeley campus square for the greatest class we ever attended.

As we surrounded the car, we became conscious that we were a

new community with the power and love to confront the old institutions.

Our strength was our willingness to die together, our unity.

We created our own spontaneous government. People formed
communes to make sandwiches for those surrounding the car. Committees notified the media and contacted students across the country, and we created a negotiating team in case the university was
interested.

Thirty-two hours later, we heard the grim roar of approaching
Oakland motorcycle cops behind us. I took a deep breath. "Well,
this is as good a place to die as any."

But as we prepared to meet the heavy club of the Man, the university suddenly dropped charges against our arrested brother and
agreed to "negotiate."

The deans found themselves up against the wall for the first time
in Amerika.

They didn't dig it.

Two months later, we learned a heavy bureaucrat trick: the
fucking deans were using "negotiations" as a dodge to wear us out.
Talk, talk, talk while the rules against political activity stood strong.

We got very pissed off.

Fuck this shit!

So one beautiful sunny noon, Joan Baez sang, Mario Savio orated
and a thousand people walked into the administration building to
shut the motherfucker down.

At 4 A.M. the governor, a liberal Democrat, ordered the Oakland
cops to clear the building:

800 persons were arrested, the biggest single bust in Amerikan
history.

The sight of cops on campus threw all the fence-sitters, including
the professors, right into the arms of the extremists.

Students retaliated with a strike that crippled the university.
We destroyed the university's moral authority.

The only authority left on campus was the Free Speech Movement. The Regents and deans had no power. Students could do anything we wanted.

Students became the biggest political force in the state with the
university as our guerrilla stronghold.

We held power on campus because we were the majority there.

But off-campus the politicians, courts and cops were hollering for our balls.

> *The war against Amerika*
> *in the schools*
> *and the streets*
> *by white middle-class kids*
> *thus commenced.*

ABBIE HOFFMAN

SOURCE: From Revolution for the Hell of It *by Abbie Hoffman. Copyright © 1968 by The Dial Press, Inc. Reprinted by permission of the publisher.*

At first I thought throwing out money at the Stock Exchange was just a minor bit of theater. I had more important things to do, like raising bail money for a busted brother. Reluctantly, I called up and made arrangements for a tour under the name of George Metesky, Chairman of East Side Service Organization (ESSO). We didn't even bother to call the press. About eighteen of us showed up. When we went in the guards immediately confronted us. "You are hippies here to have a demonstration and we cannot allow that in the Stock Exchange." "Who's a hippie? I'm Jewish and besides we don't do demonstrations, see we have no picket signs," I shot back. The guards decided it was not a good idea to keep a Jew out of the Stock Exchange, so they agreed we could go in. We stood in line with all the other tourists, exchanging stories. When the line moved around the corner, we saw more newsmen than I've ever seen in such a small area. We started clowning. Eating money, kissing and hugging, and that sort of stuff. The newsmen were told by the guards that they could not enter the gallery with us. We were ushered in and immediately starting throwing money over the railing. The big tickertape stopped and the brokers let out a mighty cheer. The guards started pushing us and the brokers booed. When we got out I carried on in front of the press.

"Who are you?"

"I'm Cardinal Spellman."

"Where did you get the money?"

"I'm Cardinal Spellman, you don't ask me where I get my money."

"How much did you throw out?"

"A thousand dollars in small bills."

"How many of you are there?"

"Two, three, we don't even exist! We don't even exist!"

We danced in front of the Stock Exchange, celebrating the end of money. I burned a fiver. Some guy said it was disgusting and I agreed with him, calling my comrades "Filthy Commies."

The TV show that night was fantastic. It went all over the world. TV news shows always have a pattern. First the "serious" news all made up, of course, a few commercials, often constructed better than the news, then the Stock Market Report. Then the upswing human interest story to keep everybody happy as cows. Our thing came after the Stock Market Report, it was a natural. CBS, which is the most creative network, left in references to Cardinal Spellman; I was surprised at that. Every news report differed. Some said we threw out monopoly money, some said twenty-thirty dollars, some said over $100, some said the bills were all ripped up first. It was a perfect mythical event, since every reporter, not being allowed to actually witness the scene, had to make up his own fantasy. Some had interesting fantasies, some boring. One tourist who joined the exorcism got the point: "I'm from Missouri and I've been throwing away money in New York for five days now. This is sure a hell of a lot quicker and more fun."

May 20, 1967

DAVID DELLINGER

SOURCE: David Dellinger, Revolutionary Non-Violence *(Indianapolis: Bobbs-Merrill, 1970). Reprinted by permission of* Liberation.

Numerous participants in the civil rights movement and in the less cut-and-dried antiwar demonstrations (such as the August 1965 Assembly of Unrepresentative People, the activities of the Resistance, the demonstrations at the Pentagon in the fall of 1967 and at the Chicago convention, the Oakland Stop the Draft Week, and the struggle over the People's Park in Berkeley) have reported experiencing something of the same liberating dynamics. It is sometimes difficult for people who have these experiences to hold onto their conviction that they are the key to the building of a new society, given the pressures from both the right and sections of the left to think that all power grows out of the barrel of a gun. But they are what gives hope and distinction to the movement.

. . .

After Chicago, the movement has taken to the offensive. For the moment at least, the problem is not to avoid surrendering to threats and intimidations (as Senator McCarthy and Allard Lowenstein did when they told their followers to stay away from Chicago) but to mount an offensive without mimicking the self-righteous disregard for free speech, human rights and life itself which characterizes the power elite. It is one thing to have a justifiable contempt for the "law and order" which the establishment attempts to use as a noose around our necks. As Dick Gregory has said: "Law and order is a new word for nigger"; it is a device for strangling the creative energies of the movement and restricting our activities to token actions which the establishment can handle quite nicely, thank you. But it is another thing to have contempt for human beings and their rights, even if they oppose us.

Even the concept of "free speech" becomes suspect, because meaningful access to the mass media is by no means free. The economic resources of the power elite, the domination of the public's airwaves by multimillion dollar corporations (both the networks and the sponsors), the power of the government to coöpt prime time (directly and indirectly) put us in a position comparable to that of a David with a slingshot who is engaged in a "fair fight" with a modern army of tanks, flame-throwers and heavy artillery.

In the rhetoric of the black liberation movement heroes play an important role. Malcolm X is viewed by Black liberation leaders as the first new black radical of the 1960's, hence he is a hero and a paragon for other black leaders. Malcolm was a martyr to the cause of black liberation; others in the movement are also viewed as martyrs. Huey P. Newton was tried and imprisoned for the alleged murder of a white policeman; he is considered a martyr although he has been released. Other blacks in prison are considered martyrs, especially George Jackson, who was shot and killed by guards during an apparent prison escape attempt at San Quentin.

ELDRIDGE CLEAVER

SOURCE: *Eldridge Cleaver*, Post-Prison Writings and Speeches (1969)
Copyright © 1968, 1969 by Eldridge Cleaver. Reprinted by permission of
Cyrilly Abels, Literary Agent.

Before Malcolm, time stands still, going down in frozen steps into
the depths of the stagnation of slavery. Malcolm talked shit, and
talking shit is the iron in a young nigger's blood. Malcolm mastered
language and used it as a sword to slash his way through the veil
of lies that for four hundred years gave the white man the power of
the word. Through the breach in the veil, Malcolm saw all the way
to national liberation, and he showed us the rainbow and the golden
pot at its end. Inside the golden pot, Malcolm told us, was the tool
of liberation. Huey P. Newton, one of the millions of black people
who listened to Malcolm, lifted the golden lid off the pot and
blindly, trusting Malcolm, stuck his hand inside and grasped the
tool. When he withdrew his hand and looked to see what he held,
he saw the gun, cold in its metal and implacable in its message:
Death-Life, Liberty or Death, mastered by a black hand at last!
Huey P. Newton is the ideological descendant, heir and successor
of Malcolm X. Malcolm prophesied the coming of the gun to the
black liberation struggle. Huey P. Newton picked up the gun and
pulled the trigger, freeing the genie of black revolutionary violence
in Babylon.

The genie of black revolutionary violence is here, and it says
that the oppressor has no rights which the oppressed are bound to
respect. The genie also has a question for white Americans: which
side do you choose? Do you side with the oppressor or with the
oppressed? The time for decision is upon you. The cities of America
have tested the first flames of revolution. But a hotter fire rages in
the hearts of black people today: total liberty for black people or
total destruction for America.

. . .

Suddenly the room fell silent. The crackling undercurrent that for
weeks had made it impossible to get one's point across when one
had the floor was gone; there was only the sound of the lock clicking
as the front door opened, and then the soft shuffle of feet moving
quietly toward the circle. Shadows danced on the walls. From the
tension showing on the faces of the people before me, I thought the

cops were invading the meeting, but there was a deep female gleam leaping out of one of the women's eyes that no cop who ever lived could elicit. I recognized that gleam out of the recesses of my soul, even though I had never seen it before in my life: the total admiration of a black woman for a black man. I spun round in my seat and saw the most beautiful sight I had ever seen: four black men wearing black berets, powder blue shirts, black leather jackets, black trousers, shiny black shoes—and each with a gun! In front was Huey P. Newton with a riot pump shotgun in his right hand, barrel pointed down to the floor. Beside him was Bobby Seale, the handle of a .45 caliber automatic showing from its holster on his right hip, just below the hem of his jacket. A few steps behind Seale was Bobby Hutton, the barrel of his shotgun at his feet. Next to him was Sherwin Forte, an M1 carbine with a banana clip cradled in his arms.

THE BLACK PANTHER

SOURCE: From "State of the Struggle," The Black Panther, January 8, 1972, p. A. Reprinted by permission of the Black Panther Party. Copyright January 8, 1972 by Huey P. Newton.

The over-riding events of our struggle took place last year in the prisons, the maximum security camps of the United States. Certainly no other event fell so heavily upon us than the brutal murder by San Quentin Prison guards of the Field Marshal of the Black Panther Party, George Jackson, on August 21st. Comrade George had offically joined the Black Panther Party in 1968, after Huey P. Newton (the leader of our Party) was shot and arrested in Oakland and sent to prison. Prior to that Comrade George had inspired and induced unity among the prisoner class that none before had been able to achieve. The California prisons seemed to literally vanguard the over-all struggle of those inside the U.S. maximum security camps to be liberated. George had been the prime initiator of the progressive, revolutionary prison movement, teaching and educating for eleven years of incarceration. As the Field Marshal of the Black Panther Party, he better organized and developed the active struggle inside and outside the maximum prisons. He became known as one of the Soledad Brothers, having been falsely

236

charged for the murder of a Soledad prison guard in 1970. The Soledad Brothers' trial is still in progress, only they are two now, Fleeta Drumgo and John Clutchette. George's writings reached everywhere, into so many minds, that his death last year signalled a new level of struggle. Around the world, from progressive countries, organizations, individuals, came angry and bitter words, and even firmer dedication and solidarity. We say, of course, therefore, that George Jackson lives!

Counter-Elitism White intellectual leaders of the "new left" are curiously reticent to assert their leadership directly in the movement. They seem to rely on their symbolic leadership, attained as a result of media exposure rather than organizational talents. Thus they avoid the responsibilities of leadership while enjoying the perquisites of spokesmen for the movement. Black liberation leaders, on the other hand, readily assume a leadership posture. Their counter-mythology (above) emphasizes heroism and their counter-elitism emphasizes discipline. They use Leninist concepts of "revolution as a profession" and "the vanguard party." They also use the concepts of Frantz Fanon, who developed a Freudian-Marxian analysis of colonialism in Africa. Fanon himself denied the relevance of his concepts to blacks in America,* and other authors regard his ideas as elitist and impractical in a mass movement.† But they have rhetorical value, which is their principal utility to the black liberation movement.

*Frantz Fanon, The Wretched of the Earth (New York: Grove Press, 1968), p. 216.
†Martin Oppenheimer, The Urban Guerrilla (Chicago: Quadrangle books, 1969), pp. 52, 60.

TOM HAYDEN

SOURCE: From Trial by Tom Hayden. pp. 91, 106–107, 109–110, 112–113. Copyright © 1970 by Tom Hayden. Reprinted by permission of Holt, Rinehart and Winston, Inc.

We said that our trial, unlike any other, provided an opportunity for a collective offensive by our generation against Nixon, Agnew and the Justice Department. It was true: the audience was part of the Conspiracy, all with a real stake in turning back repression. They knew it and they felt it.

We were not leaders in command of legions of youth; we were a myth in which millions could participate. We were symbols of what millions were going through themselves. It was not a one-way flow of energy between the Conspiracy and its supporters. We were moved and shaped by the collective rising anger of these thousands of others.

. . .

Too many people looked up to us, regarded us as a rock group, wanted posters and The Word. There were many good people who came to work on the trial with the hope that it would be a communal project with fantastic individual possibilities; but our personalities, and the structure of the trial itself, did not allow that. The truth is that although we served an important revolutionary purpose for six months, we discovered a lot that was wrong about ourselves. Even though our identity was on trial, even though our habits were truly radical compared to those of bourgeois society, that hardly meant that our identity and habits were revolutionary by our own standards. In different ways we all came to sense our own limitations.

Most of these limits stemmed from the fact that the seven of us are white middle-class males, accustomed to power and status in the Movement. The Youth International Party, all myth aside, is run by two persons, Jerry and Abbie. The National Mobilization, in its prime, existed as a coalition which revolved around Dave Dellinger. Rennie has functioned time and again as the brilliant director of an office-centered organizing project, and I have always been more of an independent catalyst than an equal member of any collective group.

. . .

Our male chauvinism, elitism and egoism were merely symptoms of the original problem—the Movement did not choose us to be their symbols; the press and government did. The entire process by which known leaders become known is almost fatally corrupting. Only males with driving egos have been able to "rise" in the Movement or the rock culture and be accepted by the media and dealt with seriously by the Establishment. (There are a few isolated women who as exceptions prove the rule: Bernadine Dohrn and Bernadette Devlin are seen as revolutionary sex objects, Janis Joplin and Grace Slick as musical ones, Joan Baez and Judy Collins as "beautiful and pure.")

The first step in this power syndrome is to become a "personality." You begin to monopolize contacts and contracts. You begin making $1000 per speech. With few real friends and no real organization, you become dependent on the mass media and travel in orbit only with similar "stars."

The media interest in Yippies illustrates this process frighteningly. Random House not only publishes *Woodstock Nation* but takes part in the put-on with a cover illustration in which their own Madison Avenue building is shown being blown up. Simon and Schuster is pleased to advertise Jerry's book, with his approval, as "a Molotov cocktail in your very hands," "the *Communist Manifesto* of our era" and "comparable to Che Guevara's *Guerrilla Warfare.*" Who is using whom? Publishing a book with revolutionary content is certainly possible under capitalism, but what does it mean when a corporation joins in an advertising put-on about the destruction of its own system? It could only mean that the corporate executives and advertisers sense something familiar and manageable in this revolution. In Jerry's book especially what must seem familiar is the marketing of a personality. The book consists mainly of interesting episodes from Jerry's life. Jerry becomes the Important Person as his history of the Movement unfolds; other people disappear. Women are unmentioned (although a photo of his wife Nancy's smiling face bobs across two full pages of Quentin Fiore's "medium-is-the-massage" layout). The content is in contradiction with its own Yippie philosophy. Leadership ideally is supposed to be shared, or even to be "non-leadership," but here it is embarrassingly self-centered, deliberately and consciously marketed.

There is much of value in this book, just as there is in the music of the Rolling Stones. But there is finally something unreal. For the Rolling Stones, "street fighting" is a lyric, not a reality which they support or participate in themselves. The irony will be if Jerry—or any of us, since we all are like him in one way or another—ends up like the Stones and other rock celebrities. In the Yippie world, toy guns are carried around for media effect and books are the only Molotov cocktails. But will they really "do it"? If not, then the theatre of personality finally will become acceptable to the weird appetite of American culture. Impossible? At the trial's end, we were seriously planning to sell movie rights to big commercial producers, and Abbie (whose *Revolution for the Hell of It* was sold to MGM) was declaring, "Let them have Washington, D.C.; we're going to take over Hollywood."

. . .

We are, after all, products of the '60s. The styles and forms of that time were perhaps as necessary as they were problematic. In a white movement that arose from the nothingness of the '50s, it was no accident that leadership went to articulate, aggressive males, and no doubt this pattern will continue for some time. But forms die, or at least change, and the test of a revolutionary may be how well he or she adapts to new possibilities. Among these possibilities are the growth of a radical feminism which is justifiably enraged at male political power; and new, younger radicals (both men and women) like the Weathermen and White Panthers whose political attitudes stem from a much deeper alienation than what we experienced in the early '60s. From women comes the insight that our power is "male" in origin, a power that involves conquering and subduing others, as opposed to a power that is collective and respectful of people. From the younger revolutionaries in general comes the insight that our pressure politics, our peace mobilizations and our theatrics, legitimate in raising issues in the '60s, are inadequate to the task of surviving and making revolutionary changes in the '70s.

To continue as revolutionaries we will have to abandon the old forms and become part of the new possibilities. One of the most revolutionary decisions possible is for leadership to refuse to consolidate its own power and to choose instead to follow new vanguards. Only by making such a decision will we be relevant to the future.

ABBIE HOFFMAN
SOURCE: From Revolution for the Hell of It *by Abbie Hoffman. Copyright © 1968 by The Dial Press, Inc. Reprinted by permission of the publisher.*

This reluctance to define ourselves gives us glorious freedom in which to fuck with the system. We become communist-racist-acid-headed freaks, holding flowers in one hand and bombs in the other. The Old Left says we work for the CIA. Ex-Marines stomp on us as Pinkos. Newport police jail us as smut peddlers. Newark cops arrest us as riot inciters. (These four events were all triggered by passing out free copies of the same poem.) So what the hell are we doing, you ask? We are dynamiting brain cells. We are putting people through changes. The key to the puzzle lies in theater. We are theater in the streets: total and committed. We aim to involve people and use (unlike other movements locked in ideology) any weapon (prop) we can find. The aim is not to earn the respect, admiration, and love of everybody—it's to get people to do, to participate, whether positively or negatively. All is relevant, only "the play's the thing."

As soon as you do anything in this country you become a celebrity. It's not really the same as being a leader. You can only stimulate actions. Stopping them or controlling them is something leaders can do. I'm not a leader. Nobody is under my command. I haven't the vaguest idea how to stop a demonstration, say, except to go home. I'm really not interested in stopping anything, so I'm not a leader. But this celebrity thing has certain problems. Using false names just tends to increase the myth after a while. Sometimes I do now, and sometimes I don't. If I can get away with it, I do.

Q. Will you use a false name on the book?

A. If I can get away with it.

Q. Isn't this celebrity or star system alien to your visions of a new society.

A. Most definitely. I find as you get more and more well known you get less personal freedom. You spend more time doing other people's things than your own. You know, people calling in the middle of the night with their problems. Imagine this scene: You are trying to steal some groceries and some old lady comes up and says how much she likes what you're doing. That's why I use disguises, so I can keep in shape by having to hustle without the myth. The day I can't shoplift, panhandle, or pass out leaflets on my own is the day I'll retire. The myth, like everything else, is free. Anybody can claim he is it and use it to hustle.

. . .

The first duty of a revolutionist is not to get caught. I discovered how to survive in the midst of chaos in Chicago. Use disguises, use different names, when you want to take care of business ditch your followers, bodyguards, reporters and establish good alibis. Reject all references to yourself as a leader. If you have to exert leadership let it be natural, arising out of the situation rather than your past history. The enemy always goes after the leaders. You should adopt the attitude that survival is the principal goal of the vanguard. You should avoid going to jail at all costs. If you are caught and put in jail, it is your revolutionary duty to escape. Going to jail presents people with the model of masochistic theater. Getting killed is the risk involved in living a revolutionary life to the fullest. I prefer death to prison.

The first line of defense is to turn on the enemy. Middle-of-the-roaders, cops, mothers, everybody should be hustled into the revolution. Under the uniform (the opposite of our costumes) of a cop exists a naked human being. Cops don't like to work, and have sex hang-ups just like everybody else. Ask one why he bothers working for a wife and kids that don't respect him. Ask him if he's getting laid enough. Take a lesson from Tokyo Rose, she was a damn good pool-hustler. When you are trying to turn people onto the *free* society the first question you ask, even if you don't verbalize it, is: "What do you want?" What if the person answers "I want to kick the shit out of kids like you"? Build him a boxing ring.

Never explain what you are doing. This wastes a good deal of time and rarely gets through. Show them through your action, if they don't understand it, fuck 'em, maybe you'll hook them with the next action.

Run, don't walk, to the nearest revolution. Wear out your shoes, get used to being exhausted. Eat only what you need and stay healthy if possible.

When you meet a brother, never preach to him. Only exchange information such as date, time, place, and so on. Always respect the style of a brother. If he is doing your thing, you should not even waste time talking to him. Never preach to the already committed.

Always create art and destroy property. Become a work of art. Art is the only thing worth dying for.

Never forget that ours is the battle against a machine not against people. If, however, people behave like machines, treat them as such. If a machine slips on a banana peel we all laugh. If a person slips on a banana peel we help him off the ground. Our job is to line the streets of the country with banana peels.

Remember that the people you are trying to reach often know more than you. Learn from them. Last winter I spoke at a high school in Port Washington, New York. Two kids from junior high school, age fourteen and fifteen snuck into the room to listen to the rap. At the end the kids came up and told me I didn't know much. I asked them what they were into. "We sleep outside each night preparing ourselves for guerrilla fighting in the suburbs," they responded. One of the kids had been arrested four times in demon-

strations and was about to be suspended for refusing to get a haircut.
I went to school that day in Port Washington.

DAVID DELLINGER
SOURCE: From David Dellinger, Revolutionary Non-Violence *(Indianap-olis: Bobbs-Merrill, 1970). Reprinted by permission of* Liberation.

Our role as leaders was minimal. And the movement will not help
build an egalitarian future, with grass-roots initiative and responsibility, unless it cherishes these qualities now, by rotating its leaders
and not relying unduly on any of them. The demonstrators knew
why they came to Chicago, and it wasn't to play "follow the leader."
If the government thinks it can cut off a few heads and kill the
body, it is in for a shock.

ELDRIDGE CLEAVER
SOURCE: From Eldridge Cleaver, Post-Prison Writings and Speeches.
*Copyright © 1968, 1969 by Eldridge Cleaver. Reprinted by permission of
Cyrilly Abels, Literary Agent.*

. . . A new black leadership with its own distinct style and philosophy will now come into its own, to center stage. Nothing can stop
this leadership from taking over, because it is based on charisma,
has the allegiance and support of the black masses, is conscious of
its self and its position and is prepared to shoot its way to power
if the need arises.

BOBBY SEALE
SOURCE: From Seize the Time, *by Bobby Seale. Copyright © 1968, 1969,
1970 by Bobby Seale. Reprinted by permission of Random House, Inc.*

One day I went over to his house and asked him if he had read
Fanon. I'd read *Wretched of the Earth* six times. I knew Fanon was
right and I knew he was running it down—but how do you put ideas
like his over? Huey was laying up in bed, thinking, plotting on the
man. I knew what he was doing. He used to tell me how he was
plotting to make himself some money on the man. He was always

involved with day-to-day survival like the average brother on the block.

He said no, he hadn't read Fanon. So I brought Fanon over one day. That brother got to reading Fanon, and man, let me tell you, when Huey got ahold of Fanon, and read Fanon (I had been always running down about how we need this organization, that organization, but never anything concrete), Huey'd be thinking. Hard. We would sit down with *Wretched of the Earth* and talk, go over another section or chapter of Fanon, and Huey would explain it in depth. It was the first time I ever had anybody who could show a clear-cut perception of what was said in one sentence, a paragraph, or chapter, and not have to read it again. He knew it already. He'd get on the streets. We'd be walking down the street and get in some discussion and argument, Huey would be citing facts, citing that material, and giving perception to it. At that time he was giving the same basic concepts as he's giving now, but now he's in a wider and broader area, because he's had a lot of experience in leadership in the Black Panther Party. His development now is at the head of the revolutionary struggle. But he always had this vast ability to do things along with a proper perspective, and he could run it down and get things going.

. . .

All the passages that Fanon has covered, Huey covered. We used to underline them. I wish I had the books right now with the passages we underlined: everything that Fanon said about violence and the spontaneity of violence, how spontaneous violence educates those who are in a position with skills to lead the people to what needs to be done. Fanon ran the cultural nationalists down *cold*. He talked about them like they were *dogs*. This is why many of the cultural nationalists have really, in fact, thrown Fanon's book to the side. Malcolm X talked about organization and doing things, and righteously going out there and doing it. The cultural nationalists, on the other hand, wanted to sit down and articulate bullshit, while Huey P. Newton wanted to go out and implement stuff.

This is very important. This is the difference, the line of demarcation, in fact, between the revolutionaries and those who are jiving in the confines of the ivory walls, the ivory towers of the college. Huey and I began to talk about a lot of things. We really began to get very intense in how this thing was going to go and how we thought it should go. We had been rejected by people at San Francisco State, Merritt College, and on the Berkeley campus, because we talked and emphasized the necessity of arming the people with guns. The cultural nationalists and many of the leading white liberals, they look at it like, "You can't pick up guns. It's impossible to pick up guns." This is what they want to emphasize. This is what you could infer from all their rhetoric. But Huey said, "No, you must pick up guns, because guns are key."

ELDRIDGE CLEAVER

SOURCE: From Eldridge Cleaver, Post-Prison Writings and Speeches. Copyright 1968, 1969 by Eldridge Cleaver. Reprinted by permission of Cyrilly Abels, Literary Agent.

This book [*The Wretched of the Earth*], already recognized around the world as a classic study of the psychology of oppressed peoples, is now known among the militants of the black liberation movement in America as "the Bible."

Written by a black man who was born in Martinique and educated in Paris, who reached the apex of his genius in the crucible of the Algerian Revolution, Fanon's book is itself an historical event. For it marks a very significant moment in the history of the movement of the colonized peoples of the world—in their quest for national liberation, the modernization of their economies, and the security against the never-ending intrigues of the imperialist nations.

During a certain stage in the psychological transformation of a subjected people who have begun struggling for their freedom, an impulse to violence develops in the collective unconscious. The oppressed people feel an uncontrollable desire to kill their masters. But the feeling itself gives rise to myriad troubles, for the people, when they first become aware of the desire to strike out against the slavemaster, shrink from this impulse in terror. Violence then turns in upon itself and the oppressed people fight among themselves: they kill each other, and do all the things to each other which they would, in fact, like to do to the master. Intimidated by the superior armed might of the oppressor, the colonial people feel that he is invincible and that it is futile to even dream of confronting him.

When the revolutionary impulse to strike out against the oppressor is stifled, distortions in the personality appear. During the Algerian Revolution, Fanon worked in a hospital in Algeria. A psychiatrist, there he was able to observe carefully Algerians who had caved in psychologically under the pressures of a revolutionary situation. *The Wretched of the Earth* contains an appendix in which Fanon introduces several of these case histories, tracing the revolutionary impulse and attempts to evade it through the psyches of his patients.

Not all of Fanon's patients were Algerian colonial subjects. French policemen who were bothered by the brutality with which they were surrounded and in which they were involved. French soldiers who had inflicted despicable tortures on prisoners, were often confronted with situations in which their rationalizations broke down and they found themselves face to face with their own merciless deeds.

The rare significance of this book is that it contains the voice of a revolutionary black intellectual speaking directly to his own people and showing them the way to harness their forces. Fanon teaches that the key factor is to focus all the hatreds and violence on their true target—the oppressor. From then on, says Fanon, be implacable. The same point is made by Leroi Jones in his play, *Dutchman*, when his character, Clay, screams to the white woman who had tormented him, "A little murder will make us all sane again" [Speaking of black people *vis à vis* whites]. What this book does is legitimize the revolutionary impulse to violence. It teaches colonial subjects that it is perfectly normal for them to want to rise up and cut off the heads of the slavemasters, that it is a way to achieve their manhood, and that they must oppose the oppressor in order to experience themselves as men.

In the aftermath of Watts, and all the other uprisings that have set the ghettos of America ablaze, it is obvious that there is very little difference in the way oppressed people feel and react, whether they are oppressed in Algeria by the French, in Kenya by the British, in Angola by the Portuguese, or in Los Angeles by Yankee Doodle.

French philosopher Jean-Paul Sartre wrote an introduction to this book, which, he says, needed no introduction by anyone. Sartre's introduction is itself a masterpiece. Interpreting Fanon's thought for a white audience, Sartre has rendered a valuable service in driving home to the reader that this is a book he dare not pass up. *January 15, 1967*

THE BLACK PANTHER

SOURCE: From "Pigs Threaten Well-Being of the Supreme Servant of the People," The Black Panther, February 20, 1971, p. 2; and "State of the Struggle," The Black Panther, January 8, 1972, p. C. Reprinted by permission of the Black Panther Party. Copyright February 20, 1971 and January 8, 1972 by Huey P. Newton.*

From the time that Huey P. Newton and Bobby Seale first stepped onto the streets of Oakland, California in 1966, armed against the oppressors of the People, the Black Panther Party has suffered such a variety of attacks, that it would require a future historian to give a complete account. Not only has our Party been said to be both racist and integrationist at the same time, or communist and reformist, hoodlums or gun-toters, etc.; but, we have suffered innumerable attacks against our very lives by every enforcement agency of the Empire's regime and its hired and authorized agents.

But it has been and is our prime task to serve and meet what we believe to be the true interests of all the people. And we have studied, theoretically and practically, the best means to attain this goal. And we have tried to expose, theoretically and practically, to all the people what we have learned. And we have suffered these attacks because we have put forward every energy we have to serve the true interests of the People.

And this is why the Black Panther Party is called and is the Vanguard of Revolution in the Empire of the United States. And the masses of people have stated this—here in the Empire and in other communities of the world, in Vietnam, in China, in Korea, in South America, in Africa. But those who know best the threat the Black Panther Party presents to the continued existence of the American Empire and its various political regimes—Nixon's at present—those who know best that the Black Panther Party is "the greatest threat to the internal security of the U.S." (J. Edgar Hoover) and, is, therefore, in the vanguard of the People's Revolution in America are those of the Empire's ruling circle itself.

And it was the leader of our Party, Huey P. Newton, who, taking the lessons that Malcolm had so eloquently stated, tired and angry as every black and oppressed person is, who by himself, at that time,

*Since publication of these articles the Black Panther Party has dropped the use of all titles.

challenged the very foundations of this decadent, vicious and rotten society. Arming himself against dogs to whom killing, raping, robbery and all kinds of treacherous deeds had become more than familiar acts, but which deeds became the American Institution over the centuries, Huey P. Newton set forward the supreme example of his very life to bring this message to as many people as possible. It was this supreme example and offer of his life to expose the truth for even a moment that has brought the many hundreds of thousands of people around the world to respect and support the organization he founded. And the hatred the world's pigs feel for the Party is pinpointed at our founder.

. . .

The unity between those outside and those inside the maximum security prisons was certainly strengthened and took tremendously progressive steps. The unity and solidarity among oppressed peoples is the key to our salvation. Therefore, the unfortunate events surrounding the defection from the Black Panther Party (in February) of the former Minister of Information, Eldridge Cleaver, served to temporarily disrupt that unity. However, from that event came many positive results. There was the building up, as never before, of the Black Panther Party sponsored People's Survival Programs, Free Shoes, Free Breakfasts, Free Food, Free Commissary for Prisoners and Bussing to Prisons Programs, Free Health Clinics, Free Clothing, etc. These survival programs served to not only meet our basic needs, but to unify our efforts to survive while struggling for complete liberation.

Alienation In the rhetoric of alienation the counter-cultural motif of new radicalism becomes evident. The influence of Marcuse is strong in the rhetoric; the identity of the young as culturally "deviant" is a badge of honor; and the concept of "dehumanization" is used in criticizing society. All of these themes are derived from intellectual radicalism and cultural rebellion since 1960.

Both white and black radicals regard persecution of the Black Panther Party as the focus of repression in American society. They suggest that white skin saves the "new left" leaders from the full brunt of repression. The full force of capitalist evil is felt by the Panthers, according to the rhetoric. Panther leaders strike back with rhetoric based on themes such as the "criminal system" which engages in "official murders." Thus the perceived repression is turned around and directed back, rhetorically, at the society and the government.

TOM HAYDEN

SOURCE: From Trial *by Tom Hayden. Copyright © 1970 by Tom Hayden. Reprinted by permission of Holt, Rinehart and Winston, Inc.*

Putting our identity on trial caused them to expose their own.

Normally in America oppressors appear to be flexible, even friendly persons. Only when their power is threatened are we given a glimpse of the paranoia, the rigidity, the violence at their core. This threat to power can occur with little or no provocation from those whom they oppress. The mere fact that the oppressed are becoming conscious of their own needs is enough to shake any system which for its maintenance depends primarily on attitudes of conformity and submission.

The American system, perhaps more than any other, controls people through manipulation rather than force. Advertising, the mass media, schools, electoral politics, the church, all serve to create a belief that this is the best of all possible societies, that no alternative ways of life are really achievable. Blacks, the Cubans, the Vietnamese are all shattering the image that the world is one-dimensional, and now even white youth is creating a dimension of its own. In this conflict, our identity itself is the alternative, reaching people on a deeper level than rhetoric or blueprints ever could. We are living proof that life can be different. Our very existence, therefore, is a threat to the social order. Our appearance, because we strip away all illusion, produces the total revelation of our oppressors as well.

ABBIE HOFFMAN

SOURCE: From Revolution for the Hell of It *by Abbie Hoffman. Copyright © 1968 by The Dial Press, Inc. Reprinted by permission of the publisher.*

The message: Property is the enemy—burn it, destroy it, give it away. Don't let them make a machine out of you, get out of the system, do your thing. Don't organize students, teachers, Negroes, organize your head. Find out where you are, what you want to do and go out and do it. Johnson's a commie, the Kremlin is more fucked up than Alabama. Get out. Don't organize the schools, burn them. Leave them, they will rot. . . . The kids are getting stoned. We're all talking now. Lots of resistance. Kid says to me, "I like what you're saying and I'm going to drop out in a year." "What the hell you waiting for?" "Well, I want to finish school first." Reminded me of an SDS picket line I saw on a campus last year, protesting the tests used to determine draft status. Most of the demonstrators put their signs down and went in to take the test. These are the potential revolutionists? *Eich meir* a revolution!

. . .

You want to get a glimpse of what it feels like to be a nigger? Let your hair grow long. Longhairs, that new minority, are getting the crap kicked out of them by cops all over the country, and with the beatings and jailings comes the destruction of flower power. Cops Eat Flowers painted in large white letters last fall on Second Avenue and St. Marks Place signaled the end of flower power. As the kids pour back into the Lower East Side they bring with them tales of police harassment previously reserved only for blacks. Two hundred kids busted on Boston Common for "idleness." Three kids arrested for vagrancy in Nevada (even though they all had money) and held fifty days before they even had a trial. Kids arrested in Indiana get their hair cut and then are thrown out of the jail without even going to trial. In Florida a head shop was smashed by the police and the owners were told bluntly, "We don't want your kind around here. Get your ass out of town." Anyone who takes to the road going cross-country literally takes his life in his hands.

. . .

It's really quite interesting to stand on the corner of Avenue A and 10th Street and watch the scores of relatives with puzzled expressions on their faces, scurrying to and fro. Here and there is a bounty hunter or plainclothesman querying the local gossips. The parents are really a sight, plowing through incense-burning, rock-blasting psychedelic shops, "Please, Mary, won't you come home; we all love you." About two sets of parents a week make their way to my apartment. Somehow I have this reputation for being "in the know." They are referred by the police or shopkeepers. We talk a little. Sometimes I get personal. "What drugs was she using?" "Oh, Janie would never think of taking drugs." There never was a parent who believes his kid uses drugs and I've never met a kid in the Lower East Side who didn't use drugs before he got here. It seems America has a failure of communication going. *It seems America has lost her children.* They come down here or to Haight-Ashbury or to the stops in between. An underground railroad exists. The runaways are hidden in crash pads, communes, apartments, in country communities. They let their hair grow, change their style of dress, and vanish. The pictures that are stuck on police-station walls, printed in underground newspapers, or thrown in my wastebasket, are of different people. A nice school photo. Girl with lipstick, pert dress with white collar. Boy with tweedy sportsjacket, windsor knot in his tie, hair parted on the right side. Where have all the neckties gone? Are the runaways going back? I don't know. Ask them. I'll tell you one thing—I sure as hell ain't, they'll have to kill me first.

DAVID DELLINGER

SOURCE: *David Dellinger,* Revolutionary Non-Violence *(Indianapolis: Bobbs-Merrill, 1970). Reprinted by permission of Liberation.*

As nearly as uninformed citizens who are not in on government secrets can ascertain, the purpose of these attacks and wild charges is not simply to destroy the Black Panther Party. From the public statements of top officials, one may deduce that an additional pupose is to manufacture an atmosphere in which a drastic general crackdown would seem justified. By discrediting the Panthers and then establishing their conspiratorial ties with the antiwar movement and the Yippies, the Government would be able to move significantly in the direction of political suppression of insurgent groups. Apparently it believes that such a move is necessary in order to continue the present unpopular foreign policy (with or without withdrawal from Vietnam) and to keep blacks, students, and other rebels in line.

ELDRIDGE CLEAVER

SOURCE: *From Eldridge Cleaver,* Post-Prison Writings and Speeches *Copyright © 1968, 1969 by Eldridge Cleaver. Reprinted by permission of Cyrilly Abels, Literary Agent.*

I am a political prisoner, and an examination of the circumstances resulting in my imprisonment will reveal this fact to you or to anybody else. I realize that I have just asserted an awkward claim, because I know that other people have already examined the circumstances of which I speak and have drawn the conclusion that, indeed, I should be right where I am. But I do not intend to argue their side of the story, which I not only consider wrong, but perfidious and criminal. Because certain people had to do certain things in order for me to be, at this moment, sitting in this cell. People talked about me and my activities and then they issued orders. Other people moved to carry out those orders. Those who fastened the handcuffs to my wrists, the shackles around my legs, the chain around my body, put me into a car, transported me to this place and turned me over to the keepers here, were mere functionaries, automatons, carrying out their "duties" in Adolf Eichmann's spirit. I speak, rather, of the decision makers, those whom you have appointed and charged with making decisions in this area. They are the guilty ones, the conspirators, whose decisions and orders I bring to your attention.

. . .

This piggish, criminal system. This system that is the enemy of people. This very system that we live in and function in every day. This system that we are in and under at this very moment. *Our* system! Each and every one of your systems. If you happen to be from another country, it's still your system, because the system in your country is part of this. This system is *evil*. It is criminal; it is murderous. And it is in control. It is in power. It is arrogant. It is crazy. And it looks upon the people as its property. So much so that *cops*, who are public servants, feel justified in going onto a campus, college campus or high school campus, and spraying mace in the faces of the people. They beat people with those clubs, and even shoot people, if it takes that to enforce the will of the likes of Ronald Reagan, Jesse Unruh, or Mussolini Alioto.

THE BLACK PANTHER

SOURCE: From State of the Struggle The Black Panther, *January 8, 1972, p. E. Reprinted by permission of the Black Panther Party. Copyright January 8, 1972 by Huey P. Newton.*

Nowhere, however, does the U.S. commit more brutal and vicious murders than where it continued to do so in its aggressive

war against the Vietnamese People. The U.S. Army and other
agencies have killed and continue to murder thousands of innocent Vietnamese people. However, even the government's clever
way of lying did not conceal its viciousness when Lt. William
Calley was convicted for crimes against the Vietnamese people,
and then exonerated by the personal, Presidential order of Richard
Nixon. While Calley went free, Black G.I.'s who had refused to
participate in Nixon's war were being persecuted.

Absolutism Contrast is used as a
rhetorical device in new radical
rhetoric as in old radical rhetoric.
However, the alternative to the old
system—the old politics, the
repressive government—is a new
freedom. The revolutionary culture
of the new radicals is portrayed as
a liberating spirit, not a stifling
model of a static socialist society.

DAVID DELLINGER

SOURCE: *David Dellinger,* Revolutionary Non-Violence *(Indianapolis:
Bobbs-Merrill, 1970). Reprinted by permission of Liberation.*

But the problem of having an increasingly cruel and irrational
enemy that has contempt for human life and makes a cynical
mockery of the democratic values it claims to believe in is the
danger of becoming cruel and irrational oneself in the act of com-
batting the enemy. Because "they" are vicious and wrong and
"we" are humane and right, it is easy to conclude that whatever
we do is justified. For the most part this did not happen in Chicago,
but it has happened more than once in the history of revolutionary
movements. And some of the conclusions people are drawing from
the battle of Chicago point dangerously in that direction. One has
only to talk to some of the participants—and to read some of the
reports in the underground press which exaggerate and extol the
violence of our side while forgetting to mention the reasons for our
being there—to realize that it can happen here.

There is a heady sense of manhood that comes from advancing
from apathy to commitment, from timidity to courage, from pas-
sivity to aggressiveness. Anyone who has been forced to yield
ground or surrender his rights in the face of the superior force
and legal backing of the occupying armies of the state would surely
be thrilled to stand side by side with an aroused body of comrades

in resisting the police assaults. Anyone who has stood helplessly by in a poor neighborhood while the police abused a suspect, or anywhere when his comrades in the movement were being taken off to kangaroo courts and jails could not but respond favorably to the occasions in Chicago when the police were denied their intended vitctims.

There is an intoxication that comes from standing up to the police at last. There is an even greater sense of satisfaction that comes from feeling oneself a functioning part of a larger whole whose members act together not only to protect one another but to serve a larger purpose as well. All the things that William James wrote about in his famous essay on the need for a moral equivalent to war were at work among the resisters in Chicago. Ordinarily, a society which has frustrated the natural community of mankind and deprived its citizens of a more social purpose than money-grubbing, offers them a counterfeit sense of community and national purpose in a holy war against a foreign enemy. In Chicago, for once, a generation which sees through the false idealism and ugly purposes of the U.S. aggression in Vietnam found alternate, more meaningful satisfaction in a heroic battle in which righteousness was clearly on their side. Now it is our responsibility to see that righteousness continues to be on our side, both in the objectives for which we continue to struggle and in the spirit and activities by which we carry on that struggle. This will not be achieved by moving backwards into the old-style nonviolence, which seemed content with symbolic actions and token victories even when war and oppression continued undiminished. But neither will it be achieved by falsely concluding that the need of the movement is to stockpile weapons and increase the violence in the next encounter.

Some people are saying that the time has come when we must fight "by any means necessary." But some means that seem necessary at the moment end by degrading and corrupting the movement. Tactically they provide the enemy with ready-made excuses for its most repressive actions. They confuse and alienate people whose eyes are just being opened to the viciousness of the system and who should be providing not just cover and support but recruits for the movement. We came off well in Chicago. It was a clear-cut victory because the police acted abominably and our people showed courage, aggressiveness and a proper sense of values. But if street fighting breaks out when the police are restrained and if we act contemptuously of other people's rights, the sentiments of those who should be our allies could turn against us. More important, we will begin to lose sight of our objectives and develop a movement style which attracts lovers of violence rather than lovers of justice and brotherhood.

JERRY RUBIN

SOURCE: From Do It! by Jerry Rubin. Copyright © 1970 by the Social Education Foundation. Reprinted by permission of Simon and Schuster.

AN ACID VISION:

The Democratic Convention opens behind barbed wire. Props include tear gas and bayonet-bearing paratroopers, rushed back from Vietnam.

Millions mill in the street searching for the government they've lost. Their attention is drawn to the sky.

It's a bird.

It's a plane.

No, it's super-LBJ, airlifted into the besieged hall.

Suddenly a handkerchief is waved from an upstairs window.

The Democratic Party surrenders.

The yippies take over.

Ecstasy

Vision ends.

The Festival of Life vs. the Convention of Death: a morality play, religious theater, involving elemental human emotions—future and past; youth and age; love and hate; good and evil; hope and despair. Yippies and Democrats.

The media prepared to transfix the consciousness of the entire world on Chicago for five whole days. *Our* chance to touch the world's soul. The right act at the right time: instantaneous communication. Nobody could pretend Chicago wasn't happening. Local disruption becomes global war between good and evil.

The mission: freak out the Democrats so much that they disrupt their own convention. And meanwhile demonstrate to the world the alternative: our own revolutionary youth culture.

HUEY P. NEWTON

SOURCE: From "Eulogy Delivered by Huey P. Newton, Supreme Commander, Black Panther Party, at the Revolutionary Funeral of Comrades Jonathan Jackson and William Christmas, St. Augustine's Church, 27th and West Streets, Oakland, California, August 15, 1970," The Black Panther, Vol. V, No. 8 (August 21, 1970), p. 13. Reprinted by permission of the Black Panther Party. Copyright August 21, 1970 by Huey P. Newton.

While it is viewed as a tragedy, and many would weep for Jonathan Jackson and William A. Christmas, the Black Panther Party serves notice that it is not brothers Jonathan Jackson and William A. Christmas for whom we should weep. They have achieved freedom and we remain slaves. If we must weep let it be for those of us who remain in bondage.

The Black Panther Party will follow the example that was set forth by these courageous revolutionaries. The people refuse to submit to the slavery and bondage that is required in order for us to live a few more years on the planet earth. *If the penalty for the quest for freedom is death–then by death we escape to freedom.*

Without freedom life means nothing. We have nothing to lose but our shackles and freedom to gain. We have gathered today not only to give respect to Comrades Jonathan Jackson and William Christmas, but also to pledge our lives to the accomplishment of the goals exemplified in the actions of brothers Jonathan Jackson and William Christmas.

There are no laws that the oppressor makes that the oppressed are bound to respect.

Laws should be made to serve people. People should not be made to serve laws. When laws no longer serve the people, it is the people's right and the people's duty to free themselves from the yoke of such laws.

Oppressed people in general, and Black people in particular, have suffered too long and we must draw the line somewhere. There is a big difference between thirty million unarmed Black people and thirty million Black people armed to the teeth.

We are not alone. We have allies everywhere. We find our comrades wherever in the world we hear the oppressor's whip. People all over the world are rising up, the high tide of revolution is about to sweep the shores of America—sweeping away the evil gentry and corrupt officials.

Our comrades Jonathan Jackson and William A. Christmas have taught us a revolutionary lesson. They have intensified the struggle and placed it on a higher level.

A picture is worth a thousand words but action is supreme. Comrades Jonathan Jackson and William A. Christmas have made the ultimate sacrifice. They have given the revolution their lives.

15

OLD FUNDAMENTALISM

Sources of Rhetoric Two leaders who dominate the contemporary expressions of the old fundamentalist movements, Billy James Hargis and Robert Welch, have written books which are the principal sources of rhetoric for their movements. Hargis wrote *Communist America . . . Must It Be?* in 1960 and *The Real Extremists— The Far Left* in 1964, just as the radical right movements were attaining prominence and influence in American politics. Robert Welch "wrote" the *Blue Book* in 1958 when he delivered a two-day speech to the founders of the John Birch Society and later had the speech transcribed and printed.

In addition to these books, Hargis and Welch publish periodicals. The Christian Crusade publishes a newspaper called *Christian Crusade Weekly*, and the John Birch Society publishes a monthly magazine called *American Opinion*. Hargis seems to maintain firm editorial control over his *Weekly* while Welch leaves the editing of *American Opinion* to his staff. However, it is clear that both periodicals reflect the ideology of the leaders of the old fundamentalist movements.

Counter-Mythology As a religious movement, old fundamentalism stresses the Christian doctrines of salvation and mission. As a political movement, old fundamentalism stresses nationalism and patriotism. The combination of these two sources is a mythology of "Christian Americanism" and national destiny. The fundamentalism of Billy James Hargis is expressed through a religious mythology of American history. He views the "founding fathers" as saints leading a pilgrimage to the Promised Land. The political fundamentalism of Robert Welch leads him to compare America with Rome. He laments the decline of "American civilization," which has become tainted with internationalism.

BILLY JAMES HARGIS

SOURCE: *From Billy James Hargis,* Communist America . . . Must It Be?
(Tulsa: Christian Crusade, 1960), pp. 30–31. Reprinted by permission.

America is a Christian country. The men and women who braved an uncharted wilderness to carve out this Republic, were rich in faith. With a Bible under one arm, and a musket under the other, they were willing to fight for their faith and their freedom as well as talk about it.

The doctrine of separation of Church and State is very precious to the American people. Like many other things, it is a misunderstood and misinterpreted doctrine today in America. Our founding fathers came from countries where the state government and the ecclesiastical machine of the predominant church were the same. Usually, the head of the State was the head of the Church. This, of course, is still true in many countries of the world today. In Great Britain, the Queen is not only head of the government, but is head of the Church. In many countries, such as Switzerland, when you pay your taxes, you automatically pay your tithes. There is no free-will or voluntary contribution to the Church, for support of the Church is identical with support of the government.

Our forefathers felt they could improve upon this system. It was especially hard for minority groups. Take for example, the men and women who sailed the Atlantic on the Mayflower to found this Republic. Previously, they had lived in Great Britain. It was contrary to their belief to support the Church of England which they were forced to do, as long as they lived in the country. It was also contrary to their belief to attend services of the Church of England. They were independently minded. The crown of England, and the people looked upon our Pilgrim Fathers as a sect or a cult, and they were the object of bitter criticism and severe persecution. These people of faith fled to the Netherlands for religious refuge. However, as in the case of England, there was no difference between Church and State in that land, although they were afforded much better treatment and understanding by the people and the government there. Pooling their resources, these courageous forefathers purchased a ship and left the ports of Holland enroute to the new nation which was to become known as the United States.

I have knelt in prayer in the little church in Amsterdam, Netherlands, where these men and women dedicated and sanctified their lives to the service of God on the night before they set sail. On each subsequent visit to the Netherlands since my original visit in 1953, I have knelt and prayed in that sacred little cathedral hidden from the city streets of Amsterdam and enclosed by ancient Dutch homes. A simple plaque on the outside of the church announces to the tourist that this was the place the Founding Fathers of America dedicated their lives to the building of a new nation prior to leaving the Netherlands.

Their frail vessel, which had been purchased by great sacrifice, became inadequate by the time they reached the English Channel. So, they purchased another ship, the Mayflower, and completed their voyage. Just before they reached American shores they agreed on the form of government that would become the basic law and philosophy of America, and set it down in writing so that all future generations of Americans might never forget why our founding fathers endured such hardship to establish this Republic. The Mayflower Compact, November 11, 1620, states, that it was undertaken for "the glory of God and advancement of the Christian faith." Therefore, let it be remembered that separation of Church and State simply means that there will be no official church in the U.S. but that all may be free to worship God, according to dictates of their conscience.

ROBERT WELCH

SOURCE: From Robert Welch, The Blue Book pp. 52–53. (Belmont, Mass.: Robert Welch, Inc., 1961). Reprinted by permission.

There are few parallels in history more striking than the way Italy was settled by Greek pioneers, who simply took over from the aborigines already there, and developed the new nation and new civilization of Rome, and the way America was settled by pioneers from Western Europe who developed a new nation and a new civilization here. In its earlier centuries America not only did not regard itself as a part of the European organism at all, but became fiercely proud of its differences from Europe, and of its indigenously vigorous customs, culture, and destiny of its own. The American civilization was every bit as much of an entirely new and different civilization from the old and ancestral one of Western Europe, as was Rome a new civilization distinct from Greece.

And this American civilization, at the turn of the present century, was only three hundred years old. It had the strength and vigor and promise of a healthy young man in his late teens. There was no reason on earth for any such organism to be attacked by, and start succumbing to, the cancerous disease of collectivism at that stage of its young manhood, with its whole lifespan of accomplishment before it. And any of the natural or fortuitous attempts of the disease to get a foothold in the American social body—such as the virus implanted by Edward Bellamy with his *Looking Backward*, or by Upton Sinclair with his *Jungle*, or even the more pretentious concoctions of Thorstein Veblen—would have been so easily repulsed by the strong and growing organism that none of them would have left even a scar.

But we have the cancerous disease of collectivism firmly implanted now, nevertheless. We have people feeling that nothing should be done by them, but everything for them, by the government. Its disastrous ravages are quite far advanced. And we have it, basically, because of too long and too close an association with a parent that was dying of the disease; that was old enough and weakened enough for the virus to be rampantly active throughout this parent's whole environment.

When Woodrow Wilson, cajoled and guided even then by the collectivists of Europe, took us into the first World War, while solemnly swearing that he would never do so, he did much more than end America's great period of happy and wholesome independence of Europe. He put his healthy young country in the same house, and for a while in the same bed, with this parent who was already yielding to the collectivist cancer. We never got out of that house again. We were once more put back even in the same bed by Franklin D. Roosevelt, also while lying in his teeth about his intentions, and we have never been able to get out of that bed since.

Counter-Elitism "Expertise" is the ostensible basis of the authority of the old fundamentalist leaders. Billy James Hargis regards himself as a self-educated expert, qualified to identify the Communist conspiracy in American life by virtue of spiritual inspiration: "I have never claimed educational attainments, but I do claim to know the mind of God."*

Robert Welch is an "expert" who disdains academic credentials; he bases his claim to authority on his business background. Both men feel that they offer Americans a precious commodity: the truth which will awaken America to the Communist conspiracy before it is too late.

Weekly Crusader, March 9, 1962, p. 7.

BILLY JAMES HARGIS

SOURCE: From Billy James Hargis, The Far Left (Tulsa, Okla.: Christian Crusade, 1964), p. 5. Reprinted by permission.

I believe in Jesus Christ as the promised Messiah, the Savior of all believers, whether they are Jew or Gentile, and in His divinely authorized Church, the body of the believers. I believe in America, her freedoms, her ideals and in her traditions. To me, America is one of the greatest gifts that God has ever given man, outside of the gift of His only begotten Son and his divinely-inspired Bible. The spiritual traditions and ideals of freedom of Americanism are, I believe, the greatest of any nation in history.

I believe in the Constitution of the United States, and in the Constitution of the fifty Republics that make up these United States. I believe that Communism violates all of our freedoms that we have enjoyed as Americans. I believe that Communism is opposed to our American ideals, transgresses our traditions, is weakening our nation's unity, and is wrecking our American way of life. To me, it is an inevitable fact that if Communism triumphs, Americanism will die.

My sole objective in writing this book on the "Far Left" is to help save America from a godless, despotic dictatorship which is based on bloodshed, barbarism, suppression and slavery, all of which are un-Christian, un-American and unpalatable to freedom-loving men. I am convinced that every real American, if he but knew the truth, would strive to defend his nation from Communists who, utilizing their weapons of intrigue and infamy, are imposing upon our country their profane pattern of serfdom.

ROBERT WELCH

SOURCE: From Robert Welch, The Blue Book (Belmont, Mass.: Robert Welch, Inc., 1961) pp. 5, 35, 158–159. Reprinted by permission.

I personally have been studying the problem increasingly for about nine years, and practically full time for the past three years. And entirely without pride, but in simple thankfulness, let me point out that a lifetime of business experience should have made it easier for me to see the falsity of the economic theories on which Communism is supposedly based, more readily, than might some scholar coming into that study from the academic cloisters; while a lifetime of interest in things academic, especially world history, should have given me an advantage over many businessmen, in more readily seeing the sophistries in dialectic materialism.

So I have felt, rightly or wrongly, that my grasp of Communist purposes, and even of their methods, should have been more rapid than that of some of my patriotic friends who have gradually become staunch anti-Communists. Yet almost every day I run into some whole new area, where the Communists have been penetrating and working quietly for years, until now they are in virtual control of everything that is done in that slice or corner of our national life.

. . .

The only thing which can possibly stop the Communists is for the American people to learn the truth in time. It is to contribute my small bit to such an awakening that I have given up most of my business responsibilities and most of my income, in order through my magazine and speeches to bring some inkling of the truth to as many people as I can reach. I do not expect nor deserve any slightest applause or sympathy for this sacrifice. I mention it at all for just one reason only—which is to show how deadly serious the situation appears to me.

You may think I am an alarmist. Frankly I am. For in my opinion, based on many years of intensive study of the methods, the progress, and the menace of the Communist conspiracy, there is ample reason for extreme alarm; and I hope to make *you* alarmists too. It seems to me that all you need, to cause you to share my alarm, my fears, and my determination, is simply to get a map of the world and *Look At The Score*! And the first thing for you to do, as a newly awakened alarmist, is to become better informed about many things that we cannot cover here.

. . .

It is my fervent hope that The John Birch Society will last for hundreds of years, and exert an increasing influence for the temporal good and the spiritual ennoblement of mankind throughout those centuries. For I am staking my whole aspiration to play my part, in forwarding man's one increasing purpose, on whatever can be accomplished through The John Birch Society. I want no other title than that of its Founder, and have no other ambition for anything resembling fame or historical remembrance.

The John Birch Society is to be a monolithic body. A republican form of government or of organization has many attractions and advantages, under certain favorable conditions. But under less happy circumstances it lends itself too readily to infiltration, distortion and disruption. And democracy, of course, in government or organization, as the Greeks and Romans both found out, and as I believe every man in this room clearly recognizes—democracy is merely a deceptive phrase, a weapon of demagoguery, and a perennial fraud.

For withstanding the stresses and strains of internal differences and external animosities, throughout changing political climates over long periods of time; for the building of morale and loyalty and a feeling of unified purpose and closely knit strength; for effective functioning in periods of crisis and a permanence of high dedication throughout more peaceful decades; for these and many other reasons The John Birch Society will operate under completely authoritative control at all levels. The fear of tyrannical oppression of individuals, and other arguments against the authoritative structure in the form of governments, have little bearing on the case of a voluntary association, where the authoritative power can be exercised and enforced only by persuasion. And what little validity they do have is outweighed by the advantages of firm and positive direction of the Society's energies. Especially for the near future, and for the fight against Communism which is the first great task of the Society, it is imperative that all the strength we can muster be subject to smoothly functioning direction from the top. As I have said before, no collection of debating societies is ever going to stop the Communist conspiracy from taking us over, and I have no intention of adding another frustrated group to their number. We mean business every step of the way.

Alienation A major preoccupation of old fundamentalist rhetoric is an all-pervasive "communist conspiracy." This theme is used to discredit American institutions and elites such as the mass media, the government, political parties, educational institutions, and liberal Protestant churches. The "communist conspiracy" is seen as the basis of governmental policies, foreign and domestic. It leads to fears about the security of the middle class, and about the "insiders" who are secretly controlling elites, Republican as well as Democratic.

BILLY JAMES HARGIS

SOURCES: 1. From The Far Left *(Tulsa, Okla.: Christian Crusade, 1964)* p. 11. 2. From Communist America . . . Must It Be?*(Tulsa, Okla.: Christian Crusade, 1960), p. 21.* 3. Ibid., *pp. 38–39.* 4. From The Far Left, p. 19. 5. From "Politicians Mislead the People," Christian Crusade Weekly, *February 20, 1972, p. 1. Reprinted by permission.*

1.

In America, the seeds of confusion and disunion are spawning and spreading, and Communism is growing. In their efforts to wean Americans from Americanism, Communists devilishly revile and defile everyone whose opinions and convictions differ in any way from their own. Their subtle, sinister schemings sway and mislead many Americans who in ignorance or weakness yield or submit to Communism their previous loyalty to God, to country, and to their fellow men. We have no right to give up our country to the Communist conspiracy without a battle.

2.

If the average American citizen doubts that his beloved country is in mortal danger, that his wife and children are on the verge of the embrace of Communist rape and enslavement, let him look anywhere about him. Let him look at what is happening in his own church denomination, in his labor union, in his school system, at his place of entertainment, the books he reads, the movies and television shows he enjoys; let him look at his newspaper, which he has always believed to be one of his great guardians of liberty; let him look at the 1960 complexion of the Congress, and the rulings past and present of the United States Supreme Court.

It is as Lenin wrote, the "shoots" of Communism, "are to be seen literally everywhere."

It is when they may be seen "literally everywhere" that deadly danger is at hand. America is marked for Communism.

America needs to take a hard look at Communism, and especially at itself, and what has happened within itself. Communism, and what has happened, cannot be shrugged off by anyone wanting to live as a free man or woman. The American people need to see communism for what it really is, whether disguised as liberalism, socialism, progressivism, or modernism. The American people need to take a hard look at the strange happenings within America, and take action with historic and characteristic forthrightness and determination.

Never has America been in greater danger.

NEVER!

3.

America is being sold out by treasonous, traitorous leaders. America is being surrendered to the enemy by a deceived people. America's salvation is an immediate return to the faith of our fathers, and the declaration of that faith in the Bible, the word of God. America must return to the faith which proudly declares, "I am not ashamed of the gospel of Christ for it is the power of God unto salvation to everyone that believeth."

America's destruction is in satanic Communism. America's salvation is in the faith of our fathers, in Jesus Christ, the Son of God.

4.

The unfortunate thing is, as this volume will prove, millions of Americans who would greatly resent being charged with pronounced communistic leanings are actually promoting its apostolate through membership in various organizations and other associations.

When you talk of Communism internally, one of the first challenges from the liberals invariably is, "But the Communists represent so few Americans. There are probably less than 25,000 of them." We must understand in dealing with Communism internally that the size of the Communist Party itself is not important. It will never be large. Even in Soviet Russia slightly more than one per cent of the people belong to it. Outside of the Soviet Union, the Communist Party wants trained men who will seek to get into every sort of organization, interest themselves in it and work themselves toward the top so that they may steer it into the direction of Communist sympathy. There are many such agents in the United States.

5.

It has been said over and over that President Nixon's accomodation of the left-wing element and its goals in this country and throughout the world is a political maneuver.

Having been raised in an era of professional politicians, I, for one, buy this argument. Nixon, rightly or wrongly, felt he had to placate the Left-Liberal element in this country in order to be re-elected in 1972.

His enthusiastic support for unilateral disarmament; his suicidal

Red China policy; his blundering mistake in supporting pro-Red Chinese Pakistan in the Indian-Pakistan War; his determination to send military aid to avowed enemies, such as Communist Yugoslavia and Communist Chile, prove that the man had something in mind, besides what benefits the nation.

Writing off old allies, like Chiang Kai-shek, and propping up shaky Communist regimes, like Tito's in Yugoslavia and Allende's in Chile, could not be interpreted as a foreign policy that holds America's interest first.

Admittedly, his march to the Left in 1971 has gotten a lot of the Liberal news media off his back and has dampened the spirits of the Left-Liberal Marxist agitators on college campuses. In short, his new Left-Liberal decisions have bought him a little time, but I seriously wonder if he has gained enough political support among this element for re-election.

I'm sorry that I didn't live during the days of Teddy Roosevelt and some of the other *non-professional politicians.* It would have been good to live in an era where the national president was dedicated to America's interest and not his own political future.

ROBERT WELCH

SOURCE: From The Blue Book *(Belmont, Mass.: Robert Welch, Inc., 1961), pp. 32–34. Reprinted by permission.*

Now we see exactly the same principle at work on the whole front of our domestic economy. Although our danger remains almost entirely internal, from Communist influences right in our midst and treason right in our government, the American people are being persuaded that our danger is from the outside, is from Russia military superiority. And under the excuse of preparing to match that military might, of defending ourselves from this threat of outside force; in other words, under the guise of fighting Communism, we are being stampeded into the biggest jump ever towards, and perhaps the final jump right into, socialism and then the Communist camp.

Of course Sputnik did many things for the Soviets. It gave them, no matter how undeserved, a whole new level of prestige in the scientific world. It put very valuable ammunition into the hands of the world-wide Communist-sponsored groups, which in the United States were called Committees For A Sane Nuclear Policy, and into the hands of all of the Cyrus Eatons and Bertrand Russells and other "let's surrender" boys. And it indirectly enabled the pro-Communists in the chancelleries of Western Europe to increase their pressures on Adenauer in many ways.

But we are talking at this point about the usefulness of Sputnik to the Communists and their socialist allies, through its impact on the psychology of the American people with regard to their domestic affairs. This, in my opinion, was the most important ultimate effect of Sputnik, as planned by the Soviets, and as now gradually being realized by them. Here are the Communists' aims for the United States—to be achieved, they hope, through the leftward momentum of the attitude induced by Sputnik and all of its auxiliary propaganda. (1) Greatly expanded government spending, for missiles, for so-called defense generally, for foreign aid, for every conceivable means of getting rid of ever larger sums of American money—as wastefully as possible. (2) Higher and then much higher taxes. (3) An increasingly unbalanced budget, despite the higher taxes. When these notes were first put together many months ago, I expected a deficit of ten billion dollars at least, in the fiscal year of 1958–1959, despite all of the talk at that time about a balanced budget. Today well informed people, even within our government, are talking about a deficit of fifteen billion. (4) Wild inflation of our currency, leading rapidly towards its ultimate repudiation. (5) Government controls of prices, wages, and materials, supposedly to combat inflation. (6) Greatly increased socialistic controls over every operation of our economy and every activity of our daily lives. This is to be accompanied, naturally and automatically, by a correspondingly huge increase in the size of our bureaucracy, and in both the cost and reach of our domestic government. (7) Far more centralization of power in Washington, and the practical elimination of our state lines. There is a many-faceted drive at work to have our state lines eventually mean no more within the nation than our county lines do now within the states. (8) The steady advance of Federal aid to and control over our educational system, leading to complete federalization of our public education. (9) A constant hammering into the American consciousness of the horror of "modern warfare," the beauties and the absolute necessity of "peace"— peace always on Communist terms, of course. And (10) the consequent willingness of the American people to allow the steps of appeasement by our government which amount to a piecemeal sur-

render of the rest of the free world and of the United States itself
to the Kremlin-ruled tyranny.

There is what Sputnik and all of its side decorations are really
about. If the Communists can succeed in making us domestically
a communized nation, it will not be too difficult a final move for
them to pull us right into the world-wide Communist organization,
ruled by the Kremlin. And unless we can have enough of an awakening in this country, and enough of a rebellion against the appeasement policies of our government outside and its communizing policies inside America, the Communists are going to succeed in
accomplishing every one of these means to their final end, and that
final goal as well.

AMERICAN OPINION

SOURCES: 1. From Gary Allen, "The Politics of Dollars and Sense,"
American Opinion, Vol. XIV, No. 7 (July-August 1971), p. 18. 2. Gary Allen,
"Middle Class," American Opinion, Vol. XIV, No. 11 (December 1971),
pp. 35, 18. 3. Medford Evans, "The Presidency," American Opinion, Vol.
XIV, No. 11 (December 1971), pp. 39–40. Reprinted by permission.

1.

Mr. Nixon calls all this "a new American revolution . . . as profound,
as far-reaching, as exciting as that first revolution almost 200 years
ago." Balderdash! President Nixon's "new" revolution is rooted in
the one of 1848. It is certainly not American. As "Liberal" commen-
tator John P. Roche, a former national chairman of the A.D.A., observed in his syndicated column of February 11, 1971:

A keystone of Marxist thought is the concept of the "withering
away of the state," a doctrine that suggests that once the Socialist
revolution has occurred, the state—a repressive capitalist enterprise—will simply have no function and disappear. Under President Nixon's auspices, we are witnessing the Republican version
of this theory, at least as far as the national government is concerned.

And, just as in the Soviet Union, the Nixon decentralization is
totally illusory; a complete reversal of truth. In making his proposal
the President even used the Communist slogan, "Power to the People"—the battle cry of the Black Panthers and other revolutionary
groups, taken directly from a little red book titled Thoughts Of

Chairman Mao.* Just as "Power to the People" in Communist China means "Power to the Communist Dictators," so the revenue sharing proposals of Mr. Nixon's program to bring "Power to the People" means "Power to the President." In Communist countries they call it "democratic centralism." Theoretically, the power in a Communist state resides in the "soviets," the local governments. But, as every child knows, the real power is in the Politburo. Richard Nixon is creating his own Politburo.

Meanwhile our people are growing weary and restless. The primary diversion during the past decade of Leftward escalation has been the Vietnam War. President Johnson could not clear it with the *Insiders* to bring that war to a close, so he wisely declined to face the electorate for another term. Mr. Nixon has apparently arranged to make it at least appear that the war in Indochina is being ended. As he does, he is moving to complete the program which will, if he succeeds, socialize America. The United States must be completely in the hands of a central authority before the conspirators will dare to move for World Government.

How long do we have? Establishment spokesman James Reston declared in his internationally syndicated column for the *New York Times* of May 21, 1971: "Nixon would obviously like to preside over the creation of a new world order, and believes he has an opportunity to do so in the last 20 months of his first term." My guess is that we have it in our power to stop him. It will not, however, be an easy task. We will certainly need your help.

2.

The middle class is surrounded. Below is a growing proletarian army of welfarists who demand more and more socialism. Above the middle class are the elite "intellectuals" who are supported by the financial elite. The elite at the top, like those at the bottom, are also pushing socialism, but for a different reason. The Establishment is promoting anything which demoralizes the middle class.

. . .

Remember that Russia possessed only a small middle class, and it was quickly destroyed after the Revolution. But the enormous middle class in the United States is another matter. The Communists realize that we must be destroyed before a revolutionary *coup d'état* is possible. The war of the Left on the American middle class is therefore all-out war, taking a diversity of shapes and forms. We are under siege. Yet while middle-class Americans are troubled and frustrated over high taxes, inflation, the interminable war in Southeast Asia, crime in the streets, runaway welfare, an exploding drug problem, the alienation of youth, and many darkly complementary trends, few realize that these upsetting developments are not only related but are fronts in a coordinated assault.

One of the most obvious and consequential attacks on Mr. Middle American is aimed at his pocketbook. The middle class is simply being taxed into oblivion. In 1900, the cost of running the federal government amounted to a bargain $6.90 per head. At that time the government did little more for the people than protect them from foreign and domestic predators and provide a court system. Naturally the nation prospered, and the middle class mushroomed. As the decades passed, Uncle Sam was gradually transformed into Big Daddy. By 1950, the cost of the federal government was $303 per capita. In 1970, as Big Daddy more and more evolved into Big Brother, the expense of operating the federal government was $956 for every man, woman, and child in America.

There's more. A decade ago, according to the tally keepers at *U.S. News & World Report,* state and local taxes totalled $39 billion. Today they cost us $97 billion—which figures out to approximately $475 for each individual assessed by your friendly state and local politicians. The grand total for taxes is approximately $1,430 per year for every living, breathing, human in America. And it must be kept in mind that a large number of those are primarily tax absorbers, not taxpayers. According to the U.S. Chamber of Commerce, an average jobholder in the private sector not only cares for his family but must support through his taxes almost one-fourth of a welfare recipient, and one-half of a person on Social Security.

It is extremely important to the elitists whose aim is to destroy the middle class that most of us do not recognize how much we really are paying in taxes. Expropriation is concealed to keep it as painless as possible. Withholding from our paychecks, for example, is done on the theory that what is never seen is seldom missed. Many even get some of their money back from the government, and look upon it as a windfall.

3.

The *Insiders* are inside America, and show thoroughly American masks to the outside. Our last six Presidents—Roosevelt, Truman, Eisenhower, Kennedy, Johnson, Nixon—could never have led this country so far toward national dissolution if they had not every one presented, each in his own way, an image of 105 percent Americanism. Not one of them is imaginable in Europe. Moreover, all of them served in the Armed Forces prior to becoming President, and all exuded an aura of superpatriotism, which was not necessarily insincere in a subjective sense just because it was objectively inconsistent with the main trend of all their administrations toward surrender of national sovereignty to a new world order—where 200 million Americans would certainly be swallowed up when the principle of "one man, one vote" was applied to a homogenized world population of 3.5 billion (equals 3,500 million).

No President has been more thoroughly "American" in style than Richard Nixon, who indeed owed his emergence into the limelight to that spirit of chauvinistic anti-Communism which, like it or not (I liked it), suffused the electorate circa 1950. Richard Nixon got Alger Hiss a couple of years before Joe McCarthy got Owen Lattimore. (It seems now that Hiss was more expendable than Lattimore, while Nixon was certainly more convertible than McCarthy.) The importance of the pro-American, anti-Communist image which Nixon established twenty-odd years ago is brought out by Robert Welch in *A Timely Warning*: "There are strange things going on today, my friends, in this race of the Great Conspiracy to establish its *novus ordo seclorum*. But one of the strangest of all is that reasonably informed and sensible anti-Communists can still regard Richard Nixon as on their side in the struggle which now engulfs the whole human race and will determine its fate for a long time to come."

That belief that Nixon is on their side is what has enabled him to lead them to embrace the malignancy in Peking, to accept genocidal school-busing in the United States, and to hail as a proud achievement the imposition of economic fascism in America.

The iconoclasm of events may destroy Nixon's image within the year, and he may well not be President of the United States after January 1973. But whether he succeeds himself or whether he is succeeded by another, the danger to the country is that the citizens will again accept an image of patriotism for the ugly reality. Americans will not elect a man who openly advocates, as the so-called "Peace" candidates generally do, surrender of American interests to a foreign power, but we might elect, as we more than once have elected, a man who demands dollars for defense while double-dealing with the very enemies against whom any major defense would be needed.

If our whole election scene is indeed stage-managed and rigged by *Insiders*, as we have so much reason to suspect, then it seems likely that such far-out peaceniks as Senator George McGovern, not to mention partyless freaks of the counter-culture, are played into prominence by the media *in order* to create a backlash in favor of men who seem by contrast to be temperate but staunch patriots. Certainly Richard Nixon himself benefited in 1968 by the revulsion with which Middle America viewed on television the antics in Chicago. Interestingly enough, the crazies made no comparable attempt to stultify the Republican Convention. The New Left demonstrators did not, on balance, help such figures as Senator Eugene McCarthy; they helped Richard Nixon.

Absolutism Polarization as a rhetorical device is highly evident in the rhetoric of the old fundamentalists. It is expressed in stark alternatives; the phrase "light versus darkness' is used by both Hargis and Welch. This rhetoric is consistent with the counter-mythology illustrated earlier: if America is the highest expression of Christian civilization, then any threat to it such as the "Communist conspiracy" is a force of darkness, a satanic evil to be resisted at any cost. Conveniently, a means of staving off this darkness is available: membership in the Christian Crusade or the John Birch Society.

BILLY JAMES HARGIS

SOURCE: From Billy James Hargis, Communist America . . . Must It Be? *(Tulsa, Okla.: 1960), pp. 6–7, 175–176. Reprinted by permission.*

The people of China are not our enemies. The Communist dictatorship that enslaves the masses of China is our enemy. The people of Yugoslavia, Czechoslovakia, or any Communist occupied land are not our enemies. Our enemies are the Communists who have taken control of these governments by unfair, under-handed methods and now subject the people to slavery and tyranny such as this world has never seen since the dawn of civilization.

This battle against Communism is Christ versus anti-Christ; light versus darkness. It is not a political battle. Because of the nature of the struggle, the church should be in the forefront in the fight against Communism, rather than being an apologist for godless Communism, the case in far too many instances, as I will discuss later in this book.

. . .

And, you can join organized movements dedicated to exposing Communism. Unless movements like Christian Crusade are permitted to continue and grow, the doors to the churches you build now will be closed by God-hating Communists before they have a chance to develop. Your membership in such organizations will mean personal sacrifice, for you will be called upon to give your time, your energies and your wholehearted support to fighting Communism. The reward? The knowledge that the dreams your children hold dear will be realized, the compensation that you will live to see your child grow up in freedom, knowing that he will be able to kneel in the church of his choice without the threat of reprisal. Every war takes money for ammunition. The arms in our fight against Red infiltration is truth. It takes money to print pamphlets exposing Communism. It takes funds to combat propaganda. Where does the money come from? From the pockets of Americans who are willing to sacrifice to keep their freedom. It is only through this help that such organizations are able to continue to fight against Communism for these organizations depend entirely upon the contributions received. A nation-wide campaign on every radio station, in every newspaper and on every television channel might spare us Communist defeat.

To read the truth about Communism and then to shrug and say let someone else help, is in reality, saying, "I am ready to surrender this country to Communism. It's all in vain."

Evidence indicates that we have become a nation that places more value on material possessions than on the greatest gifts of all— Christianity and country. A graphic illustration of this is shown in a newspaper account I read recently. A school teacher asked his students to list what they considered their most valuable possessions. Not one student put Christianity or country first. In fact, the words "Christianity" or "country" did not even appear on the list!

And, yet, I cannot believe that if the majority of Americans knew what is happening in their nation that you would not find one Christian who would not stand up and fight openly.

I heard a man say recently, "I am willing to sacrifice all, even my life, if need be." Thank God for the man with this spirit. For if we are to survive, if we are to live FREELY under God's guidance, we cannot "turn away sorrowfully." Can it be done without sacrifice? NO. There is no hope without sacrifice. And, if we are unwilling to do our part . . . then, God have mercy on a nation whose people would not sacrifice to keep their freedom.

ROBERT WELCH

SOURCE: From The Blue Book (Belmont, Mass.: Robert Welch, Inc., 1961), pp. 38–39, 170. Reprinted by permission.

In fact I wish to end this grim argument today on quite a religious note. For whether you believe it or not, we are far along in a gathering crisis that is going to make us all search deeply into our beliefs, and into the values and loyalties that motivate our actions. This is a *world-wide* battle, the first in history, between light and darkness; between freedom and slavery; between the spirit of Christianity and the spirit of anti-Christ for the souls and bodies of men. Let's win that battle by alertness, by determination, by courage, by an energizing realization of the danger, if we can; but let's win it even with our lives, if the time comes when we must. Let's even keep in mind, against that time, an inspiration which we hope we shall not need. It comes from the end of a great and stirring hymn, written to inspire men to fight against a far less extensive slavery of their fellow men.

> In the beauty of the lilies Christ was born
> across the sea,
> With a glory in His bosom that transfigures
> you and me:
> As He died to make men holy, let us die to
> make men free,
> While God is marching on.
>
> . . .

For unless we can win that battle, the war for a better world will again be carried on through long and feudal Dark Ages, after we have been killed, our children have been enslaved, and all that we value has been destroyed. This is not rhetoric, and it is not exaggeration. It is a plain statement of the stark danger that is rapidly closing in on us right now.

It is the imminence and horror of this danger which drives me to so desperate a course as to offer myself as a personal leader in this fight, and to ask you to follow that leadership. It is not because I want so frightening a responsibility. And it is certainly not because I think that you gentlemen, as good friends of mine as most of you are, recognize any such qualities of leadership in me as would make me a happy choice for the role. It's just that I don't know where you, or all of us, are going to find anybody else to undertake the job. And because I know in my own mind, beyond all doubt or question, that without dynamic *personal* leadership around which the split and frustrated and confused forces on our side can be rallied, rapidly and firmly, we do not have a chance of stopping the Communists before they have taken over our country. It is not that you would choose me, or that I would even choose me, against other possibilities. It is simply that, under the pressure of time and the exigencies of our need, you have no other choice, and neither do I.

AMERICAN OPINION

SOURCE: From "Dear Reader" by Scott Stanley, Jr., American Opinion, Vol. XIV, No. 7 (July–August 1971), inside cover. Reprinted by permission.

As it turns out, we Americans don't have to go to Chad or Upper Volta or even Vietnam to stop the Communists. We can do it right here at home. James Reston, who ought to know, says that by the President's calendar we have twenty months to stop the international conspirators or face "a new world order" under Richard Nixon. If that is indeed what Mr. Nixon wants, we can say now that we mean to stop him; just as we know that James Reston of the *Times* means to help him. But we expect in these next twenty months to have a lot of help too. Yours, and your neighbor's, and the help of everyone you know. There will be millions more of us. The conspirators are now openly bragging in the *New York Times* about what they are trying to do within the next twenty months. It is time to see who stands with America and who stands against her. Let Mr. Nixon and the *Insiders* know that the battle has been joined!

NEW FUNDAMENTALISM

Sources of Rhetoric Rhetoric in this chapter is sampled from books and periodicals published by two groups: the Jesus People of Hollywood and the Christian World Liberation Front of Berkeley. Duane Pederson is the missionary to the "Jesus people" of Hollywood. His book, *The Jesus People*, and his newspaper, the *Hollywood Free Paper*, are two sources used here to represent the Southern California segment of the movement. The Christian World Liberation Front publishes *Right On*, a more intellectual paper than the *Hollywood Free Paper*. It contains occasional book and record reviews as well as serious discussions of fundamentalist doctrines. Both periodicals are devoted to fundamentalist interpretations of contemporary American life, especially the problems of youth and the counter-culture.

Counter-Mythology As a version of fundamentalism, the rhetoric of the "Jesus Freaks" returns to the revivalist theme of the Second Coming. Readers are encouraged to look for signs of the imminent return of the Messiah in the malaise of modern society. Social problems, the decline of morality, wars, and even physical events such as earthquakes are all viewed as portents of the Second Coming. Alarms about the end of the world are followed with warnings about the saved and the damned. Salvation is offered to the presumably frightened reader through the vehicle of the movement.

HOLLYWOOD FREE PAPER
SOURCES: 1. *"Earthquake Prediction,"* Vol. 3, No. 4, February 1971, p. 2; 2. *"It's About Time,"* Vol. 3, No. 1, January 1971, p. 6. 3. *"Let's Get Ready!"*, Vol. 3, No. 12, June 1971, p. 2.

1.

Jesus predicted that world conditions will get really trippy just before His return to earth. Earthquakes and other bummers like wars between nations, large-scale famine, persecution of Christians, false religious revivals, and moral degeneration—all these things are indications to tip us off that Jesus is just about to come back in person (Matthew 24). Pretty heavy, huh?

Now with all of these things that Jesus has clued us in on, isn't it pretty stupid not to take the hint and prepare for His coming? First thing you can do is to make sure that you've invited Him to take charge of your entire life. When you've done that, you've got nothing to sweat. Not even earthquakes!

Attention all Christians. It won't be long now! We've just experienced one more indication that everything Jesus said is right on. Make sure that He is Lord of your life and prepare to meet Him face to face. Get the good word out—Jesus is coming and He's coming soon!

2.

We're on the threshold of the most fantastic event of history. Nearly 2,000 years ago God stepped out of eternity into time, became man, and visited earth in the Person of Jesus Christ. Before leaving the earth, He told His disciples that He would physically return to earth at a future time in history when mankind was on the verge of destroying the entire human race. He indicated that this would take place during a thermo-nuclear war which the Bible described in great detail centuries before the atom bomb was ever heard of. He said that should He not return at the moment that He will, and bring peace to the earth, mankind would not survive this war.

His followers asked Him when this would be. He said it was not for them to know the day and the hour; but that He would give them a number of signs. When they saw these signs, they would know that they were living in the generation of His return. They would have this hope to look forward to.

3.

It almost freaks you out to watch the news these days. World conditions are getting pretty sick, to say the least. It's one thing to soothe our consciousness of what's happening by either dropping out or getting it on with our own routine trip. But we might as well face the issue and realize that world conditions are getting worse, not better.

The heavy thing about this whole situation is that somebody who had the inside scoop on what's happening laid down some heavy predictions as to what the world was going to be like towards the end of time as we know it. Dig? I mean, like, this somebody gave us an outline to check out for ourselves—so that we could tell for sure when the end of this world was approaching.

A lot of people know that Jesus came to bring liberation to man. That was His primary reason for coming. But a lot of people don't realize that this very same Jesus promised that He would return to planet earth again. That's right. But He also gave a detailed description as to where the world's head was going to be at before He'd return.

Flash on to this. Jesus said that before He returned the world scene would get so bad that men's hearts would fail them from fear—fear of what might happen to the human race (check out the ecology trip). He said that national wars and riots would be widespread. That sexual morality would reach an all-time low. That earthquakes and famines would increase with frequency. That occult mysticism and Satanism would become a fad. That knowledge and travel would increase. In fact, Jesus said a lot of heavy predictions that are significant of today. On top of all of this, He said that there would be a world-wide Jesus movement that would give the world one last chance to respond to His message of liberation before He would return. . . .

THE JESUS PEOPLE

SOURCE: From Duane Pederson with Bob Owen, The Jesus People (Pasadena: Compass Press, 1971), pp. 120–122. Reprinted by permission.

Something interesting to me is this: the Jesus People Movement is reaching a much wider group than just the street people. It is reaching into the Establishment Churches. . . . It is reaching across any and all denominational lines. . . . It is reaching across America. . . . In fact, it is reaching far beyond the boundaries of our land.

This movement of the Holy Spirit is spreading like wildfire. And I believe it is the beginning of the most powerful revival in the history of the world.

I don't like to think in terms of setting dates. But I do know that Jesus Christ will not be long in coming. This Movement—this generation—is just paving the way for Him.

To that I say only, "Praise the Lord!"

Counter-Elitism As members of a new movement composed primarily of dropouts and street people, the "Jesus Freaks" find themselves opposed to the "establishment" churches and the culture they represent. The new fundamentalist rhetoric adopts a "revolutionary" stance, claiming that Jesus was a revolutionary and a hippie. They also adopt the communal spirit of the counter-culture, alluding to the communal structure of the early Christian churches. Like the early Christians, the "Jesus Freaks" feel persecuted for their beliefs as much as for their mannerisms. They use this alleged persecution as evidence of the hostility and the evil of the society. As a reaction to hostility, the "Jesus Freaks" adopt the rhetorical stance of a "remnant," a small group of saved people who are hoping to survive the coming catastrophes. The new fundamentalists consider themselves an island of virtue in a sea of sin. This gives them a special mission to save others before the Second Coming.

RIGHT ON

SOURCES: 1. From The Street People, Selections from "Right On" *(Valley Forge, Pa.: Judson Press, 1971), pp. 10–11. 2.* Right On, *Vol. 3, No. 5, November 1971), p. 2. 3. "Perverted Imitations, Bah,"* The Street People, *p. 9. Reprinted by permission.*

1.

WANTED: JESUS CHRIST

Alias: The Messiah, Son of God, King of Kings, Lord of Lords, Prince of Peace, etc.

*Notorious leader of an underground liberation movement

*Wanted for the following charges:

—Practicing medicine, wine-making and food distribution without a license.

—Interfering with businessmen in the Temple.

—Associating with known criminals, radicals, subversives, prostitutes, and street people.

—Claiming to have the authority to make people into God's children.

*Appearance: Typical hippie type—long hair, beard, robe, sandals, etc.

*Hangs around slum areas, few rich friends, often sneaks out into the desert.

*Has a group of disreputable followers, formerly known as "apostles," now called "freemen" (from his saying: "You will know the truth and the Truth will set you free").

BEWARE—This man is extremely dangerous. His insidiously inflammatory message is particularly dangerous to young people who haven't been taught to ignore him yet. He changes men and claims to set them free.

WARNING: HE IS STILL AT LARGE!

2.

As a Christian newspaper *Right On* is to some extent anti-establishment. Since any world system right now is run by fallen men, there are always areas where Christians must stand against the system.

That we are against the establishment on some issues is not to say that we are against it in general as an unthought-out reactionary life style. I hope we are against the system only in the areas that Jesus would stand against it, but in all of those.

3.

Ever notice how whenever the people come up with something cool the ruling class always reacts and fights it, and if they can't stomp it out then they rip it off? They have their own inimitable way of distorting, perverting, commercializing and fouling up anything that's groovy.

Lately we've seen them taking our life style of clothes, hair, language, music, art, etc.—to make a profit. Now, we appreciate the fact that the ruling class recognizes that we've got something cool going, but their high handed piracy has to stop somewhere.

And, lest you think that this kind of rip-off is a new thing, let me tell you those dudes have been doing it to the people for centuries. Perhaps the classic example is what they tried to do to Jesus and His followers. The early Christians had a fantastic thing going, and the reactionary establishment got up tight. First they passed laws against them, then they hassled them and beat them up and ripped off their stuff. Finally, the ruling class plotted to bust Jesus and frame Him. They had to get Him at night when the people weren't around, because the people really dug Jesus and the ruling class was, as usual, afraid of the people. They bribed some witnesses, had a phony trial, and crucified Him. But the people were not to be denied and the murder of their leader only made them more determined. They went everywhere spreading the good news of the inner liberation Jesus provides.

The ruling class redoubled their efforts, slaughtered thousands of people who claimed to be followers of this one called Jesus, and still their members grew. So finally the ruling class did their thing. They officially embraced "Christianity," superimposed their own materialism and organization and set out to stomp out the unconditional love and forgiveness that Jesus had proclaimed. They began to produce their own revisionist, elitist, bureaucratic distortion of Christianity, proclaiming it to be the real thing. Throughout the centuries the people have rebelled and tried to get back to the real Christianity that they had going for them in the first century. Look around you! Right now, today, in Berkeley, there are groups proclaiming the people's Christianity, bringing it out from under the thumb of the ruling class. Join them and get liberated! Power to the people! All power through the Spirit!

4.

"Right On" has one line for the people: Jesus Christ holds the key to the only ultimate solution to any basic human problem you can suggest.

Too much? Well, before you split, you should know what constitutes a real Christian. All of us in the family of "Right On" writers know Jesus, and we want to share His answers with you.

We are not talking about belonging to or going to church, following the ethic Jesus taught, a religious code or rule of heart, self-righteous hypocrites, the atrocities and injustices which some men have committed in the name of Christianity, or even "good" people called Christian because they seem "nice" or moral.

We *are* talking about the change Jesus makes in lives—as shown by the kind of men and quality of life exhibited by those 1st century "Love-revolutionists" recorded in history. That life is available today—by an encounter of one's natural life with a new quality of life altogether, an experience where Jesus the Messiah, with all His power and attributes comes to live inside an individual. We *are* talking about allowing Him to replace your limited ability to love, about being totally "unhung" from one's past, including the injustices committed and the guilt experienced, and about having one's own human life linked up permanently and experimentally with the very life of God without the aid of artificial stimulants, pills, or meditation—about going through a spiritual birth just as real and permanent as was your physical birth.

Dig it! Here's how to initiate that experience. You don't have to believe a thing except that God would have to be fair enough to reward those who really want to know Him. Simply express some thoughts like these:

"God, if you're really there and can hear me right now—and although I'm skeptical: if Jesus was right and has something uniquely to do with experiencing you, I ask you, through Him, to make yourself real to me. I make no promises to you, but as best I know my own mind, I do want to experience your Spirit—I simply need you!"

That's it. The rest is up to God. "Too simple," you say. Well, if you want that to be your hang-up, that's your hang-up. All we can do is tell you we've experienced it. It has transformed the very core of our lives.

THE JESUS PEOPLE

SOURCE: From Duane Pederson with Bob Owen, Jesus People *(Pasadena: Compass Press, 1971), p. 21. Reprinted by permission.*

"*Hollywood Free Paper* supports and seeks to propagate the teachings of Jesus Christ. The only reason we do this is because we have already tried almost every means to reach God that man has thought of and at the end of this search turned to the One who said 'I am the way, the truth, and the life.' He also said 'I am come that they might have life, and that they might have it more abundantly.' (A full, complete and exciting life.)

"When you come to the time in your life that you have tried everything else and want to really start living on an eternal high, but you're not really sure if God is for real and that He loves you and wants for you to discover that love . . . Just try this—Say . . . 'God, I don't know where You are, but if You are and can hear me right now . . . even though I'm not sure what it is all about . . . if Jesus was right and is the way to knowing You, I invite You to make Yourself real to me. I make no promises, but I do want to experience Your Spirit. I need you!"

"That's it. The rest is up to God. 'Too simple,' you say . . . Well, if you want that to be your hang-up . . . that's your hang-up. All we can do is tell you we've experienced it. It has changed our lives.*

HOLLYWOOD FREE PAPER

SOURCES: 1. "As I See It," by Larry Norman, HFP, Vol. 3, No. 5, March 1971, p. 2. 2. "Can Woodstock Survive?", HFP, Vol. 3, No. 11, May 1971, p. 2. 3. "As I See It," by Larry Norman, HFP, Vol. 3, No. 10, May 1971, p. 4.

1.

The thousands of Jesus People who marched on California's state Capitol held more than a BELIEF in common. They have experienced RESULTS. Their personal prisons have been blown open. Their problems have begun to leave. They've experienced GOD-LIBERATION. The love of God and the peace of Jesus. The freedom of the Holy Spirit.

They greet one another as brothers and sisters and embrace spontaneously when the love of God overflows in them. They're alive: and will tell you that they thought they were alive before, but didn't know what alive really was until they met Jesus.

This personal liberation brings with it an ironic peace. A peace that does not diminish under persecution or imprisonment.

2.

What is cool, though, is that God has created one, and only one, community that is for real. There is absolute love and oneness and unity and unselfishness existing in this community and it is found in the supernatural dimension of His Spirit.

Every single person who has invited Jesus to be Lord over his life, has God's Spirit living inside of him right now. That makes him an automatic member of this special community.

3.

In the excitement of birth it is important not to overlook growth. Why are we, who are in the movement, so quick so encourage the act of conversion and then consistently neglect "follow-up." If we do not provide fellowship during the first few months of growth, the convert's hope in Jesus often dissolves or is displaced by lack of

---

*Note that the last half-dozen sentences in this excerpt are almost identical to the last two paragraphs of the previous one, which is from a different source. There seems to be some cooperation among new fundamentalists in their use of rhetoric. [Ed.]

direction. And if we allow new Christians to fall away a first time, it will be difficult to renew them to repentance a second time.

Is there no burden within the established church for the movement of the street Christian: the Jesus People, the Jesus Freaks? Where are the workers and elders needed to help the new flock grow strong and scripturally sound? Well, we like children lead each other as the blind lead the blind while criticize our immaturity and find fault with our doctrine? Neophytes need support and guidance. And while the Jesus People may need the stability and Biblical background of the church, the church itself could certainly use the energy and joy of the children.

Alienation New fundamentalist rhetoric uses the theme of alienation to frame the message of salvation. Both the personal problems of the individual and the social problems of the nation are viewed as symptoms of sin and apostasy. The solution of these problems will come with salvation. A reassertion of the Christian basis of social and national life follows from this view of the world. The Jesus movement, according to the rhetoric, is saving the nation by fighting against Satan. Since social problems such as war, pollution, crime, and drug abuse are all evidence of the evil machinations of Satan, it follows that the Jesus movement is fighting against these problems in the most effective way. Changes in personal fortune or national destiny are possible only through the conversion of individuals to fundamentalist Christianity, not through social change. Pollution, for example, can be solved by internal changes in individuals that will cleanse away "soul pollution." War and violence are manifestations of man's evil nature; only through salvation of the individual can this evil be overcome. The peace movement is misdirected, according to this view, because it does not focus on morality. The Jesus movement will bring peace to individuals and nations. Thus the new fundamentalists divert the energies of youth from the more mundane movements which attack social problems directly.

RIGHT ON

SOURCES: 1. "Dear America," Right On, Vol. 3, No. 26, July 4, 1971, p. 1. 2. "Peace March," by Frank Hermann, Right On, Vol. 3, No. 6, December 1971, p. 7. Reprinted by permission.

1.

Dear America:

I'm feeling kind of bad. I know the usual thing to say is "Happy Birthday," but to let it go at that seems kind of plastic right now.

You see, since I saw it was your birthday coming up on the 4th of July, and especially since you're getting up there in years, I started thinking about your life over these many years. I wanted badly to tell you on your birthday about how mellow and peaced out you were at this ripe old age.

But, like I said, I've been feeling kind of bad as I've been thinking about it all. Now I don't want to take anything away from you. You really have put together some good things for a lot of people now and then. And a lot of the problems you have had to face . . . well, you aren't the only one that hasn't been able to solve them. So I want you to know that I'm not interested in putting you down.

But I gotta tell you: when I look at you and rap with you, it is obvious that you aren't doing too well. You're not mellow and peaced out like I was hoping you would be. Your physical condition is pretty bad. Some say it's almost beyond hope! Part of you isn't getting enough food! Part of you isn't getting enough air and water! In other obvious ways you seem to be coming apart into many pieces, all uncoordinated and in a constant hassle rather than being harmoniously together.

But America, it isn't your broken and sick body that worries me most! It is your spirit, your soul, that worries me most! The body problems, the obvious physical and social needs, are very critical. But they won't be solved unless your attitude and total world-view is changed. I'm really feeling bad about you, America. A few people still wave your flag and insist that you are fine. But I think a lot more agree that the hour is critical and that some major changes in your condition are inevitable.

Some people are suggesting that all your problems are physical and some surgery as well as a change in diet will take care of you. I think they are right those changes being needed, but they don't go far enough and deal with your spirit problems. Some people are suggesting that you need a more active sex life. Some people are suggesting that there is no hope and you should just shoot up and turn up the music and try not to think at all.

But I gotta tell you, America, that the radical change that you need is the one which will change your whole world-view and then your life-style, including the physical problems I already mentioned. And this solution is one which will work on every cell, every atom, of your body. In fact, for your condition to improve, this solution will *have* to affect many of your cells: it can't remain only in the mouth or even the stomach, it has to get into each cell and atom!

America, my Father told me to go ahead and offer this solution to you as a gift. Now that it is your birthday, I really want to give it to you with love from the Family. You've always been kind of unusual and unpredictable, so I really pray and hope that this gift won't be just looked at briefly and put on the shelf. I really hope that each cell will be changed spiritually and then physically by this gift.

Yes, America, I'm feeling kind of bad. But as I've been writing this birthday letter to you, I've been getting more optimistic as I have thought about the gift. It's so far out and so exciting in fact, that I want to give you a hint: it's abbreviated J.C.

Oh yeah, and have a happy birthday, America.

With love and best wishes,

The Forever Family
Berkeley, California

2.

In reality, most of the "peace movement" should be called the "anti-war" movement. Why? Because the movement exists as a reaction to a, nonetheless, evil phenomenon: the Southeast Asian War. Although the attention of the anti-war movement has necessarily been focused on stopping the conflict in Vietnam, several other evils have, directly and indirectly, been attacked. The military draft is tottering under the pressure of the movement, largely because of the courageous men who have resisted induction.

The war in Vietnam **is** coming to an end. The war is ending too slowly and at too high a cost in human life and the pressure must be sustained to keep the warlords aware of the will of the people. At the same time the anti-war forces in the U.S. have realized that the dictatorship in Greece, the arms escalation in the Mideast, and the economic colonialism practiced by the U.S. in much of the world are no less in need of opposition, to each and every instance of racism, oppression, war, and exploitation a vigorous protest should be launched.

It is, however, a shallow peace that is defined merely by the absence of physical war. It is time for the movement to recognize that it must not simply exist as a reaction to various evil phenomena. A soundly based program of peace must be found and initiated. Simply from the standpoint of the number and magnitude of the conflict situations in the world today, we are dooming ourselves if we accept the role of "reactor" to the actions of aggressors. We must step out on our own with a program of peace.

The problem with all human proposals is that their authority and perspective are limited and finite. Hence the peace movement, for all our high ideals, is frequently split and torn by conflict. The answer may bring a superficial reaction from most of us because of our educational upbringing in a shallow rationalistic humanism. Nonetheless the answer to the need for a *viable* peace program is to find a solution with transcendent, supernatural authority and perspective. We have such a solution, though it has waited nearly 2000 years to be fully implemented. It is simply to recognize the Prince of Peace as our Leader and follow His dictates. Jesus, though caricatured and rejected by many, remains our only hope for peace. He offers new life and liberation, new power and peace to all who will come to Him and make the commitment to follow Him. Do it, and then share it.

HOLLYWOOD FREE PAPER
SOURCE: From "Alternative for Revolution," Hollywood Free Paper, *Vol. 3, No. 3, February 1972, p. 3.*

Okay, so nobody's gonna hassle the fact that the straight society is a little fluked. It's pretty easy to see through their phony games. And all the religious weirdos who think they've got all the answers to everything that ever was—they're a little spacy, too!

So what are you going to do? The establishment hassles us because we don't dig their synthetic life-style. The church groupies think we need to rotate around their own little brick building and take a liturgical trip. And all their memorized answers to questions nobody even asks makes us want to shine it on to anything good they might have to say.

. . .

So what does that mean? It means we gotta get changed on the *inside* that's what! All your ecology programs, and ghetto renewal plans, and religious formulas are all a bunch of garbage until man is changed. We've had thousands of years to improve on human behavior. But we haven't managed to change anything yet. Don't give me that jazz about man is getting better. That's a bunch of flack.

. . .

When Jesus starts living His life through you things will change. I mean, like you won't want to be the bad-mouthing creep you used to be. And you won't want to pollute your environment or abuse the natural function of living either. He takes you off your spinning wheel and puts your head back together.

Jesus' revolutionary alternative really works. It's spiritual, not religious. Get the difference? His trip isn't plastic, and that's all! What he wants you to do is to drop out of your hang-ups and to drop into His revolutionary love. With Jesus pulling for you, you can't lose. After all, He *is* God!!

Absolutism Fundamentalist doctrines seem to merge comfortably with absolutism in the rhetoric of the new fundamentalism. The belief in heaven or hell as alternatives for eternal life is translated into either-or rhetoric. Intolerance is expressed through rhetoric which poses Christ and Satan as the only alternatives; any belief system that is not orthodox Christianity must be inspired by the devil. Mystical and spiritual cults are regarded as pagan and thus demonic. The political beliefs of the new left are regarded as misleading; they are also viewed as Satanic. To soften the harshness of this absolutism, the "Jesus Freaks" allow for the prodigal sons to return to the fold. They see this return as their mission. They seek to salvage lost souls who have strayed into other belief systems and other causes during their wild youth.

HOLLYWOOD FREE PAPER
SOURCES: 1. "Shootin' Up Satan," HFP, Vol. 4, No. 3, January 1972, p. 3. 2. "Spiritual Warfare," HFP, Vol. 3, No. 13, June 1971, p. 2.

1.
If you're not into drugs there are plenty of other trips to inject into your system. One of the heaviest things that dudes are shooting up today is spiritual mysticism. But that's nothing new. People have been shooting up Satan for centuries. It's just that every now and then the culture as a whole gets hip to Satan and then he really has a field day.

But whenever that happens, God always counteracts with a positive spiritual revolution. Would you believe, that's what's happening right now? Well dig, 'cause that's what's happening!

This happens because there are two spirit worlds. One's an upper and the other is a super-downer. Nope, we're not talking about white magic and black magic. Both of those trips are part of the same spirit realm. We're talking about the positive Spirit (God's Spirit) and the negative spirit (Satan's spirit). The first one is into genuine love, the other is into self-love. Dig? The first is for real and the other's phony.

2.

It is necessary then, first of all, that we recognize the reality of the warfare now in progress. The Book of Ephesians gives attention to the warfare we are talking about. After dealing with various phases of the Christian's life on earth, the apostle says, "Finally, my brethern, be strong in the Lord, and in the power of his might. Put on the armour of God, that ye may be able to stand against the wiles of the devil. For we wrestle not against flesh and blood, but against principalities, against powers, against the rulers of the darkness of this world, against spiritual wickedness in high places" (Eph. 6:10—12). The Twentieth Century translation of this twelfth verse is helpful: "For ours is no struggle against enemies of flesh and blood, but against all the various powers of evil that hold sway in the darkness around us, against the spirit of wickedness on high."

Our tendency is to overlook the spiritual aspect of our warfare. Too often our battles are fought on a carnal plane, person against person, or organization against organization. I may have good reason to disagree with a man and his methods, but it is not my business to fight the man. My responsibility is to fight the Devil who has caused that man to leave the paths of righteousness.

The glorious side to all this is that we battle a defeated foe. Our victory does not lie in having our minds occupied with the enemy, but rather in looking away unto Jesus, the Author and the Finisher of our faith. This gives us an enthusiasm in the fight. In all these things we are "more than conquerors through him that loved us" (Rom. 8:37).

Just as he lost in his battle with Christ, so will Satan lose in his battle with us when we learn to stand our ground against him in the grace and strength provided by our Savior.

THE JESUS PEOPLE

SOURCE: *Duane Pederson with Bob Owen,* The Jesus People *(Pasadena: Compass Press, 1971), pp. 72–73. Reprinted by permission.*

That's why Jesus People do not "preach" doctrine. Some Jesus People accept and embrace speaking in tongues. Others do not. Some have other views about other doctrines. But as a group . . . as a movement . . . we hold to only one creed: Jesus Christ.

He, alone, is the Way, the Truth and the Light. He, alone, can bring life to the one who is lost. He, alone, can bring peace and release to the one who was bound by fears and sins.

Jesus Christ was a revolutionary. Because He dared to oppose the ecclesiastical leaders of that day, to open up the windows of heaven—and allow the light of God to shine into a darkened world, and into darkened lives.

RIGHT ON

SOURCES: 1. "Up From Zen," Right On, Vol. 3, No. 27, August 1971, p. 7. 2. Right On, Vol. 2, No. 23, April 1971, p. 3. Reprinted by permission.

1.
No matter what philosophy or religion we formulate, we cannot escape the truth of what is, that we are made in the image of God. My own philosophy led me to the belief that life could only be meaningful if I lived in tension, but I could not live that way. The existentialist who says that life and all things are absurd cannot help himself from falling in love, the nihilist at some point finds an inconsistency between his logic which tells him he might as well just destroy, and some part of him which yearns to create, and to create significantly. The beginning of all truth is that God is, and that there was love and communion in God Himself before the creation of the universe. God created man in the image of His character, he created man free to be in a relationship with God, who is the source of all love and communication. Man turned away, to be his own world, to be alone, and in turning away found himself totally alone and finite. Without the sustenance of the relationship with God, in cutting himself off from the true source of love and communion, man found himself separated from everything around him and from every other man, and outside of the relationship for which he was created, man found himself without identity.

God has reached down to us and provided us with a way to come back to Him. In Christ, God and man are totally united, totally reconciled; separation is conquered, alienation is conquered, death is conquered.

It's time for us all to come home.

2.

Almost any day you can hear a political animal upbraiding the rest of the menagerie. "Get off your ass and become one of us, the pig is oppressing you!" The political animals have all sorts of delightful illusions about the perfectability of "human" systems and how creatures can pull themselves up by their own paw-straps. They are really very moral although they can't give a reason for it. And they would probably deny it if someone told them that. Not that they follow their own morality, for how can there be a morality in the zoo?

If it is simple obeying one's instincts, then no one is at fault. This must surely include the pig who is only following his own tendencies towards law and order. So what is morality based on?

More and more the answer the political animal gives is power. "Follow us or we will destroy society." But he cannot deny that right now the consensus of society is against him. It looks like his attempt to achieve freedom is a failure. He can break all the windows in the world but he hasn't changed the nature of those he wants to free. And no wonder, he hasn't been able to "free his mind," as Lennon would say.

But doesn't man have a "free will?" Sure. And he often uses it to act more inhumanly than animals. I shouldn't even have to give examples of this. But there is Vietnam, ghettos, crime, brutality, repression, and corruption.

But hasn't man made "moral progress?" Where? His moral evolution hasn't kept pace with his technological advances. Do you trust the men in whom awesome power has been placed? I don't. All it takes is a high-ranking American or Russian military official to go haywire and pow! Doomsday. For many people this is a frightening thought. But all this means is that there will be on a grand scale what we all must experience anyway—death. So the problem, inevitably, returns to living. We have seen two extremes. Those who would concern themselves solely with the "inner" life and their private group, and those who want to revolutionize the outward system. Each group forms one-half of a total picture. So why can't the two concepts merge? The answer is that they did, 2000 years ago in the teachings of Jesus! He tirelessly spoke out against the hypocrisy of the "establishment." But He had no illusions about how man could progress on his own. In fact, He said man couldn't, without God's help. And the same thing is true of man today. If you have come to a point in your life where you recognize and want to change your "animal" nature, and you are painfully aware of your inadequacy to do it, call upon Jesus to help you. If He is just a dead man you have lost nothing. However, if He is what He claims to be then you should be ready for a transformation unlike anything "human."

The choice is yours!

EPILOGUE

EPILOGUE: THE DEATH OF A REVOLUTION

Max Lerner is an intellectual and a journalist, and his syndicated column combines the best qualities of both. In this retrospective piece, Lerner looks back over the 1960's and discusses social movements in a way that is both timely and analytic. He concludes, as many other intellectuals have, that organized movements of the 1960's are defunct but that their influence continues in the 1970's. He finds evidence of radical proposals for social change in the ideology of the ecology movement and the women's liberation movement. He says that the influences of radicalism extend much further than the proposals of these special-interest reform groups. He feels that questions raised by the movements of the 1960's go to the roots of social and human life, and that these questions lead to a reawakened interest in religion. He concludes by suggesting that the future interest in ideology and social movements will be directed at religious movements such as those of the "Jesus Freaks" and of oriental mysticism.

MAX LERNER

SOURCE: The Los Angeles Times, *June 25, 1972 Section F, pp. 3–6.* Copyright, The Los Angeles Times. *Reprinted with permission.*

It is now roughly a decade since the revolutionary changes of the early 1960's began in earnest . . . this may be a good time to ask what has happened to the revolution and strike its trial balance.

There are broadly two contrasting theories. One is that all the chaos of changes adds up to a disintegration of America, not immediately but before the end of the century—its energies run down, its values corrupted, its unity split, its will to survive stymied.

The events of the last year—the new mood on the campus, the slowing down of the black revolt, the quieter atmosphere in the courtrooms, the new climate in the relations with China and Russia, the activism of the young inside the party system, the sense of new political stirrings—have confirmed my skepticism about the disintegration theories.

The other theory is that America is going through convulsive, dislocating changes which lead to many discontents, that the civilization may well fall victim to those changes and discontents, but that there is a good chance it will survive them and emerge a stronger rather than a weaker civilization.

*

I can't disprove this view, nor do I discount the opposite one. There is a law of acceleration and deceleration in history, which we understand only very murkily. Social and cultural changes seem to speed up suddenly, then slow down, but it takes considerable arrogance to be sure you know the sources of either process.

. . .

We must see the reasons in the governing facts of the life of the young. American soldiers continue to be withdrawn, the draft's impact is light, the problem of jobs and careers is real. These felt subjective factors—more than the condition of the war itself—evidently govern the actions of the students.

The three passionate movements of the '60s—the antiwar marches, the black movements, the campus revolts—still evoke deep feelings but no longer hold to the center of the stage. Each of them aimed at a radical change in the power structure. Each tried to use the students to that end. Each stirred up the dust each achieved some immediate objectives, none got its long-range ones.

*

As for the hard-core revolutionaries, they stopped at nothing in either aim or means, and achieved nothing. I include the SDS, the Weatherman, Yippies, Black Panthers. They fed on the antiwar mood, the frustrations, the enragements, the absolutes. Their tactic was to identify with each passionate movement—blacks, the students, militant women, the march on the Pentagon, the Chicago convention demonstrations—and push it to extremes. In a time of violence, they increased the violence they fed on. They developed a mystique of violence, as if there were something cleansing in it—of and for itself. At one point, in the case of the Weatherman, they even used the terrorism of bombing.

It was a short-lived, if lurid, chapter of the '60s. It got nowhere. Its extremism boomeranged and made every militant movement harder. Partly it fell victim to a policy of containment by the authorities which at times became repressive, but which never reached a full-scale repression. Mainly it ran afoul of the rage it set in motion among the large mass of ordinary people.

The antiwar movement hasn't ended the war, but it kept Mr. Johnson from running again, put President Nixon on the defensive and helped McGovern on his road to the nomination. Mostly it sparked the other attacks on the power structure, gave a special passion to the passionate movements and served as their accelerator and multiplier. Its chief effect, however, wes the erosion of authority all through the society, for war itself is actually the enemy of all authority, and eats away respect for law and the social fabric.

The movement of the blacks (and this applies to some other ethnic movements as well) had three aspects. One was revolutionary nationalism. It exploited, if it didn't spark, the inner city riots. It hurt itself badly by a violence of brother against brother. There seems to be a law of fractional revolutionary politics that the violence turns inward and becomes fratricide. In the end, the black people themselves rejected it.

J. K. Obatala, a professor of pan-African studies, wrote recently in The Times that "there never was a black revolution" in the '60s, that it was mostly radical rhetoric and symbolism and that "the campuses continued to be training grounds for the traditionally conservative Afro-American middle class."

This strikes me as too sweeping. It doesn't do justice to the second aspect of the black movement—the prideful assertion of black identity, which doesn't have to be either separatist or violent in order to have meaning for young blacks and give them a new sense of self-confidence. Malcolm X and Martin Luther King Jr. became folk heroes not because one was a revolutionary and the other a champion of nonviolence, but because both of them touched a deep—even religious—pride of identity in their people. To call that "middle class" is to narrow it unnecessarily.

The third aspect is the concrete gains that the black movements have made—economic, legal, political, educational. As I interpret what engrosses the black students today in their studies, it is not to become "middle class" or "conservative" but to consolidate these gains and push them all the way to de facto equality in the whole of American life.

*

For the students as a whole, white as well as black, the college revolution brought some concrete gains in a constitutional restructuring of power on the campus. But when the disruption of college life by a minority became extreme, the large student majority got either angry or bored with them—or both.

What happened to the ecology revolution? It started later than the ones in the ghettos and on the campuses and drew on a broader spectrum of support and is still going strong. Instead of using violence, its aim was the opposite—to undo the violence that men had done to their environment. Alone among the passionate movements of our time, it has aimed at balance, not polarization, at healing alienations (especially of man from nature), not sharpening them.

Logically, there should have been a strong link between the protest about the city and the protest about the environment, for the shame of the cities was as much ecological blight as social blight. But this didn't work out. The leaders of the ethnic inner-city revolts showed far less interest in the problems of pollution, population and technology than they did in income, social justice and political power.

Yet the environmental problems abide. What makes the cities unlivable and ungovernable, makes them so for all, and no group has immunity from the damnation of the "unheavenly city." Similarly, the cities will not be saved except by those who have some sense of place and have put down roots into their block and neighborhood.

The pollution problem—air, water, noise, vanishing species— couldn't by itself have fed the fires of the ecology movement. Other sources of incitement have added to it and kept it alive and strong. One was the population movement, reaching an intense form in Zero Population Growth. It provided a new cause to fight for—to help people make a life by refusing to congest the living space that nature had provided. The second was the Women's Liberation

Movement, which brought a new passion to the fight for revised state abortion laws and for day-care centers.

The third was a revival of the liberal passion against the big corporations and big technology, but in a new form. It is less an attack on their monopoly position than on what they will do to the environment if left unchecked. And it has broadened out to an attack on the whole idea of economic growth.

*

Rarely has a revolution gone so fast, broadening and clarifying as it moved, without the sudden deflation and collapse of some of the more violent revolutions of the past decade. But the general acceptance of its antipollution demands has dulled its cutting edge. Those who thought it might be an important issue in the 1972 elections have turned out wrong. Pollution has become a no-no for everyone.

But the ecology revolution can't subsist only on saying no. It must say yes to some things. It should say yes not only to the conserving of natural resources, but to the kind of technology which can put new energy resources to use, can cope with pollution and relieve human drudgery.

It should say yes to all forms of social creativeness and moral imagination, which shape an environment within and beyond the natural environment. It is right to limit runaway technology and economic growth. But if there is no growth, every social problem becomes stickier, every group claim and demand harder to fulfill, every conflict harder to resolve. The problem is not to stop growth, but control it, and thus achieve balance within man's natural and social environment.

Whatever happened to the new culture? I think it is still going on, and that there is a nub of truth in the vision Charles Reich had in "The Greening of America," although he didn't foresee some of its forms. He called it Consciousness III, which was pretty gimmicky. Theodore Roszak had called it the counterculture, which was more descriptive. Other names emerged, like the adversary culture, the hippie culture, the drug-and-rock culture, the new barbarians. After a time, the writers began to settle for the simplest of all—the new culture.

From the start, the fact has been there—that the rebellions of the young have not been what was at first most clamant and most visible, the assaults on the power structure, but that more deeply they have been assaults on the value structure and on cultural life-styles. There was so much noise in all the marchings, posturings, invectives, demonstrations, seizures of buildings, invasions of class-rooms, manifestos, "non-negotiable demands," rock-throwing, hel-met-wearing, even bomb making and bombing, that for a time, we couldn't hear the quieter message.

The message was simple and forceful, and when the noise died down, we made it out. It was that something had gone wrong, not just with the corporations, the Army, the ghettos, the way power was distributed, but more crucially with the way people live their lives, and with the purposes they live for. Something so fundamen-tal has gone wrong, the young people were saying, that to set them-selves off from us they had to look different, dress differently, take on a new outer profile as a badge of differentiation.

But the break was sharper than the outer profile, and deeper than the surface perceptions of the New Left and the new journalism and the new activisms. The young people themselves didn't understand it for a time, while the antiwar fervor and the civil-rights fervor caught them up and engaged their energies, and the ecological movement, and the Women's Liberation Movement.

All of these were important causes, and there was camaraderie in pursuing them. But the fact was that these were lonely young people, and a little insecure despite all their bravado. While one cause succeeded another, it was the camaraderie that counted, it was the sense of being wanted and useful, of finding human warmth and meaning together. But when the causes were over, the loneli-ness and insecurity remained.

Hence the continuance of the drug culture, which in some form is likely to remain part of the new culture during the rest of the de-cade. In another part of the forest, however, the new culture is being undercut by new developments. Many young people, coming out of college, are returning to the career market, working in the professions. Some of them plan to use their careers, in law, medi-cine, journalism, to further the cause they care about. Others are playing their careers straight, much as their fathers and older brothers did before the revolutions. This is especially true of a whole new generation which has entered the community colleges, with a strong vocational interest. The current projection is that by the end of the decade, more than half the American student bodies will be in these community colleges. And while their outer profile—hair, jeans, dirty sneakers—is like that of students in the '60s, their value system is almost a "straight" one.

The students coming out of the elite and state universities are more likely to fashion a new "new culture," quieter, less militant, with values closer to what the recent Daniel Yankelovich study of values calls the "new naturalism." They tend to live closer to the land, with or without formal marriage, making a Thoreau-like living by escaping to career roles and working on and off as artisans, simplifying their lives outside the career system even while they work politically "within the system."

But the root question remains. What was it that went wrong? Surprisingly for an irreverent generation, the answer seems to lie in the area of religion. When science and technology wore away the protective strata of traditional religion, the older culture crumbled. The new religious movement—the "Jesus freaks," the new mysticism and occultism, the vogue of Oriental religions, the practice of meditation and transpersonal disciplines, the drug mystique—all attest to a search again for the wonder and mystery of life. It would be a rich jest of history if the "greening" of America turned out to to be a quest for a repair and a renewal of the broken religious connection.

DATE DUE

APR 1 5 1993		
DEC 1 2 1997		

DEMCO 38-297